THE OTHER SIX DAYS

THE OTHER SIX DAYS

*Vocation, Work, and Ministry
in Biblical Perspective*

R. Paul Stevens

WILLIAM B. EERDMANS PUBLISHING COMPANY
GRAND RAPIDS, MICHIGAN / CAMBRIDGE, U.K.

REGENT COLLEGE PUBLISHING
VANCOUVER, BRITISH COLUMBIA

First published in 1999 in the U.K. by Paternoster Press
under the title *The Abolition of the Laity*
Paternoster Press is an imprint of Paternoster Publishing
P.O. Box 300, Carlisle, Cumbria, CA3 0QS, UK

This edition published jointly 2000 in North America by
Wm. B. Eerdmans Publishing Co.
255 Jefferson Ave. S.E., Grand Rapids, Michigan 49503 /
P.O. Box 163, Cambridge CB3 9PU U.K.
www.eerdmans.com
and by
Regent College Publishing
an imprint of Regent College Bookstore
5800 University Boulevard, Vancouver, B.C. V6T 2E4

Printed in the United States of America

05 04 03 02 01 00   5 4 3 2 1

Library of Congress Cataloging-in-Publication Data

Stevens, R. Paul, 1937-
The other six days: vocation, work, and ministry
in biblical perspective / R. Paul Stevens.
p.   cm.
Includes bibliographical references and indexes.
Eerdmans ISBN 0-8028-4800-1 (pbk.: alk. paper)
Regent ISBN 1-57383-175-1 (pbk.: alk. paper)
1. Laity. 2. Lay ministry.   I. Title.

BV4400.S716 2000
262'.15 — dc21
00-041733

Contents

PART I

A PEOPLE WITHOUT 'LAITY AND CLERGY'

Chapter 1

Doing People Theology

> At bottom there can only be one sound and sufficient theology of the laity, and that is a 'total ecclesiology' . . . it will also be an anthropology, and even a theology of creation in its relation to Christology.
>
> Yves Congar[1]

This book makes an outrageous proposal. Should the laity be abolished?[2] Can it be? As Yves Congar once said, there will always be laypersons in their place in the church: kneeling before the altar, sitting under the pulpit and having their hand in their purse.[3] Throughout almost all of its history the church has been composed of two categories of people: those who 'do' ministry and those to whom it is 'done'. Lay people are the object not the subject of ministry. They receive it, pay for it, promote it and perhaps even aspire to it. But they never quite become ministers for reasons that are deep in the church's soul: theological reasons that will be explored in this book, structural and cultural reasons that have been explored in many contemporary books on the subject.[4] In

---

[1] Y. Congar, *Lay People in the Church: A Study for a Theology of the Laity*, xvi–xvii. Extracts from this book are used with the permission of the publisher, Geoffrey Chapman, an imprint of Cassell & Co.

[2] The phrase 'the abolition of the laity' was first coined by Elton Trueblood in a chapel address in 1935 and incorporated into his first book, *The Essence of Spiritual Religion* (1936); see Tony Campolo, 'The Quiet Revolutionary', *Christianity Today* 35.2 (February 1991), 22–4.

[3] Congar, *Lay People in the Church*, xi.

[4] P. Collins and R. Paul Stevens, *The Equipping Pastor*; B. Hull, *The Disciple-Making Pastor*; G. Martin and L. Richards, *Lay Ministry:*

spite of the fact that the clergy–lay division in the church finds no basis in the New Testament, it persists tenaciously.

Most efforts at recovering the New Testament vision of every member ministry are half-measures. They focus on the Christian *in the church* – lay preachers, lay pastoral care-givers and lay worship leaders. What is needed is a comprehensive biblical foundation for the Christian's life in the world as well as the church, a theology for homemakers, nurses and doctors, plumbers, stockbrokers, politicians and farmers. Recovering this, as Gibbs and Morton said decades ago, would be like discovering a new continent or finding a new element.

This, of course, raises the question of what is theology and what is applied theology, matters about which there is no agreement among theologians, though in passing I note that the word 'theology' was hardly ever used in the sense of unapplied theology until the Enlightenment.[5] My central concern in this book is to recover a truly biblical basis for the theological enterprise, especially as it

---

[4] (continued) *Empowering the People of God*; G. Ogden, *The New Reformation: Returning the Ministry to the People of God*; R. Paul Stevens, *The Equipper's Guide to Every Member Ministry: Eight Ways Ordinary People Can Do the Work of the Church*; F.R. Tillapaugh, *Unleashing the Church*.

[5] Definitions abound. Stanley Grenz says that 'theology is intellectual reflection on the faith commitments we have as Christians as informed by Scripture, carried out in a specific historical-cultural context for the purpose of living for the glory of God' (from a lecture at Regent College). J.I. Packer says that theology is for 'achieving God's glory (honour and praise) and humankind's good (the godliness that is true humanness) through every life activity' (a lecture at Regent College). John Stott says 'theology is a serious quest for the true knowledge of God, undertaken in response to his self-revelation, illumined by Christian tradition, manifesting a rational inner coherence, issuing in ethical conduct, resonating with the contemporary world and concerned for the greater glory of God' (J.R.W. Stott, ' "Theology" A Multidimensional Discipline', in Donald Lewis and Alister McGrath [eds.], *Doing Theology for the People of God: Studies in Honor of J.I. Packer*, 17–18 [3–19]). For a history of the use of the term 'theology' see Y. Congar, OP, *A History of Theology*. For a careful delineation of theology, doctrine and dogma see A.E. McGrath, *The Genesis of Doctrine: A Study in the Foundations of Doctrinal Criticism* (Oxford: Basil Blackwell, 1990), 1–13.

relates to the ordinary person not only in the church but the world. In this chapter I will adapt the famous words of Lincoln and I will introduce a theology *of* the people, *for* the people and *by* the people, taking each preposition as illuminative of the theological enterprise as it relates to the whole people of God.[6]

1. 'Of ' the Whole People of God: Beyond Clericalized Theology

As mentioned above Yves Congar, the French Catholic, said, rightly, 'at bottom there can be only one sound and sufficient theology of the laity, and that is a "total ecclesiology"'.[7] But to obtain this 'total ecclesiology' we must deal with some persistent misunderstandings.

First, we look in vain in the New Testament for a theology of the laity. There are neither laypersons nor clergy.[8] The word 'laypersons' (*laikoi*) was first used by Clement of Rome at the end of the first century, but was never used by an inspired apostle in Scripture to describe second-class, untrained and unequipped Christians. It ought to be eliminated from our vocabulary. 'Laity', in its proper New Testament sense of *laos* – the people of God – is a term of great honour denoting the enormous privilege and mission of the whole people of God. Once we were not a people at all, but now in Christ, we are 'a chosen people, a royal priesthood, a holy nation, a people [*laos*] belonging to God' (1 Pet. 2:9; Ex. 19:6).

The word 'clergy' comes from the Greek word *klēros*, which means the 'appointed or endowed' ones. It is used in Scripture not for the leaders of the people but for the whole people.[9] Ironically the church in its constitution is a people without laity in the usual sense of that word, but full of clergy in the true sense of that word – endowed, commissioned and appointed by God to continue God's own service and mission in the world. So the church does not 'have'

---

[6] Macquarrie outlines his book on this basis. J. Macquarrie, *The Faith of the People of God: A Lay Theology*.

[7] Congar, *Lay People in the Church*, xvi.

[8] A. Faivre, *The Emergence of the Laity in the Early Church*, 7–8.

[9] Col. 1:12; Eph. 1:11; Gal. 3:29.

a minister; it is ministry, God's ministerium. It does not 'have' a mission; it is mission. There is one people, one trinitarian people, one people that reflects the one God who is lover, beloved and love itself, as Augustine once said,[10] and one God who is sender, sent and sending.

Throughout almost all of its history the church has been composed of two categories of people, those who are ministers and those who are not. Ministry has been defined as what the pastor does, not in terms of being servants of God and God's purposes in the marketplace, the church, the home, the school or professional office. Going into 'the Lord's work' means becoming a pastor or missionary, not being co-workers with God in his creating, sustaining, redeeming and consummating work in both the church and the world.

Second, the result of this regrettable state of affairs is that writing a theology of the so-called laity is normally a compensatory thing – trying to correct the imbalance, to elevate the non-clergy layperson, usually at the expense of the clergy layperson. One of the first to write such a compensatory theology in modern times was Yves Congar, a person who had a profound influence on Vatican II. Where Congar's theology leads, though, is toward an ecclesiology in which distinction and ranking is inevitable. The fundamental assumption he brings to his otherwise ground-breaking study is that the church is not only the community that God has brought into being; it is also the means by which the Lord brings humankind into fellowship with himself.[11] For this purpose the hierarchy is essential.[12] Thus he ends up proposing a complementary relationship of clergy and laity,

---

[10] J. Moltmann, *The Trinity and the Kingdom*, 32.

[11] 'Whilst Protestantism was making the Church a people without a priesthood and Catholic apologists were replying by establishing the rightfulness of priesthood and institution, the Church in more than one place was finding herself reduced to a state of a priestly system without a Christian people. Thus it was that of the Church's two aspects which Catholic tradition requires to be held together – that in which the Church is an institution that precedes and makes its members, and that in which she is the community made by its members – the theological treatises practically ignored that one according to which a role of the laity could be *a priori* conceivable' (Congar, *Lay People*, 47).

[12] Ibid., 110.

through which alone the *plērōma* (fullness) of the church can be experienced.[13]

Shortly after Congar first wrote his 'study' Hendrik Kraemer penned *A Theology of the Laity*. This too has the bearing of a compensatory strategy and fails to provide what Congar sees as so necessary: a biblical understanding of the whole people of God (a total ecclesiology), one people loving and serving God in both the church and the world.[14]

So a theology of the whole people of God should neither be clerical nor anticlerical. What we should embrace is a-clericalism –

---

[13] St John Chrysostom uses the term *plērōma* for the relationship of the faithful with their bishop. The hierarchy and the people are like husband (head) and wife – a couple (Congar, *Lay People*, 284–5).

[14] Kraemer has several strengths: (1) He corrects Congar in noting that in Scripture women are not only among 'the saints' but are truly minister/servants; (2) he rightly insists that the traditional trilogy of 'prophet, priest and king' do not adequately sum up Christ's purpose and ministry – insisting that *diakonos* (servant) does this better; (3) he clearly notes the problem of layperson as object of ministry rather than subject; (3) he develops helpfully the idea that the church *is* ministry and *is* mission, not merely having these as elected and occasional activities; (4) he implicitly suggests that the traditional marks of the church (the Word of God preached and the administration of the sacraments) are not sufficient to identify the true church, if mission and ministry to the world is lacking.

But Kraemer has several deficiencies: (1) He roots his ecclesiology exclusively in the service of Christ so that the church is a Christocratic community, substantially neglecting the Father and the Spirit, a fully trinitarian foundation for peoplehood ('a total ecclesiology'); (2) in his passion to get the people of God engaged with the world Kraemer resolves the essence of the church as 'projection' through service/mission in the world, neglecting the central biblical truth that the purpose of the church is derivative of the purpose of all creation to worship and bring glory to God, something that is not restricted to worship services in the institutional church on Sunday mornings.

Others in recent years who have written theologies of the laity include M. Gibbs and T. Ralph Morton, *God's Frozen People: A Book for and about Ordinary People*; R. Mouw, *Called to Holy Worldliness*; R. Banks, *All the Business of Life: Bringing Theology Down to Earth*, 119–47, republished as *Redeeming the Routines*; G. Ogden, *The New Reformation*; W.J. Rademacher, *Lay Ministry: A Theological, Spiritual and Pastoral Handbook*.

one people without distinction except in function, a people that transcends clericalism.[15]

Third, a theology of the whole people of God must encompass not only the life of God's people gathered, the *ekklēsia*, but the church dispersed in the world, the *diaspora*, in marketplace, government, professional offices, schools and homes. Here I affirm Yves Congar's call for a theology of the laity that is not only a total ecclesiology but also an 'anthropology, and even a theology of creation in its relation to Christology'.[16] It must be a theology that encompasses earthly realities and expounds the menial, the trivial and the necessary: washing, cleaning, maintaining the fabric of this world, play, games, art, leisure, vocation, work, ministry, mission and grappling with the principalities and powers. It must help us understand and experience sexuality, family and friendship. It must show us the place of sabbath and sleep. It should help us live blessedly with the automobile, travel, the telephone, computer and e-mail.

Finally, a theology of the whole people of God must take the contemporary situation seriously. The work of theology is never finished. It is elliptical in nature with one focus on the timeless word of God and another on the context. So today we must consider the end of Christendom and the prevailing postmodern culture.[17] Ellen T. Charry puts this brilliantly:

Now that Christianity is disestablished and the general populace more familiar with secularism or modern expressions of paganism than with Christianity, theologians should undertake to demonstrate that the apostolic faith has resources for and presents the promise of a version of

---

[15] J.R.W. Stott, *One People: Helping Your Church Become a Caring Community*, 41. Stott suggests a fourth alternative – coexistence – and argues that this is fundamentally the view of Y. Congar and the Roman Church following Vatican II.

[16] Congar, *Lay People*, xvi–xvii.

[17] See S. Grenz, 'Star Trek and the Next Generation: Postmodernism and the Future of Evangelical Theology', *Crux* 30.1 (March 1994), 24–32. See also D.L. Guder (ed.), *The Missional Church: A Vision for the Sending of the Church in North America*.

human selfhood that is both dignified and honorable. In other words, knowing *and* loving God should again locate people in the world.[18]

So a theology *of* the whole people of God must expound the unity of the people of God, exploring the meaning of the dispersed life, as well as the gathered life, of the people of God. This book is essentially concerned with a theology of the *whole* people of God: a people without the distinction of laity and clergy (Part I), summoned and equipped by God (Part II), for the life of the world (Part III). But, at the same time, it will serve a second, subsidiary purpose: a theology *for* the whole people of God. Theology, as we shall see, is inherently practical.

2. 'For' the Whole People of God: Beyond Unapplied Theology

A theology *for* the so-called laity is normally considered as communicating to the 'ordinary' Christian, untrained in academic theology, how the great truths of the faith impinge on his or her life. Sometimes this amounts to a 'watered down' systematic or biblical theology – putting the cookie jar on a lower shelf. But at its best, a theology *for* the laity is what theology is all about: the continuous and dynamic task of translating the word of God into the situations where people live and work. Biblical theology is practical to its core and it is heretical to promote, as theological institutions have for decades, unapplied theology.[19]

---

[18] Ellen T. Charry, 'Academic Theology in Pastoral Perspective', *Theology Today* 50 (April 1993), 90 (90–104).

[19] It is widely acknowledged that practical theology is the Cinderella of the seminary. Don Browning says 'throughout its history [applied theology has been] the most beleaguered and despised of the academic disciplines'. He proposes that historical, systematic and practical theology (in the more specific sense of the term) should be seen as subspecialities of the larger and more encompassing discipline called *fundamental practical theology* (D. Browning, *A Fundamental Practical Theology: Descriptive and Strategic Proposals* [Minneapolis: Fortress Press, 1991], 3, 7–8).

To most ordinary people formal academic theology seems abstracted from life, a matter lamented by Lesslie Newbigin who notes how the work of scholars makes it appear to the ordinary Christian that no one untrained in their methods can really understand anything the Bible says. 'We are,' he says, 'in a situation analogous to the one about which the great Reformers complained...'[20] What would recovering a theology *for* the whole people of God mean?

First, there is more to the practicality of theology than the relevance of its theory. <u>Theology, it is often said, is practical because it is the basis of faith-filled action and life</u>. It helps people gain the truth of God to meet their fundamental need of knowing God and relating rightly to the world. But, in this view applied or practical theology is essentially the delivery mechanism – communicating to and persuading people of the truth and their need to act on it.[21] This is the old linear way of doing theology: first you get the theory and then, when you have banked the truth, you apply the truth, usually, in the case of theological education, after you graduate from a seminary. But what if the action is part of the truth? What if all action is theory-laden and all theory is action-laden? And what will we do with the words and works of Jesus, who, as Alister McGrath says, is the 'primary *explicandum* of Christian theology . . . something and someone who requires to be explained'.[22] Jesus said, 'If anyone chooses to do God's will, he will find out whether my teaching comes from God' (Jn. 7:17). The Hebrew word for 'know' is the same word as 'intercourse'. As Robert Banks says, to invite someone to take a course on a subject is to invite intercourse with the subject.[23]

Of course the term 'applied theology' does not appear in the Bible. But the idea of linking thought with action, of relating faith and life, of joining doctrine with ethical practice, the idea that

---

[20] L. Newbigin, *Foolishness to the Greeks: The Gospel and Western Culture* (Grand Rapids: Eerdmans, 1986), 142–3.

[21] This is the view expounded in K.S. Kantzer, 'Systematic Theology as practical Discipline', in Lewis and McGrath, *Doing Theology*, 24 (21–41).

[22] McGrath, *The Genesis of Doctrine*, 1.

[23] In a lecture at the Coalition for the Ministry in Daily Life, Chicago, 1993.

divine truth involves love of God and neighbour, is so fundamental that the only theology that is truly Christian is one that has been applied.

Many of Jesus' words emphasize that obedience is the organ of revelation.[24] In Luke 16:31 Jesus asserts that if people are not acting on the light they have (the law and the prophets) 'they will not be convinced even if someone rises from the dead', thereby suggesting that his own resurrection will have little evidential value to those who are not executing their knowledge. Francis of Assisi once said, 'Humankind has as much knowledge as it has executed.' That means that what you really know – in the fully biblical and Hebraic sense – is what you live. Lesslie Newbigin puts this aptly: 'Because the ultimate reality in the Bible is personal . . . we are brought into conformity with this reality not by a two-step process of theory and practice . . . but by a single action comprised of hearing, believing, and obeying.'[25]

Second, throughout the history of Christian theological activity the separation of theory and practice did not take place until fairly recently. Since the founding of the church up to the eleventh century, theology was not the *basis* of practical action but was itself essentially practical. In her recent work *By the Renewing of Your Minds*, Ellen Charry describes her experience of working through the writings of Paul, Athanasius, Basil of Caesarea, Augustine, Anselm, St Thomas, Dame Julian, and John Calvin. She confesses that the divisions in the modern theological curriculum made less and less sense.[26] She calls for a recovery of 'sapience' – engaging God in love so that knower and known are connected emotionally, something largely lost in modernity when theology became the intellectual justification of the faith.[27] So theology as practical theology, and theology as spiritual theology, were disconnected,

---

[24] See Jn. 15:10; 8:31, 8:39; 8:51.

[25] L. Newbigin, *Proper Confidence: Faith, Doubt and Certainty in Christian Discipleship* (Grand Rapids: Eerdmans, 1995), 38–9.

[26] E.T. Charry, *By the Renewing of the Minds: The Pastoral Function of Christian Doctrine* (New York: Oxford University Press, 1997), viii.

[27] Ibid., 4. E. Charry does a careful analysis of Augustine's distinction between *scientia* (rational judgement on the acts of God) and *sapientia* (delight in the grace of God) particularly in Books XII–XIV of *The City of God*. *Scientia* was knowing about God's grace and *sapientia* was loving

fragmented. Understanding the history of this fragmentation of theology is critical, though I can only deal with this in broad strokes.[28]

Theology in the primitive church was integrated with and arose within the life of local Christian communities or monasteries. It related to practical issues and questions arising from the liturgy and life of the people of God.[29] It was a practical *habitus* – the disposition of the soul, lived truth, *phronēsis*, practical wisdom.[30] It did not separate theory and practice. One did not study theology for three years, banking information about God and then, upon graduation, apply this in the field. Congar notes that 'up to the end of the twelfth century theology is essentially and, we may truthfully say, exclusively biblical'.[31]

It remained this way well into the eleventh century even when the universities emerged, these being at first attached to monasteries and cathedrals. But by the twelfth century, as universities became

---

[27] *(continued)* God as a result of that grace. It is the difference between the knowledge of faith and the wisdom of love, loving being the greater. She comments: 'Today our situation is vastly different. Professional theologians are trained in universities or university-oriented doctoral programs guided by secular scholarly norms. They often see their task as articulating the structure of the Trinity or of Christ or of the logic of salvation as set forth historically, or as clarifying the grounds for and mechanism of faith on the human side. Rarely are these tasks harnessed to the goal of *sapientia* as Augustine understood his own pastoral responsibilities.'

She also notes that Peter 'Lombard criticized Augustine for promoting love of God over rational speculation on eternal matters, the precise opposite of modern criticism of the Bishop of Hippo' ('Academic Theology in Pastoral Perspective', 90–96).

[28] I acknowledge my indebtedness for some of this reflection to R.L. Maddox, 'The Recovery of Theology as a Practical Discipline', *Theological Studies* 51 (1990), 650–72.

[29] Maddox notes that a good example of this was St Basil's *On the Holy Spirit*, trans. David Anderson (Crestwood, NY: St Vladimir's Seminary Press, 1980), which analysed the interrelations of the Godhead in dealing with the question of whether Christians should pray to the Holy Spirit.

[30] E. Farley, 'Interpreting Situations: An Inquiry into the Nature of Practical Theology', in L.S. Mudge and J.N. Poling, *Formation and Reflection: The Promise of Practical Theology* (Philadelphia: Fortress Press, 1987), 18 (1–26).

[31] Congar, *A History of Theology*, 51.

more independent, academics adopted an Aristotelian model of thinking which aimed at demonstrating rational knowledge and ordering it for its own sake. Theology became a speculative science, especially with Thomas Aquinas,[32] thus marking the end of the agreement that theology was in its essence practical, though not so in the Eastern Church until much later.[33]

As theology became increasingly reduced to logical, rational formulae, issues of application, matters relating to the real life of people in the world became relegated to a single section of the comprehensive textbooks, as they are today. Applied theology is seen as a subset of systematic theology, along with ethics, missiology and other subsidiaries. In spite of the protest of the Franciscans, practical theology became marginalized while academic theologians pursued a rigorous dispassionate analysis of the truth. Theology was pursued in the universities, while practical theologians, largely centred in the monasteries, pursued Christian spirituality, exemplified in Thomas à Kempis's *The Imitation of Christ*. We should see these works as theologies *for* the people of God and even theologies *by* so-called laypersons,[34] even though they are normally considered as classics of spiritual theology. The Reformation was itself a reaction to the

---

[32] E. Charry describes how Thomas Aquinas argued that sacred doctrine is a form of *sapientia* even though it is not infused with the Holy Spirit, thus becoming possible to make accurate theological judgements without having faith. 'Thus, Aquinas dissolved Augustine's distinction between knowledge and wisdom as the distinction between knowledge and love of God and set subsequent theology on a path that took academic theology to be objective knowledge independent of the knower's disposition, or relation to the material learned, or even confession of Christian faith. Here precisely is the gateway by which sapiential theology gave way to academic theology' ('Academic Theology in Pastoral Perspective', 97).

[33] See A. Schmemann, *Church, World, Mission* (Crestwood, NY: St Vladimir's Seminary Press, 1979), 129–44. In the nineteenth century Eastern Orthodoxy established contacts with Western university theology.

[34] I acknowledge my indebtedness to Dr John Toews's reflection on the emergence of 'lay' theologies in the early centuries of the church, including Origen's school, monastic learning (which was usually 'lay' though largely unconnected with life in the world), the works of Peter Waldo that were a protest theology, and the Franciscans, who reacted against the dominant Dominican schools.

medieval church and Luther once said, 'True theology is practical . . . speculative theology belongs to the devil in hell.'[35]

By the eighteenth century pastoral theology emerged as a separate discipline from moral theology and was concerned with poimenics – the activities of the pastor. By the nineteenth century the clerical captivity of applied theology was almost complete. So in most modern seminaries practical theology has frequently been reduced to how-to courses, often measured by effectiveness and success in church growth, irrespective of whether such actions are normatively Christian and without adequate theological reflection.[36] And 'pure' theology has been reduced to the God-talk of Job's miserable comforters: rational, objective and abstracted.

Can theology be healed? There are some encouraging signs of renewal.

Third, we are witnessing a recovery of theology as *phronēsis* – practical wisdom, especially with many contemporary theologians including the liberation theologies of Segundo, Gutiérrez and Bonino and the indigenous theologies of people groups throughout the world.[37] For all the problems of these theologies – matters carefully critiqued by evangelicals for their flawed hermeneutic and what Stott calls, in the case of liberation theology, their 'dangerous innocence'[38] – they have, nevertheless, recovered

---

[35] *Luther's Works*, ed. T.G. Tappert (55 vols.; St Louis: Concordia, 1955–86), LIV, 22, quoted in Maddox, *The Recovery of Theology*, 654.

[36] C. Dykstra, 'Reconceiving Practice', in B. Wheeler and E. Farley, *Shifting Boundaries: Contextual Approaches to the Structure of Theological Education* (Louisville, KY: Westminster/John Knox Press, 1991), 35–66 (55). See also E. Farley, *Theologia: The Fragmentation and Unity of Theological Education* (Philadelphia: Fortress Press, 1983); J.N. Poling and D.E. Miller, *Foundations for a Practical Theology of Ministry* (Nashville: Abingdon Pess, 1985); M.L. Stackhouse, *Apologia: Contextualization, Globalization and Mission in Theological Education* (Grand Rapids: Eerdmans, 1988).

[37] See S. Amirtham and J.S. Pobee (eds.), *Theology by the People*, 3–5. These authors note the emergence of black theology, African theology, feminist theology, Korean Minjung theology, these theologies emerging from small Bible study groups, base communities and indigenous churches.

[38] ' "Theology" A Multidimensional Discipline', 3–19.

something essential. This was expressed by Henri Nouwen when he visited Peru. He said, '*theologia* is not primarily a way of thinking, but a way of living. Liberation theologians do not think their way into a new way of living but live themselves into a new way of thinking.'[39]

So we are now in a better situation to define theology in a way that conserves its essentially practical nature. This was done brilliantly by the Puritan William Perkins, who said that theology is the 'science of living blessedly forever'.[40] Years before him Martin Luther confessed, with respect to the way that his trials, controversies and sufferings had made him a theologian of the cross: 'It is through undergoing the torment of the cross, death and hell that true theology and the knowledge of God come about . . . The cross alone is our theology' (*CRUX sola est nostra theologia*).[41] It is precisely this 'theology-wrung-out-of-life' which underlies Luther's celebrated statement concerning the qualifications of a true theologian: 'living, or rather dying and being damned make a theologian, not understanding, reading or speculating.'[42]

Only a curricular revolution can remedy this bifurcation so that we will not only think theologically but live theologically. If all the disciplines of the theological academy were consistently taught in the direction to which the Bible points – faith active in love – with theory and practice interdependently linked, rather than merely placed in a linear way, would there be any need for a separate discipline called applied theology?

What is theology *for* the whole people of God? Not merely 'watered-down' and popularized systematics but rather, as William Perkins said, 'the science of living blessedly forever'. It explains and

---

[39] H. Nouwen, *Gracias! A Latin American Journal* (Maryknoll, NY:Orbis Books, 1983), 159, quoted in Lewis and McGrath, *Doing Theology*, 13.

[40] *A Golden Chain* (1592), in I. Breward (ed.), *The Courtenay Library of Reformation Classics*. III. *The Work of William Perkins* (Appleford, UK: The Sutton Courtenay Press, 1970), 177 (169–259).

[41] *D.M. Luthers Werke. Kritische Gesamtausgabe* (Weimer, 1993–), V.176.32–3, quoted in A.E. McGrath, *Luther's Theology of the Cross: Martin Luther's Theological Breakthrough* (Oxford: Basil Blackwell, 1985), 152.

[42] Ibid., V.163.28–9, quoted in McGrath, *Luther's Theology*, 152.

empowers the life of the ordinary believer in the world. But it means even more: it sees acts of faith as not only applying but discovering doctrine. In 1949 Ian Fraser wrote a seminal article in the *Scottish Journal of Theology*, entitled 'Theology and Action'. In this, he says: 'Obedience to the living God must always surge beyond present theological containing walls. When Abraham went out, he knew not whither he went. The business of theology is not to circumscribe such obedient action. It is to feed on it . . . Theology draws its very life from worship, and in that life draws its nourishment from obedience.'[43]

It is precisely the question of obedience – lived truth – that gives rise to a third distinction: theology *by* the whole people of God.

3. 'By' the Whole People of God: Beyond Academic Theology

In July 1859 John Henry Newman published an article in *The Rambler*, entitled 'On Consulting the Faithful in Matters of Doctrine'. It was deemed scandalous![44] Would that the scandal could proliferate! Furthermore, William Hordern says, 'We simply do not have the alternatives of theology or no theology. Our alternatives are either to have a well thought out theology, a theology which has passed the test of critical thought, or to have a hodgepodge theology of unexamined concepts, prejudices and feelings.'[45] Let me explore this point by point.

First, everyday life positively bristles with the need for theological reflection. Existential questions faced by most people positively cry out for an earthy theology: Who am I? Where am I? What is the purpose of my life? To whom do I belong? Does my daily work have any meaning? What happens when I die? Does the planet have

---

[43] I.M. Fraser, 'Theology and Action', *Scottish Journal of Theology* 2.4 (December 1949), 414–5 (411–23).

[44] Quoted in Congar, *Lay People*, 285.

[45] W. Hordern, *A Layman's Guide to Protestant Theology* (New York: Macmillan, rev. edn, 1975), xvii, quoted in Lewis and McGrath, *Doing Theology*, 29.

a future? The theological task is not only to exegete Scripture but to exegete life, and to do these together.[46]

Alister McGrath offers a searing critique of academic theology on the basis of the fact that God came down to earth in Jesus Christ:

> Theology must come down to earth, to serve the church and its mission to the world – and if it will not come down to earth, it must be *brought* down to earth by so marginalizing academic theology within the life of the church that it ceases to have any relevance to that church, in order that a theology orientated toward the pastoral and missiological needs of the church may develop in its wake.[47]

Second, many significant theologians through the history of the church have been non-clerical, non-professional theologians: Tertullian, Clement of Alexandria, Origen; and in the Eastern Church, Socrates and Sozomen.[48] The Reformation was essentially a lay movement. John Calvin in one of his letters said, 'I have never been anything else than an ordinary layman (*laicus*) as people call it.'[49] Through an 'accident in history', namely the overrunning of the Roman Empire in the West by the barbarians and the saving of religious culture by monks and priests, the Western Church reserved theological inquiry for the clergy. In the Eastern Church, however, there was less of a clerical monopoly so that even until modern times important chairs of theology are held by laymen though sadly not by laywomen.[50]

Commenting on community theologizing in the Indian summer of the ancient world, William Frend notes that theology was the ruling passion of the Christian provincial. In Constantinople, the capital of the Empire, points of doctrine were argued in the bazaars, marketplaces and public baths, not by theologians but by

---

[46] See Patricia O'Connell Killen and John de Beer, *The Art of Theological Reflection* (New York: Crossroad, 1995).

[47] Alister McGrath, *The Enigma of the Cross* (London: Hodder & Stoughton, 1987), 174, quoted in Lewis and McGrath, *Doing Theology*, 14.

[48] Congar, *Lay People*, 308.

[49] Kraemer, *A Theology of the Laity*, 25.

[50] Congar, *Lay People*, 309.

educated ordinary Christians. Gregory of Nazianzus states in 379, 'If in this city you ask anyone for change, he will discuss with you whether the Son is begotten or unbegotten.'[51] (In the twentieth century the layman C.S. Lewis is conspicuous for his theologizing.)

There is risk in this, as Alister McGrath shows in his study *The Genesis of Doctrine*. While the religious life of the monasteries birthed the concept of Mariology, popular piety gave rise to the dogma of the assumption of Mary.[52] Theology has been done by thoughtful and educated Christians who are not part of either clergy or academy.

Third, theology is being done today by ordinary people. Like the character in Molière's play who was surprised to learn that he was speaking prose all the time, the serious but non-clergy Christian may be surprised to find he or she is doing theology much of the time.[53] This 'people' theology proliferates in films and books, as well as private conversations: vernacular theology, spur-of-the-moment theology, off-the-cuff theology and indigenous theology.

For example, my young granddaughter was told by her 'atheist' friend that there is no God and no heaven. 'Well', she said, 'if there's no heaven, then what's the point of dying?' – pure theology!

In the film *A Man for All Seasons* Thomas More says to his daughter, 'When a man takes an oath, he's holding his own self in his own hands. Like water. And if he opens his fingers *then* – he needn't hope to find himself again.' More is reflecting on the nature of the human person, on words and vows.

This is theology being done 'from the bottom up'. Much of the theology being done is inadequate but it is being done! Indigenous theology, on-the-spur-of-the-moment theology, while often

---

[51] W.H.C. Frend, 'The Church of the Roman Empire', in Stephen Charles Neill and Hans-Ruedi Weber, *The Layman in Christian History: A Project of the Department on the Laity of the World Council of Churches*, 70 (57–87).

[52] McGrath, *The Genesis of Doctrine*, 11.

[53] M. Gibbs and T.R. Morton, *God's Lively People*, 41. See also 'A People's Theology', in R. Banks, *All the Business of Life* (Sutherland, Australia: Albatross Books, 1987), 119–47.

reactionary, often reveals some unexplored dimensions of Christian truth.[54]

Fourth, this theology from below is not simply a curiosity but is fundamental to the whole theological endeavour. It is remarkable that in his prolegomena Karl Barth affirms that through the centuries what he calls 'irregular dogmatics' has been the rule – theology done as a free discussion of the problems of proclamation. 'Regular dogmatics' has been the exception. He includes Athanasius and Luther in the former, in contrast to Melanchthon and Calvin in the latter. Barth counsels against the disparagement of the one by the other. Indeed he concedes that regular dogmatics – in the theological school and with a concern for completeness and rational consistency – 'has always had its origin in irregular dogmatics, and could never have existed without its stimulus and cooperation'.[55]

In contrast, the 'trickle down' process of theological instruction in the academy and pulpit gives 'predigested' truth without the privilege of dialogue and participational learning. Ray Anderson touches a nerve when he says, 'Intimidated by the claims of biblical scholars and theologians whose own professional careers are evaluated and affirmed by other scholars, the church acquiesces by surrendering its role in determining its own theological agenda.'[56]

Fifth, to recover a theology by the whole people of God the theological task must be relocated. The academy must work with the congregation, the home, and the marketplace. For example, in the case of the congregation, our understanding of what constitutes theological education begins to change when a congregation

---

[54] The consideration of an in-built, precognitive response to challenges is explored in several secular books: A. Heller, *Everyday Life* (London: Routledge & Kegan Paul, 1984); E.S. Tauber and M.R. Green, *Prelogical Experience* (New York: Basic Books, 1959); D.A. Schon, *The Reflective Practitioner: How Professionals Think in Action* (New York: Basic Books, 1983); and W.L. Sullivan, *Work and Integrity: The Crisis and Promise of Professionalism in America* (San Francisco: HarperCollins, 1995), 172–9.

[55] Karl Barth, *Church Dogmatics*, trans. G.W. Bromiley (4 vols; Edinburgh: T. & T. Clark, 1956–77), I.1.278.

[56] R.S. Anderson, *The Praxis of Pentecost: Revisioning the Church's Life and Mission*, 194.

redefines its primary arena of ministry as the daily life of its members rather than in-house service.[57] By definition a marketplace is a place where things – goods, services, information – are exchanged. As part of my own learning I spend two weeks a year in the marketplace. One course required in the Master of Divinity programme at Regent College places every student for twenty hours alongside an ordinary Christian in the workplace, listening to the questions, praying, and trying to discover how the church can equip people for full-time ministry in the world.[58]

Sixth, to recover a people theology professional theologians have a crucial role. They too are part of the community contributing their research and historical perspective. The temptation to distort the whole gospel is always present and professional theologians can bring the full scope of God's redemptive purpose to bear on new movements. This must be theology done by the whole people of God, not merely one part. John Macquarrie calls this 'co-theologizing'. In one sense it may be improper to call this the democratizing of theology because it is not about *kratos* (power), nor about rights, nor even about redressing an imbalance, but rather recovering a fellowship of doing theology together.[59] Could we call

---

[57] J.C. Hough and B.G. Wheeler, *Beyond Clericalism: The Congregation as a Focus for Theological Education* (Atlanta: Scholars Press, 1988). A complete issue of a journal was dedicated to exploring the reorientation of seminary education to lay people and developing a philosophy of lay theological education in the church. Especially helpful is the article by J.P. Dever, 'As the Church Moves into the Twenty-First Century: Some Extended Observations', *Review and Expositor: A Quarterly Baptist Theological Journal* 93.1 (winter 1996), 11–25.

[58] There are other contexts for theological reflection: lay institutes, theological colleges, parachurch movements and informed networks.

[59] Robert Banks's arguments for academic theologians joining with ordinary people are as follows: (1) ordinary Christians can best identify their everyday concerns; (2) ordinary Christians already have some elements of an everyday theology; (3) a workable theology of everyday life requires practical testing by ordinary Christians. He notes how the great theologians Augustine, Luther and Calvin, and the Puritans, had a practical cast in their theology partly because it was wrung out of suffering, service and engaging problems. See Banks, *All the Business of Life*, 119–31.

this demo-theologizing or koino-theologizing? We have much to learn about this from believers in the developing world.[60]

In contrast to the dichotomizing of theology and practice in the theological academy today, the New Testament presupposes a community in which every person is a theologian of application, trying to make sense out of his or her life in order to live for the praise of God's glory: theology of, for and by the whole people of God.

This volume builds on and is indebted to previously mentioned works. But it also draws on the rich experience and often perceptive reflections of faculty colleagues, friends and students at Regent College.[61] This will be apparent in many references and notes at the bottom of each page. It is a people project. Some of this theological work has been literally hammered out during my carpentry and business years, as well as complemented and challenged by indigenous theologies of churches in the developing world among whom my wife and I serve each year. It is only 'together with all the saints' (Eph. 3:18) that we can know how wide, long, high and deep is the love of Christ. And love, as we shall see, is the essence of the ministry and mission of the people of God – no more and no less. Theology is the science of living the life of love blessedly forever.

In the chapters following we will develop a biblical description of the people of God, a people without laity or clergy. Then we explore how this people is summoned and equipped by God in vocation, work and ministry. Finally, we consider what it means for

---

[60] W.A. Dyrness, *Learning about Theology from the Third World* (Grand Rapids: Zondervan, 1990); *Invitation to Cross-Cultural Theology: Case Studies in Vernacular Theologies* (Grand Rapids: Zondervan, 1992); *Emerging Voices in Global Christian Theology* (Grand Rapids: Zondervan, 1994). See also R. Paul Stevens, 'Marketing the Faith: A Reflection on the Importing and Exporting of Western Theological Education', *Crux* 28.2 (June 1992), 6–17.

[61] I am particularly grateful for the contributions (and in some cases manuscript critique) of Don Anderson, Robert Banks, Klaus Bockmuehl, Stephen Daly, David Falk, Gordon Fee, Don Flow, David Gaskell, Stan Grenz, Stella Griffin, Poul Guttesen, James Houston, James Packer, Charles Ringma, Ian Stackhouse, David Taylor, and Siew Li Wong.

this people to be given for the life of the world as prophets, priests and kings, as a missionary people grappling with the powers.

I pray that these thoughts will help pastors to equip the saints (Eph. 4:11–12); college professors who need a textbook that engages ordinary Christians with the high calling of Christ; and thoughtful followers of Christ who want to make sense of their lives as they try to balance what feels like three full-time jobs: church ministry, daily work and family. The book can be used as a basis of study in small groups or classes using the guide at the end of each chapter. As will become immediately apparent, this book is my story.

For further study/discussion

1. Identify the theology expressed in each of the following:

   - a secular film
   - a contemporary worship song (we sing our real theology)
   - a traditional hymn (for example, one of Wesley's)
   - a novel you have read
   - a piece of contemporary art (for example, one by van Gogh)

2. Write down the questions you bring to this study in the three areas explored in this chapter:

   - a theology of the laity
   - a theology for the laity
   - a theology by the laity

3. Meditate on the haunting words of Jesus at the end of the Sermon on the Mount where he uses the word for practical wisdom, *phronēsis*:

   Not everyone who says to me, 'Lord, Lord,' will enter the kingdom of heaven, but only he who does the will of my Father who is in heaven. Many will say to me on that day, 'Lord, Lord, did we not prophesy in your name, and in your name drive out demons and perform many miracles?' Then I will tell them plainly, 'I never knew you.'

   Therefore everyone who hears these words of mine and puts them into practice is like a wise man who built his house on the rock. The rains came down, the streams rose, and the winds blew and beat against that house; yet it did not fall, because it had its foundation on the rock (Mt. 7:21–5).

Chapter 2

Reinventing Laity and Clergy

Theology is not a private reserve of theologians. It is not a private affair for professors . . . Nor is it a private affair for pastors . . . Theology is a matter for the church. It does not get on well without professors and pastors. But its problem, the purity of the church's service, is put to the whole church. The term 'laity' is one of the worst in the vocabulary of religion and ought to be banished from Christian conversation.

Karl Barth[1]

In the spring of 1975 I became a layperson. I was trained in a seminary, ordained and served with my wife in various churches and parachurch movements. But that spring I resigned from the leadership of a wonderful church, put on my nail belt and began working as a carpenter, doing business while planting a church among street people in the city of Vancouver. Understandably my pastor colleagues, to say nothing of the congregation, were confused.

1. A People without 'Laity'

What a slippery term we have to define. Depending on the specific church context 'lay' is defined by *function* (does not administer the Word and sacraments), by *status* (does not have a 'Rev.'), by *location* (serves primarily in the world), by *education* (is not theologically

---

[1] *Theologische Fragen und Antworten* (1957), 175, 183–4, quoted in R.J. Erler and R. Marquard (eds.), trans. G.W. Bromiley, *A Karl Barth Reader* (Grand Rapids: Eerdmans, 1986), 8–9.

trained), by *remuneration* (is not full-time and paid), and by *lifestyle* (is not religious but occupied with secular life) – usually in terms of negatives! Generally laypersons are considered to be assistants to the pastor rather than the other way around. For example, Georgia Harkness cites a survey taken among twelve thousand members of the Methodist denomination in the United States in which she offered four options:

Laypersons are
i.   members of the people of God called to a total ministry of witness and service in the world;
ii. those who are ministered to by the clergy who are the true church;
iii. people in part-time Christian service;
iv. non-ordained Christians whose function is to help the clergy do the work of the church.

She notes that 59.9 per cent marked the fourth option.[2]

With scientific precision the Catholic theologian Karl Rahner defines laypersons both negatively and positively. Laypersons are understood negatively as (1) those who are not in the hierarchy of the church, without proper hierarchical powers either legal or liturgical – thus eliminating the few so-called lay popes from the category; and (2) as people distinguished from those in the religious life, monks and nuns who have taken the vows of the Evangelical Counsels. Positively, Rahner defines laypersons as (1) those who remain in the world and have specific tasks in society that determine their 'status' in the church; and (2) (positively again) laypersons in the church are called, adopted, commissioned and blessed persons fully functioning as co-operators of the grace of God in and through the church's life because of their baptism and confirmation.[3]

Protestants fare little better in spite of the rich heritage of the Reformation and its clarion call to the 'priesthood of all believers'. In place of the twofold alternatives to laity in the Catholic communion, based on function (the priesthood) and life (the religious

---

[2] G. Harkness, *The Church and Its Laity*, 15–16.
[3] Karl Rahner, *Theological Investigations*. II. *Man in the Church*, trans. Karl-H. Kruger (22 vols.; New York: Crossroad, 1961–91), 319–30.

– monks and nuns), Protestants define 'lay' as non-ordained, unpaid and untrained. Even Morton and Gibbs's layman type B, who functions as a voluntary clergy person (the 'ideal' church member who lives for and in the church), is still a layperson.[4] The parachurch movements that are proliferating everywhere are, in one sense, an amazing spread of Kingdom ministry by ordinary Christians but one can hardly claim that parachurch staff are laity since they are professional religionists, remunerated for their service and, to a large extent, theologically trained, even though they usually lack formal ordination.[5]

So Protestants have their own hierarchies: the cross-cultural missionary at the top, followed by parish priests and pastors, then youth workers and parachurch ministers (including seminary professors). Below the clergy–lay divide (and in descending order of religious value) are people-helping professionals (e.g. teachers, doctors and nurses), homemakers, tradespeople, business people, politicians and marginally valuable occupations (such as law and stockbrokering). Should such distinctions be eliminated?

When you enter the church today there are two 'peoples' – laity, who receive the ministry, and 'clergy' who give it. But when we enter the world of the New Testament we find only one people, the true *laos* of God, with leaders among the people.

New Testament authors rejected two disparaging 'laity' words available to describe the people of God under the newly reconstituted covenant. The first was the Greek word *laikos*, 'belonging to

---

[4] Gibbs and Morton, *God's Lively People*, 20.

[5] Ironically, recent articles from the World Council of Churches lament not only the loss of the Department of the Laity in 1971 but real laypersons in the mainline churches as traditional forms of congregational life disintegrate under the pressure of postmodernity. In contrast to this Konrad Raiser notes, 'The increasing number of evangelical, fundamentalist and charismatic groups and new religious movements are largely supported by "lay people" in the classical sense, but the Christian base communities and the movements critical of society or of the churches which have sprung up around the churches – not least the women's movement – are also essentially the result of lay initiatives' ('Laity in the Ecumenical Movement: Redefining the Profile', *Ecumenical Review* 45.4 [October 1993], 378 [375–83]).

CONTEMPORARY CHURCH-VIEW

NEW TESTAMENT CHURCH-VIEW[6]

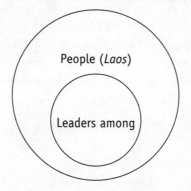

the common people'.[7] It is not used at all in the New Testament. Clement of Rome at the end of the first century was the first to use it for Christians. He used 'layman' (*laikos*) in his letter to the Corinthians to describe the place of laity in worship when the presbyters were being deprived of their functions.[8] Alexandre Faivre notes both the

---

[6] I owe this drawing to Gordon Fee, '*Laos* and Leadership Under the New Covenant,' in *Crux*, Vol XXV, No 4 (December 1989): 3–13. Reproduced with permission.

[7] I regret the unfortunate mistake in *Liberating the Laity*, p. 21, where this word is used to describe the whole people of God.

[8] 'Thus all things are to be done religiously, acceptable to His good pleasure, dependent on His will. Those, therefore, that make their offerings at the prescribed times are acceptable and blessed; for, since they comply with the ordinances of the Master, they do not sin. Special functions are assigned to the high priest; a special office is imposed upon the priests; and special ministrations fall to the Levites. The layman is bound by the rules

military comparison (commander-in-chief) and the allusion to the Old Testament cultic hierarchy,[9] two obvious sources of the clergy–lay distinction that would be later institutionalized in the church. This first use of 'layman' by a Christian passed largely unnoticed and it was not until much later, with Clement of Alexandria and Tertullian that the term emerged again.[10] Remarkably Tertullian affirmed that 'where there are three gathered together, even though they are laypersons, there is the church'.[11] But in responding to heresy Tertullian noted that the heretics 'at one time put *novices* in office; at another time, men who are bound to some secular employment . . . For even on laymen do they impose the functions of priesthood.'[12]

---

[8] *(continued)* laid down for the laity. Each of us, brethren, must *in his own place* [his emphasis] endeavour to please God with a good conscience, reverently taking care not to deviate from the established rule of service' (Clement of Rome [1 Clement 40:5]).

Remarkably the only occasion where 'lay people' is used in the NIV (2 Chron. 35:5,7) refers to this exact situation: the people of God that were not of the priestly tribe of Levi. In fact this English translation skews the meaning of the original pejoratively and should be translated 'the rest of the people'.

[9] Faivre, *The Emergence of the Laity*, 15–24.

[10] In 'An Exhortation to Chastity', in the context of affirming a monogamous priesthood, Tertullian writes: 'Well, then, you will say, it follows that all whom the Apostle does not mention in this law are free. It would be folly to imagine that lay people may do what priests may not. For are not we lay people also priests? It is written: *He hath made us also a kingdom, and priests to God and His father.* It is ecclesiastical authority which distinguishes clergy and laity, this and the dignity which sets a man apart by reason of membership in the hierarchy. Hence, where there is no such hierarchy, you yourself offer sacrifice, you baptize, and you are your own priests. Obviously, where there are three gathered together, even though they are laypersons, there is the church' (*The Ante-Nicene Fathers* (10 vols.; Grand Rapids: Eerdmans, 1974–76), IV.7.54 (50–58).

[11] Ibid., 53. Tertullian also maintained that in the absence of a bishop, presbyter or deacon, a layperson could administer baptism: 'even laymen [and excluding women] have the right; for what is equally received can be equally given. Unless bishops, or priests, or deacons, be on the spot, *other* disciples are called *i.e. to the work*' (*On the Power of Conferring Baptism* III.17.677) 669–76.

[12] *On Prescriptions Against Heretics*, III.41.263(243–65).

The term does not appear either in the writings of Justin Martyr (AD 150), for whom the title 'Christian' was sufficient,[13] or in those of Irenaeus (AD 180).[14]

The second word in the Greek language for 'laity' is *idiōtēs*, root of the English word 'idiot'. It means 'layperson in contrast to an expert or specialist'. This word is never used by an inspired apostle to describe Christians! In Acts 4:13 members of the Jewish Sanhedrin expressed their amazement at the powerful preaching of these 'unschooled, ordinary men' (in this case the *idiōtai* were Peter and John). The word is also used in 1 Corinthians 14:23 to describe the person from outside the church who comes into a Christian meeting totally uninitiated and cannot understand what is going on. Here *idiōtēs* refers to people who are not yet Christians. So neither of the two available negative words – *laikos* and *idiōtēs* – is used to describe ordinary Christians. Instead two other words are employed.

The laos of God

The Greek word *laos* originally meant 'the crowd' and 'the people as a nation'. It was eventually employed in the Greek translation of the Old Testament (LXX) as the universal designation for 'the people of God' translating the Hebrew *'am*. In Acts 15:14 James at the apostolic council makes the deliberate connection of the Old Testament national Israel with the newly reconstituted people of God in Christ: 'Simon has described for us how God at first showed his concern by taking from the Gentiles a people [*laon*] for himself.'[15] Strathmann notes, 'This was for Jewish ears an astounding and even a revolutionary saying, though the way had been prepared for it in Old Testament prophecy.'[16] This word may be properly translated 'laity' but to do so we would need to reinvent the word. It does not

---

[13] Faivre, *The Emergence of the Laity*, 26–35.

[14] Ibid., 35–40.

[15] Acts 15:14; 18:10; Rom. 9:25ff.; 2 Cor. 6:16; Tit. 2:14; Heb. 4:9; 8:10; 13:12; 1 Pet. 2:9ff.; Rev. 18:4; 21:3.

[16] Strathmann, '*laos*', in G. Kittel and G. Friedrich (eds.), *Theological Dictionary of the New Testament*, trans. and ed. G.W. Bromiley (10 vols.; Grand Rapids: Eerdmans, 1964–76), IV, 29–57.

mean 'untrained' or 'ordinary' but 'the people of God' – a truly
extraordinary people.[17]

While we observe in the church today two classes of people
separated by education, ordination[18] and intonation, we discover in
the New Testament one ministering people with leaders, also
members of the *laos*, serving them to equip the people for the work
of the ministry (Eph. 4:11–12).[19] The people of God (*laos*) is one
people composed (miraculously) of Jews and Gentiles, men and
women, rich and poor, bond and free – all being together the
chosen inheritance of God. Further, as Gordon Fee notes, there is
a remarkable continuity with the people of God under the Old
Covenant with respect to peoplehood, but a remarkable discontinuity with the Old Testament *with regard to leadership*.[20] Simply put,
there were clergypersons under the Old Covenant but, under the
New, these functions are abolished, or rather universalized in
the *laos* of God. The reason has to do with the lordship and
mediatorship of Christ and the gift of the Holy Spirit. This is
apparent from the New Testament use of the word 'clergy'.

Should distinctions be eliminated? Yes. Can they be? This is a
much harder question because of entrenched clericalism.

---

[17] Note that *laos tou theou* is the universal term in the New Testament for
the church. *Laos* used without a complement (as in Mt. 1:21) refers
to the nation and sometimes simply a crowd (Acts 6:12), according to
Ceslas Spicq, OP, '*laos*', in *Theological Lexicon of the New Testament* trans.
and ed. by J.D. Ernest (3 vols.; Peabody: Hendrickson, 1994), II.371–4.

[18] Ordination as a rite or ceremony that conferred power or office simply did not exist in the New Testament. See M. Warkentin, *Ordination:
A Biblical, Historical View*, 172. Luther said: 'Of this sacrament the church
of Christ knows nothing; it is an invention of the church and of the
pope' (*Luther's Works*, ed. Theodore G. Tappert [55 vols.; Philadelphia:
Fortress Press, 1955–86], XXXVI.106). For a theological/philosophical
defence of ordination see Thomas F. Torrance, 'The Ministry', in R.S.
Anderson (ed.), *Theological Foundations for Ministry*, 405–29. I will
consider ordination in Chapter 6.

[19] See Fee, '*Laos* and Leadership', 3–13. Some of the following thoughts
are developed in this fine article.

[20] Ibid, 6.

2. A People without 'Clergy'

In common speech 'clergy' is a term used to describe a religious official, a member of a religious order, or a pastoral leader of a church or denomination. Four dimensions seem to be implicit in the contemporary concept of clergy: (1) the *vicarious* function – service is rendered representatively not only on behalf of, but instead of the people; (2) the *ontological* difference usually associated with absolute ordination – namely that a person *becomes* a priest or religious in virtue of ordination and not in virtue of character, and therefore a cleric cannot resign from ministry; (3) the *sacramental* function whereby since Cyprian (AD 200–258) the term *sacerdos* is used routinely for the bishop 'leaning heavily on the image of the priesthood in the Hebrew Scriptures';[21] and (4) the *professional* status which implies a quasi-unique function with social significance, specialized functions which are interchangeable and with the assumption that a well-trained professional can do it better than an amateur or volunteer.[22] One unacceptable definition of clergy is that these are leaders who earn their living by the gospel or who engage in religious service for remuneration.[23] But we look in vain in the New Testament for such distinctions.

— apostles

A church full of clergy

Remarkably the Greek word *klēros*, the word from which our English 'clergy' is derived, is used to describe aspects of being the whole people of God. The term originally means a 'lot', 'share', or 'portion assigned to someone', and was used in the Old Testament for the inheritance in the promised land.[24] This term gets transferred to the New Testament from the Greek translation of the Old Testament. Peter and John use this word when they tell Simon Magus he

---

[21] W.J. Rademacher, *Lay Ministry*, 56.

[22] See R. Paul Stevens, 'Professions/Professionalism', in Robert Banks and R. Paul Stevens, *The Complete Book of Everyday Christianity*, 805–9.

[23] See R. Paul Stevens, 'Financial Support', in Banks and Stevens, *The Complete Book*, 419–22.

[24] See W. Foerster, '*klēros*' in Kittel and Friedrich, *Theological Dictionary of the New Testament*, III, 763 (758–64).

has 'no part or share [klēros] in this ministry, because your heart is not right before God' (Acts 8:21; cf. Deut. 12:12). But here is the new thing in Christ. The Old Testament 'inheritance' is now shared by all believers. Jesus says to Saul/Paul, 'I am sending you to [the Gentiles] to open their eyes and turn them from darkness to light, and from the power of Satan to God, so that they may receive forgiveness of sins and a *place* [klēron] among those who are sanctified by faith in me' (emphasis mine, Acts 26:17–18; cf. Eph. 1:11; Gal. 3:29; Col. 1:12).

In no situation do the apostles use this term to describe appointment to an ecclesiastical office, as was the case much later.[25] With the exception of Ignatius of Antioch (who used *klēros* to describe the martyr) the term was not used for 'clergy' until the third century. Simultaneously the term 'laity' reappears. As Alexandre Faivre shows, laypersons can only exist when they have an opposite against which they can define themselves and, until the second century, there simply was no such opposite![26]

The church in the New Testament has no 'laypersons' in the usual sense of that word, and is full of 'clergy' in the true sense of that word. Alexandre Faivre says, 'The inheritance was a joint inheritance, shared equally between all the heirs.'[27] The New Testament opens up a world of universal giftedness, universal empowerment of the people of God through the gift of the Holy Spirit, universal ministry, and the universal experience of the call of God by all the people of God.

Old Testament sources

In contrast, especially the first five books of the Old Testament immerse us in a world in which the temple and the priest are central,

---

[25] Dean Fleming notes that with the case of Judas in Acts 1:17 (who was allotted his share [klēros] in the apostolic ministry) the emphasis is on Judas's defection and replacement as the fulfilment of God's plan foretold in Scripture, rather than his appointment to and defection from an ecclesiastical office. See Dean Fleming, 'The Clergy/Laity Dichotomy: A New Testament Exegetical and Theological Analysis', *Asia Journal of Theology* 8.2 (October 1994), 232–50.

[26] Faivre, *The Emergence of the Laity*, 23.

[27] Ibid., 7–8.

as witnessed by the prominence of the book of Leviticus. There is continuity between the testaments in peoplehood but radical discontinuity in leadership as shown in this chart.

Old Covenant Ministry	**New Covenant Ministry**
limited Word ministry (Jer. 31:34)	unlimited Word ministry (Acts 2:18)
externally motivated ministry ('on tablets of stone'; 2 Cor. 3:3)	internally motivated ministry ('on . . . human hearts'; 2 Cor. 3:3)
temporary and fading (inspiration; 2 Cor. 3:13)	permanent and continuous (transformation; 2 Cor. 3:18)
priestly caste and tribe (Ex. 28:1)	unlimited priesthood (1 Pet. 2:9–11)
sacerdotal mediation of priests (Ex. 30)	total/life priesthood (Rom. 12:1–2)
occasional and exceptional spiritual giftedness (Ex. 31:3)	unlimited spiritual giftedness (1 Cor. 12:7; Eph. 4:7)
unique and special 'calls' to service (1 Sam. 3)	unlimited call to service and ministry (Eph. 4:1)
limited ordination (Lev. 8,21)	universal 'ordination' to the ministry by baptism (1 Cor. 12:13)
occasional gift of wisdom – the wise person (1 Kgs. 3:16–28)	wisdom available to all (Jas. 1:5)
special representatives of the rule of God in judges, prophets, priests and kings (Judg. 3:9–10)	unlimited experience of the power, sovereignty and rule of Christ (the Kingdom of God) by all believers (Mk.1:15; Eph. 1:19–22)
cultural separation (circumcision, diet, etc.; Deut. 17:14–20; 1 Kgs. 11:1–6)	apostolic ambassadors ('all things to all men'; 1 Cor. 9:22; 2 Cor. 5:20)
national focus (Jews and proselytes; Zech. 8:20)	world mission (disciples of, to and from all nations; Mt. 28:18–20)

Several movements within Old Testament history, all presented negatively by Scripture, appear to condemn acts of self-liberation by the laity.[28] There are, however, other strands of revelation that

---

[28] Korah's rebellion (Num. 16:1–50), Nadab and Abihu's unauthorized sacrificial ministry (Lev. 10:1–3), Miriam and Aaron's revolt against Moses' leadership (Num. 12:1–15), Saul's hasty sacrifice without waiting for Samuel (1 Sam. 13:2–15), and King Uzziah's improper sacrifice in the temple (2 Chron. 26:16–21). Other similar incidents are found but these are representative of what appears to be a clerical notion of leadership and priesthood in the Old Testament.

suggest something quite different: non-clerical ministry within the Old Testament.

(1) In Exodus 19:6 God charges the whole people to become a 'kingdom of priests'. At least one Jewish scholar has asked whether the installation of Aaron and his sons as priests (Ex. 28) was perhaps an accommodation to the proven need of the people for a visible sanctuary and therefore a priesthood, since it comes after the golden calf incident. That appears to be the case with the monarchy (Judg. 8:23; 1 Sam. 8:6–9). Reuven Kimelman argues that the reality of being away from the Temple during the exile and the ultimate fall of Jerusalem provided the Jewish community with the social and theological opportunity to 'appropriate the original divine charge to become a kingdom of priests'.[29] The rabbis did not attempt to make the Jewish community into a democracy (thereby levelling the clergy) but rather to raise all the people to become priests and rabbis together – the clericalization of the laity. Perhaps, argues Kimelman, the priesthood 'resulted from the failure of the people to respond adequately to God's revelation'.[30] In any event the idea of a priest-people predated the formation of a priesthood *within* the priest-people. This Jewish vision of every member ministry was still something less than the vision of the New Testament.

(2) Moses prays that 'all the Lord's people were prophets and that the Lord would put his Spirit on them', when Joshua complains that two 'unordained' men, Eldad and Medad, are prophesying in the camp (Num. 11:26–30). We can reverently join Moses in his prayer though this is gratuitous in the light of Pentecost. The only Old Testament person of whom it is definitively stated that he was 'filled with the Spirit of God' is a craftsman – Bezalel (Ex. 31:1–5). Add to this the fact that the Nazirite vow (Num. 6:1ff.) represented one opportunity under the Old Covenant for ordinary people to dedicate themselves to live fully for God.

(3) Many of Israel's leaders *emerged* from the people: David was a shepherd chosen to become king (1 Sam. 16:1–13); Nehemiah was a pagan king's cupbearer (Neh. 1:1–2:9); Esther was a poor

---

[29] R. Kimelman, 'Judaism and Lay Ministry', *NICM Journal* 5.2 (spring 1980), 7–8.
[30] Ibid., 41.

orphaned girl who became a queen in exile; Daniel was a young man chosen for special education in the court of Nebuchadnezzar (Dan. 1). Many of Israel's prophets were 'laypersons' and not associated with sacerdotal ministry: Amos, a dresser of fig trees (Amos 7:10–15); Ezekiel, a former priest who became a 'lay' prophet in exile.

(4) Much of what we call 'ministry' occurred in the normal contexts of life: Jacob in his relationship with his family (Gen. 33:4–11); Hosea in his marriage to Gomer; Daniel through his service in a foreign court; Joseph while in prison and in Pharaoh's court in Egypt; Job in praying for his family (Job 1:5) and his friends (42:10); the Preacher in his reflection and contemplation on his life work (Ecc. 2:17–23).

(5) Joel envisions the day when God will pour his Spirit on all flesh (humankind), so that all the people of God will prophesy and bear the Word of God (Joel 2:28–32; cf. Acts 2:17–18). Finally, Isaiah envisions the day when, after the exile, all the people will again be called 'priests of the Lord' and 'ministers of our God' (Is. 61:6). Speaking to this Reuven Kimelman suggests 'the experience of the exile enables the community to perceive the contingent nature of the priesthood. While not outrightly negating it, they embark on a path leading to its eventual obsolescence.'[31]

Is there universal (people) ministry in the Old Testament? Yes. The ʿam (people of God) is one ministering people. The ʿam never signified mere spectators. It was ordinary people who killed the sacrificial animal and cut it in pieces (Lev. 1–7). The directions for worship in the Pentateuch are universal: they apply to the whole people and not merely the religious elite. Even children and aliens in the land are expected to participate in the ceremonial life of the nation (Num. 9:14).[32] Covenant life embraced not merely cultic activity but the whole of life from birth to death, permitting no dichotomy of sacred and secular. This truth, said the prophets, would one day become apparent: 'On that day HOLY TO THE LORD will be inscribed on the bells of the horses, and the cooking

---

[31] Ibid., 42.

[32] D.W. Baker, 'Piety in the Pentateuch', in J.I. Packer and L. Wilkinson (eds.), *Alive to God: Studies in Spirituality* (Downers Grove: InterVarsity Press, 1992), 36 (34–40).

pots in the Lord's house will be like the sacred bowls in front of the altar. Every pot in Jerusalem and Judah will be holy to the Lord Almighty . . .' (Zech. 14:20–21). Ultimately the blessing to the nations (Gen. 12:3) was a covenant obligation laid on the people as a whole.

Implicit Old Testament clericalism

Notwithstanding this break with the religious practice of the nations around, Israel had clergy in the sense that some leaders were required (either by God or the people) to assume a *vicarious* function. For example, Moses is required to listen to God instead of the people: 'Go near and listen to all that the Lord our God says. Then tell us whatever the Lord our God tells you. We will listen and obey' (Deut. 5:23–7). Indeed Moses' mediatorial ministry is to be continued by the prophets to be raised up after him (Deut. 18:15).

A caveat should be entered here. Moses had a unique role in the history of salvation and some of the apparent pro-clerical stories are not vindications of a clerical caste but of Moses as an appointed leader. Korah's rebellion (Num. 16:1–50) and Miriam and Aaron's revolt (Num. 12:1–15) were revolts against Moses' leadership. They were not attempts to liberate a subjugated 'laity'. Further, in acknowledging an implicit Old Testament clericalism, it must be noted that the functions of the priests were exclusive. Aaron was the first priest (Ex. 28; Lev. 8) and only his descendants were to serve as his successors. Nonetheless the original Old Testament vision of a priest-people was not entirely lost in the centuries of Old Testament clericalism until Christ broke down the clergy–lay distinction once and for all.

- In one sense the Levites were representative rather than vicarious. 'In them every firstborn, whether Ephraimite, Benjamite or member of any other tribe, worked in the service of the priest. Each was there through representation.'[33]

---

[33] E. Dyck, 'Laos and Leadership Under the Old Testament' (unpublished paper, Regent College, Vancouver, 1989), 1.

- Further there were some exceptions to this rule of Aaronic descent for the priesthood. Samuel was not a descendant of Aaron (1 Sam. 1, but see 1 Chron. 6:33–4) and yet functioned as a leading priest. So also Micah, an Ephraimite (Judg. 17:5), Eleazar, a Benjamite (1 Sam. 7:1) and Ira of Manasseh (2 Sam. 20:26).
- No leader of Israel, however surprised at being called of God, could maintain a valid ministry on the basis of an ontological difference because of that call. Kings were anointed and therefore uniquely set aside by God and for God's service. But the anointing did not leave an indelible mark on the character and spirituality of the person so anointed. Saul's case of losing spiritual reality but maintaining the office of king is among the most poignant examples in the Old Testament.
- The functions of judge, prophet, elder or king (at least for the Northern Kingdom) were not restricted to any tribe and often were undertaken by surprised candidates.
- While some prophets aligned themselves with people of power (to some extent Jeremiah with King Josiah, and Isaiah with King Hezekiah), most who joined professional guilds charged with the task of advising kings to maintain their status quo and personal well-being were judged by the canonical prophets to be false prophets. 'The true prophet was never a professional in that sense.'[34]

The overwhelming impression left by the Old Testament is not of active priests and passive recipients of such vicarious ministry, but rather a covenantal ministering people quite different from the surrounding nations. Early defence of the separated clergy often appealed to the priest–people distinction in the Old Testament. Indeed, the argument is still used. But in many ways churches have not even appropriated the many significant contributions to whole-people ministry embodied in the older covenant. These include viewing Adam and Eve as priests of creation and prototypes for the human vocation; experiencing corporateness and people-hood and not merely making ministry an individual activity; envisioning the servant of the Lord as the paradigm for ministry by the *laos* of God; seeing sabbath (the threefold rest of God, humankind

---

[34] Dyck, 'Laos and Leadership', 12.

and creation) as the goal of the salvation story; and finally making covenant the relational basis of vocation, work and ministry.

The fulfilled Old Testament

In sum, under the Old Testament the entire people were called to belong to God, to be God's people and to serve God's purposes (Ex. 19:6). But within that people only a few – prophets, priests, wise men, and princes – experienced a special call to give leadership to God's people, to speak God's word and to minister on behalf of God (e.g. Is. 6:8). Old Testament saints looked forward to the day when a new covenant would be inaugurated, a covenant through which God's law would be written permanently and unchangeably on the hearts of all the people (not just in a document), in which 'they will all know [God] from the least of them to the greatest' (Jer. 31:34), and by which God's Spirit would 'move [people] to follow [God's] decrees and be careful to keep [God's] laws' (Ezek. 36:27). The Old Testament priesthood is fulfilled in Jesus the high priest who made the once-for-all sacrifice of himself (Heb. 7:11–28; 10:1–18).

The apostles firmly believed that the promised day came with the arrival of God's son Jesus and the outpouring of God's Spirit on the day of Pentecost (Acts 2:14–21). Three great theological realities brought about the transformation of the Old Testament *laos* into a newly reconstituted people in which *all* minister: the lordship of Jesus Christ (Acts 2:36); the outpouring of the Holy Spirit on the church for ethical living and ministry (1 Cor. 12:13); and the dawning of the end, by which believers 'already' live 'in the heavenly realms' – the way things will eventually become (Eph. 1:3–4) – as they wait for Christ's second coming.[35] For this reason the apostles used the Greek word *klēros* (clergy) to describe a wholly new reality: the dignity, calling and privilege of every member of the family of God.

The church as ministering people

With the lordship of Christ, the outpouring of the Holy Spirit and the dawning of the end/last days (Acts 2:17), the whole church,

---

[35] Fee, '*Laos* and Leadership', 9.

according to Scripture, is the true ministerium, a community of prophets, priests and princes or princesses, serving God through Jesus in the power of the Spirit seven days a week. All are clergy in the sense of being appointed by God to service and dignified as God's inheritance. All have a share in the power and blessing of the age of the Spirit. All are laity in the sense of having their identity rooted in the people of God. All give ministry. All receive ministry. That is the constitution of the church. But when we step into the modern church we see something quite different.

Few business people, for example, think of themselves as full-time ministers in the marketplace. Fewer still are encouraged in this by their churches. Hardly any one gets commissioned to their service in the world except foreign missionaries.[36] It is a heretical state of affairs. Christians in the first century would have found such a state of affairs anachronistic – a throw-back to the situation before Christ came when only a few in Israel knew the Lord, when only one tribe was named as priests, when only a select few heard the call of God on their lives. How could such a gracious revolution (under the New Covenant) be reversed, leaving us with essentially Old Covenant practice?

3. The Emergence of the Clergy

While the first century was marked by a people without clergy or laity, in the second and third centuries a definite clergy–lay distinction arose largely from three influences: (1) imitation of the secular structures of the Greek-Roman world not unlike the professional–lay distinctions in the modern world;[37] (2) the transference of the Old Testament priesthood model to the leadership of the church; and (3) popular piety which elevated the Lord's Supper to a mystery which required priestly administration. Political and

---

[36] See J. Stockard, 'Commissioning the Ministries of the Laity: How it Works and Why it Isn't Being Done', in George Peck and John S. Hoffman (eds.), *The Laity in Ministry: The Whole People of God for the Whole World*, 71–9.

[37] The *laos* of the Greek city-state were distinguished from their leaders, the *klēroi* or magistrates. See also Lk. 23:13 for a parallel distinction.

theological pressures in the church also made a contribution. The founding apostles were now memories. The unsuccessful Jewish rebellion of AD 66–70 occasioned both the scattering of Christians and an exclusivist reaction in Judaism. Congregations experienced confusion over doctrine, foreshadowing the debates over Gnosticism that would take place in the late second century.[38]

The church fathers

In the face of heresy threats (Docetism, Gnosticism and Judaizing tendencies) Ignatius of Antioch (AD 50–110) appealed for the necessity of having a single bishop as the focus of unity. In the works of Tertullian (AD 197–200) we are given a structure for the church in which the laity are identified with the *plebs* (ordinary people) to be distinguished from the priestly[39] or ecclesiastical order of bishops, presbyters and deacons. But his conception of laity was the privileged and endowed people from whom the hierarchy emerge.[40] Women, however, did not have the rights of the laity![41] Clement of Alexandria also uses *laikos* for ordinary believers. He envisioned deacons and presbyters as mere imitations and steps towards the heavenly *episkopos*.[42] Origen, a layperson, discovered how difficult it was by then for a 'lay' teacher to bring a homily in the presence of bishops.[43] Yet even Origen gave the priest power to purify laypersons at the penitential level. Commenting on this development Faivre

---

[38] R.A. Norris, Jr, 'The Beginnings of Christian Priesthood', *Anglican Theological Review* 66.9 (1984), 22–3 (18–32).

[39] 'Thence, therefore, among *us* the prescript is more fully and more carefully laid down, that they who are chosen into the sacerdotal order must be men of one marriage' ('On Exhortation to Chastity', 7, [*Ante-Nicene Fathers*, IV, 54]).

[40] Faivre, *The Emergence of the Laity*, 46.

[41] Ibid., 51.

[42] Ibid., 58–9.

[43] 'Therefore, with the permission of God, and secondly of the bishops, and thirdly of the presbyters and the people, I will again give my opinion in the matter [prayer] . . . A bishop stands over all . . . (Origen, *Dialogue with Heraclides*, in W.J. Burghart, Thomas Commerford Lawler, and John D. Dillon (eds.), trans. R.J. Daly, *Ancient Christian Writers* [56 vols.; New York: Paulist Press, 1954–92], LIV, 60–61 [57–78]).

says, 'From this time onward, the layman's function was to release the priest and levite from all his material concerns, thus enabling him to devote himself exclusively to the service of the altar, a task that was necessary for everyone's salvation.'[44]

Priests within the priesthood

In the third century the Syrian *Didascalia Apostolorum* in the East devoted five chapters to the office of bishop claiming that bishops were 'priests and prophets, and princes and leaders and kings, and mediators between God and his faithful, and receivers of the word, and preachers and proclaimers thereof, and knowers of the Scriptures and of the utterances of God, and witnesses of his will, who bears the sins of all, and are to give answer for all'.[45]

Meanwhile in the West, Cyprian, bishop of Carthage (AD 249) made it clear that a member of the clergy *is not a layman*. Using the analogy of the Levites he argues that, while all Christians should avoid becoming overly involved in the world, clergy must not do so, in order to attend properly to the ministry of the altar.[46] Cyprian was convinced that a bishop was accountable to God alone.[47] He models his church order on the civil orders of the rulers of the city of Carthage.

- He makes a clear distinction between the *ordo* of bishops and the laity.

---

[44] Faivre, *The Emergence of the Laity*, 69. Not surprisingly in *The Apostolic Tradition* even the widow, appointed/ordained to serve in prayer, 'does not offer the oblation (*prophora*) nor has she a [liturgical] ministry (*leitourgia*). But ordination (*cheirotonia*) is for the clergy (*klēros*) on account of their [liturgical] ministry (*leitourgia*). But the widow (*cheira*) is appointed for prayer, and this is [a function] of all [Christians]' ('Of Widows', *The Apostolic Tradition* 11:1–5, in G. Dix and H. Chadwick [eds.], *The Treatise on the Apostolic Tradition of St. Hippolytus of Rome* [London: The Alban Press, 1991], 20–21).

[45] *Didascalia Apostolorum*, trans. R.H. Connolly (Oxford: Clarendon Press, 1929), 80.

[46] Faivre, *The Emergence of the Laity*, 106–7.

[47] Rademacher, *Lay Ministry*, 565.

- He sacralizes the priesthood according to the Old Testament model of the sacrificial priesthood.
- He establishes a monolithic episcopate which is the same for all of Africa.
- He links ministry to sacrifice, again in the image of the Temple priesthood.
- He shapes the church as a clearly defined institution of salvation.
- He models the bishops in the image of Roman senators, thus excluding women.
- He consolidates the ruling powers of bishops through numerous episcopal conclaves.[48]

Furthermore, Cyprian argued that anyone who separates from the bishop separates from the church. In less than two centuries we have moved from a community priesthood to a separated clergy that vicariously represents both the priestly and the kingly rule of the people in Christ.[49]

Undoubtedly a strong factor in this drift into clericalism was growing popular piety, if not superstition, surrounding the Lord's Supper which increasingly came to be viewed as a repetition of the sacrifice of Jesus. To perform the sacrifice the officiant needed unique credentials. The New Testament says absolutely nothing about who should officiate at that communal meal, concentrating as it does on the importance of discerning the relational life of the community (1 Cor. 11:29) rather than the religious character of the officiant.

The mystique of the ministry

The golden-tongued orator, John Chrysostom, said, 'when you see the Lord sacrificed and lying before you, and the high priest standing

---

[48] Ibid., 59.

[49] Surveying the evidence of the first four centuries, R.A. Norris concludes that the development of the priesthood was a complex affair, a curious fusion of roles that can be summed up in being a shepherd or ruler of the people through (1) supervising the community's worldly affairs; (2) presiding over the liturgy as a high priest; (3) teaching the community ('The Beginnings of Christian Priesthood', 31).

over the sacrifice and praying, and all who partake being tinctured with that precious blood, can you think that you are still among men and still standing on earth?'[50] In his famous treatise on the priesthood, Chrysostom eliminates all women from the priesthood of the church, and most men:

> But when one is required to preside over the church, and to be entrusted with the care of so many souls, the whole female sex must retire before the magnitude of the task, and the majority of men also; and we must bring forward those who to a large extent surpass all others, and soar as much above them in excellence of spirit as Saul overtopped the whole Hebrew nation in bodily stature . . . but let the distinction between the pastor and his charge be as great as that between rational men and irrational creatures, not to say even greater, inasmuch as the risk is concerned with things of greater importance.[51]

When the priest celebrates the Eucharist, Chrysostom said, 'art thou not . . . straightway translated to heaven and casting out every carnal thought from the soul, dost thou not with disembodied spirit and pure reasons contemplate the things which are in heaven?'[52] One identifies within this quote the extent to which Neoplatonism had infected the church with its heretical appeal for a disembodied spirituality, a spirituality from which the Western Church has not yet fully repented. In fact few actually see it.

Of considerable note is the difference between the Eastern Church (Orthodox) and the Western Church (Roman) on the nature of the hierarchy, a matter which Yves Congar explores in a footnote. The West emphasized the hierarchical principle of clergy leadership (evidenced in the priesthood, papal power and Mariolatry), while the East stressed the communal principle (evidenced in married priests, the importance of councils and greater mutuality). At the root of this difference is the Eastern dependence

---

[50] John Chrysostom, 'Treatise Concerning the Christian Priesthood', trans. W.R. Stephens, in P. Schaff (ed.), *A Select Library of the Nicene and Post-Nicene Fathers of the Christian Church* (14 vols.; New York: Charles Scribner's Sons, 1899–1908), IX, 46 (33–83).

[51] Ibid., 40.

[52] Ibid., 46.

on the Cappadocian fathers who developed a fully trinitarian approach to church life with the interdependence, intercommunion and interpenetration of Father, Son and Spirit (*perichōresis*, to be explored shortly), and their conviction that the Holy Spirit is given communally from God and in God, a matter behind the celebrated filioque controversy that split East and West.[53]

Progressive clericalization

From the fourth to the sixteenth centuries the clergy–lay distinction deepened.[54] Laity were those on the bottom of the clerical ladder. After his conversion (AD 312) Constantine appointed bishops as civil magistrates throughout the empire, organized the church into dioceses along the pattern of Roman regional districts, and consistently used 'clerical' and 'clerics' as a privileged class.[55] Under the Gregorian reform (1057–1123) the ministry of the entire Western Church was shaped by Roman Law. So in the period prior to the Reformation:

---

[53] Congar comments on the importance of the doctrine of the Holy Spirit in a theology of the laity, and the difference between West and East in this. 'In the one [the West], the emphasis is put on the fact that all comes from one alone and on the dependence of the body on its head for the life that animates it; in the other [Orthodox], the emphasis is on the life distributed throughout the body by the Holy Spirit, who is seen as an autonomous reality in relation to the Word. It is clear that a theology of the laity calls for a theology of the Holy Spirit, both of which would simply be a revelation of profound and authentic traditional elements' (Congar, *Lay People*, 457, n. 1).

[54] In an unpublished paper, James Houston warns against the biases we bring to 'reading history' on this matter, including reading back into the patristic period of the *fait accompli* of the Constantinian church, but ignoring the great movements of the Spirit (such as the Beguines) bringing renewal; and interpreting history from the perspective of top-down leadership rather than from that of grass-roots people ('The Amateur Status of the Christian Life: Reflections on the Dualism of the Priesthood and the Laity' [unpublished paper, Regent College, Vancouver 1989], 4).

[55] Rademacher, *Lay Ministry*, 60.

- the bishop of Rome came to be regarded as the head of the Church on earth;
- the language of worship ceased to be the language of the people;
- the clergy dressed differently and were prepared for ministry in an enculturating seminary;
- ordination became an absolute act so that congregations were no longer needed for the celebration of eucharist;
- clergy became celibate and thus distant from the normal experiences of the laity;
- the cup was removed from the laity in the eucharist.

In due course the clergy–lay distinction became institutionalized in religious orders, priestly ordination and the seminary system.[56] Even the Protestant Reformation with its call to recover 'the priesthood of all believers' did not succeed in reinstating laity as one dignified serving people.

The incomplete Protestant Reformation

Why the full implications of the Reformation were not realized in the non-Catholic community is a fascinating and important question. Some factors are as follows:

- *The Reformation was more concerned about soteriology (salvation) than ecclesiology.* The priesthood of all believers was interpreted

---

[56] Catholic scholars show that the Council of Trent defined ministry against the backdrop of Luther's radical message (AD 1517) that all believers are equally priests. Following Peter Lombard and Thomas Aquinas, the Council reaffirmed the existence of an indelible mark imprinted on the soul of a priest at his ordination, thus emphasizing the *being* of ministry instead of the *doing* of ministry. It increased the 'grades' of ministries and established seminaries to train young men destined for the priesthood to be kept free from the pleasures of the world. It is the judgement of some Catholic scholars that even Vatican II did not discontinue the levels of ministry and this has perpetuated the clergy–lay problem The laity are confined to the secular arena and are defined by *place* rather than by baptism or discipleship (ibid., 73, 79).

according to its effect on individual salvation, but with regard to the collective Christian experience it was 'business as usual'.[57]

- *The preacher replaced the priest.* The sermon became the central act of Protestant worship (the Protestant 'Christ-event'). This gave the preacher-expositor the same clerical standing as the Catholic officiant at the Mass even though he now wore a Geneva gown. The scholarship implicit in such a ministry ultimately involved taking the Bible out of the hands of the layperson again and putting it into the hands of the biblical scholar. In the evolution of Western society from AD 500 to 1500 laypersons had lost access to high culture and learned traditions. As early as the eighth century the language of scholarship and worship had ceased to be the language of the people.[58]

- *Inadequate structures for renewal.* The Reformation did not provide an ecclesiology comparable to its rediscovered soteriology. The Protestant Reformation spawned denominations that took seriously the ministry of all believers: Quakers (with no clergy);

---

[57] A remarkable exception to this was Luther's 'third service' for which he regretfully could not find any volunteers. 'The third kind of service should be a truly evangelical order and should not be held in a public place for all sorts of people. But those who want to be Christians in earnest and who profess the gospel with hand and mouth should sign their names and meet alone in a house somewhere to pray, to read, to baptize, to receive the sacrament, and to do other Christian works. According to this order, those who do not lead Christian lives could be known, reproved, corrected, cast out, or excommunicated, according to the rule of Christ, Matthew 18:15–17. Here one could also solicit benevolent gifts to be willingly given and distributed to the poor. . . . Here would be no need of much and elaborate singing. Here one could set up a brief and neat order for baptism and the sacrament and center everything on the Word, prayer, and love. In short, if one had the kind of people and persons who wanted to be Christians in earnest, the rules and regulations would soon be ready. But as yet I neither can nor desire to begin such a congregation or assembly or to make rules for it. For I have not yet the people or persons for it, nor do I see many who want it'. Martin Luther, 'The German Mass and Order of Service' in Ulrich S. Leopold (ed.), *Luther's Works*, 55 vols (Philadelphia: Fortress Press, 1965) Vol. LIII, 63–4. Used by permission of the publisher, Augsburg Fortress Press.

[58] A. Rowthorn, *The Liberation of the Laity*, 32.

Moravians (with lay missionaries); Puritans (primarily lay centred); Baptists and Anabaptists (whose preachers were usually laypersons); Disciples of Christ and Methodists (all lay oriented). But even denominations stemming from the so-called radical reformation have now 'gravitated' to the pre-Reformation clergy–lay distinction.

- *The Catholic seminary system was eventually adopted.* While important exceptions exist (and still do), the seminary system, developed in the nineteenth century, became the universal model for equipping a generation of pastors thus guaranteeing their enculturation into a clerical culture. Theological education remains, by and large, the exclusive preoccupation of those intending a career in the clergy.[59]
- *Kingdom ministry has been almost totally eclipsed by church ministry.* Ministry is viewed as advancing the church rather than the Kingdom. The letters are the primary guide; the gospels have been eclipsed.
- *Ordination is still retained almost universally for the full-time supported church worker; no adequate recognition of lay ministries in society exists.* Most denominations still regard ordination as conferring a priestly character rather than recognizing Christian character and call. No denomination ordains people to societal careers and missions.[60]
- *An adequate lay spirituality has hardly ever been taught and promoted.* While the Reformation rejected the two-level spirituality of the monastery and the common Christian, with few exceptions Protestant spirituality has mostly focused either on charismatic and 'mystical' experiences or the deeper life of outstanding

---

[59] Anthony Russell, in *The Clerical Profession*, traces the development of theological colleges in England in the mid-nineteenth century in a way that approximated the training offered other professionals so that, in addition to the theological training provided by Oxford and Cambridge for the privileged few, cathedrals established colleges in their closes. Then in 1854 Bishop Samuel Wilberforce established the first college to have a common life based on the Catholic seminaries and European monasteries (46). Regent College (Vancouver) was founded with the vision of providing theological education for the whole people of God.

[60] See G. Ogden, *The New Reformation*, 188–215.

Christian leaders, rather than exploring the holiness of the ordinary Christian in the totality of his or her life: eating, sleeping, working, buying and selling, playing, having sexual relations and dying.[61] The church has never, in the West, become free of Greek dualism which relegates bodily life to a lower level.

The same cultural and social forces at work in the first sixteen centuries (secular management models; professional–lay analogies; the tendency to deal with outside threats by increasing central government) are still at work in the modern world. The church must continuously fight the 'fleshly' predisposition to the clergy–laity model, and each generation has to enter the renewal of ministry in Christ. Commenting on the present situation, Elton Trueblood says:

> Our opportunity for a big step lies in opening the ministry of the ordinary Christian in much the same manner that our ancestors opened Bible reading to the ordinary Christian. To do this means, in one sense, the inauguration of a new Reformation while in another it means the logical completion of the earlier Reformation in which the implications of the position taken were neither fully understood nor loyally followed.[62]

---

[61] The early Puritans did better than most on this matter. It was this vision that inspired Banks and Stevens, *The Complete Book*.

[62] E. Trueblood, *Your Other Vocation*, 32.

For further study / discussion

1. Read the whole of Paul's letter to the Ephesians as a letter addressed to *the people as a whole* rather than to you personally and individually. Record your discoveries.

2. Do your own version of the survey undertaken by Georgia Harkness noted above without prejudicing people's responses by indicating what you hope the outcome will be.

3. Discuss this comment by William Diehl, former executive of Bethlehem Steel:

   . . . In the almost thirty years of my professional career, my church has never once suggested that there be any type of accounting of my on-the-job ministry to others. My church has never once offered to improve those skills which could make me a better minister, nor has it ever asked if I needed any kind of support in what I was doing. There has never been an enquiry into the types of ethical decisions I must face, or whether I seek to communicate the faith to my co-workers. I have never been in a congregation where there was any type of public affirmation of a ministry in my career. In short, I must conclude that my church doesn't have the least interest whether or how I minister in my daily work.[63]

---

[63] W. Diehl, *Christianity and Real Life*, v–vi.

Chapter 3

One God – One People

It is safe to say that unbalanced notions about either clergy or laity are due to unbalanced notions of the Church. Indeed, to be more precise, too low a view of laity is to due to too high a view of clergy, and too high a view of clergy is due to too low a view of the Church.

John Stott[1]

Abolishing the laity and recovering the dignity of the whole people of God in theory as well as practice is a tall order indeed. But why attempt it at all?

Some may regard this as merely a pragmatic response: there is too much work for one person to do in the church and 'liberating the laity' will enlist more workers for church work. Others will view the abolition of the laity as a mere spin-off of the great democratic forces at work in the world today – forces that have brought down the Berlin Wall and must inevitably destroy the wall that divides clergy and laity. While pastors in the developing world are still, by and large, held in high esteem, the situation is different in the developed West. There, pastors are often bypassed in favour of psychiatrists and psychological counsellors when real help is sought (and purchased), church consultants when expert advice is needed in church management, marriage 'chapels' when weddings are to be conducted, and funeral 'homes' when there is a death. In a postmodern culture we are developing a generation of post-church Christians who have no apparent need of the institutional church. Relationships are everything. Institutions are suspect.

---

[1] Stott, *One People*, 18.

Pastors are unnecessary. So why try to abolish the clergy if it is on the way out anyway?

It is widely acknowledged that pastors are facing an identity crisis, a crisis which may be deepened by the pastor-as-equipper emphasis now being promoted by many, including myself.[2] Simply put, if there is no single activity that is the *exclusive* prerogative of the pastor, *including equipping*, is there anything left? John Stott calls this aclericalism.[3] At least those in a sacramental tradition can cling to their officiating role at baptisms and the eucharist.[4]

Being 'unnecessary' may be a gift. It may enable one to become truly counter-cultural,[5] to go deep with God and to become a true pastor – nurturing people in the faith, directing people Godward so they are dependent on the Head of the church.[6] It may also help one to envision a God-sized ministry for the whole people of God, to identify giftedness in others and to empower the people to love and serve God fully.

The real reason for being passionate about the recovery of the whole people of God as the Lord's true ministerium and God's

---

[2] We will take up later the vexed question of the interpretation of Eph. 4:11–12 to mean that pastor-teachers are to equip the saints who will do the work of the ministry, a matter challenged by recent revisionist exegetes and those trying to argue that the ministry always refers to the administration of Word and sacrament.

[3] Stott, *One People*, 47.

[4] John Stott, after citing with approval Article XXIII of the Church of England, 'It is not lawful for any man to take upon him the office of public preaching, or ministering the sacraments in the congregation, before he be lawfully called, and sent to execute the same,' comments that this is a question of order not of doctrine. This is not satisfactory to this reader since the ordering of church life – something Luther stressed – need not exclude duly appointed members of the church from officiating. See Luther's statement in Chapter 6 of this book (p. 154), quoted from 'The Right and Power of a Congregation or Community to Judge All Teaching and to Call, Appoint, and Dismiss Teachers, Established and Proved from Scripture'.

[5] It can be argued that this is less counter-cultural in a post-Christian, postmodern age.

[6] Significantly no church leader in Scripture is ever called 'head', a title reserved for Jesus (Eph. 4:15; 5:23).

chosen missionaries is not mere expediency – it is biblical. The church is unlike any other human organization. It is unique. It is a divine (though still human) creation. Therefore a theological approach that brings Scripture constantly into tension with the realities of the age, like two foci of an ellipse, is the most needed thing to liberate the whole people of God for service in the church and the world. But first some distinctions must be made.

1. Two Peoples or One?

Clericalism is the domination of the 'ordinary' people by those ordained, trained and invested with privilege and power. In one sense clericalism was inevitable as the church tried to maintain its inspired uniqueness against all the pressures of church and world to specialize and centralize.[7] Clericalism is not only expressed in dominance through knowledge, position or exclusive right (as in sacramental ministry). It often gets expressed as disdain for the laity as unreliable, incompetent and unavailable. Increasingly in a high-tech, fast-paced society, churches are hiring professionals for everything from childcare to financial management. Such disdain is expressed in the words of Sir John Lawrence: 'What does the layman really want? He wants a building which looks like a church; a clergyman dressed in the way he approves; services of the kind he's been used to, *and to be left alone.*'[8]

Anticlericalism is the domination of the 'laity' and the rejection of ordained church leadership. This too is marked by the questions of power, authority, competence and attitudes of disdain, but now the centre has shifted to the non-clergy *laos*. Some groups reject pastoral leadership outright and take turns at the pulpit – at least all the men do – in what has been called 'the world's greatest amateur hour'. The gift of pastor-teacher to the church (Eph. 4:11–12) is neglected.

John Stott notes, however, that there is an implicit anticlericalism in the New Testament itself. Paul denounces the exaggerated deference shown to some leaders: 'One of you says, "I

---

[7] Stott, *One People*, 35.

[8] Quoted in Stott, *One People*, 36, emphasis his.

follow Paul"; another, "I follow Apollos"; another, "I follow Cephas"; still another, "I follow Christ" (1 Cor. 1:12). To this Paul answers, "What, after all, is Apollos?" (1 Cor. 3:5)'.[9]

No biblical Christian should give in to extreme anticlericalism as it is the will of God that the church should have leadership and gifted apostles, prophets, evangelists and pastor-teachers (Eph. 4:11). It is a leadership to be honoured (1 Tim. 5:17–19) and obeyed (Heb. 13:17). Widespread anticlericalism has stripped the average pastor in the West (though not so much elsewhere) from legitimate and authorized leadership and authority.

Co-existence of clergy and laity is a more common phenomenon: clergy and laity each have their place and function in a complementary way. This is by far the dominant view of the Roman Catholic Church (even since Vatican II[10]), the Eastern Church (though with a stronger emphasis on community) and most Protestant churches. But the co-existence involves two peoples separated by education, ordination, function and even culture. This becomes most evident in pastors' conferences, in seminaries and in 'lay' conferences – now no longer in vogue – that perpetuate a distinction that is a practical heresy, namely that there are two peoples. Such gatherings of separated peoples are dangerous to say the least, as they often foster laity-bashing (or laity 'handling') and clergy-bashing (or clergy 'handling').

Community (John Stott's term) is the only biblical way of describing the relationship of leaders and the rest of the people. Each member contributes to others in a diversity of functions that contributes to a rich social unity, like the loving unity through diversity found in the triune God in whose image the church, the *laos tou theou*, is created.

Images of the people of God

Laos tou theou (the people of God) is only one of the terms used in the New Testament to describe God's own family on earth. Others are:

---

[9] I acknowledge my indebtedness to John Stott's fine treatment of these options.
[10] See Stott, *One People*, 44–5.

- 'the church' (*hē ekklēsia*, a people gathered – called out, translating the Old Testament *qāhāl*, 'congregation' – 1 Thess. 1:1);
- 'saints' (*hoi hagioi*, a people dedicated to God – Acts 9:41; Eph. 4:12);
- 'chosen ones' (*eklektoi*, a people chosen by God for God's own possession – 1 Pet. 1:1; Col. 3:12);
- 'a royal priesthood' (*basileion hierateuma*, a serving people, bridge-building between God and the world – 1 Pet. 2:9–11);
- 'the household of God' (*oikō theou*, a people sharing a common life – 1 Tim. 3:15);
- 'the Israel of God' (*Israēl tou theou*, a people of promise – Gal. 6:16);
- 'the body of Christ' (*to sōma Christou*, an empowered people continuing the ministry of Jesus – 1 Cor. 12:12–26);
- 'a holy temple in the Lord' (*naon hagion en kuriō*, a people inhabited by God – Eph. 2:21–2);
- 'a colony of heaven'/'God's commonwealth' (*politeuma en ouranois*, a missionary people – Phil. 3:20; 'fellow citizens with God' – Eph. 2:19).

We should note that all of these terms are corporate. The church is not a collection of individual 'saints' but the 'saints', 'the body', 'the household'. Nor is the church merely a gathering of people by the will and election of human beings to achieve community.

Metaphors of the people of God

Frequently the New Testament uses metaphors to describe the reality that the church has her life in God. God is the Vinedresser (the vine), the Shepherd (sheep/flock), the Father (household/family), the Builder (temple/building) and the Head (the body of Christ).[11] Especially in the last metaphor (the body of Christ), there is nothing to suggest that Christ has delegated his authority to certain church members who have responsibility for the ministry of others. The Head does not tell the hand to tell the foot what to do. The Head is connected to the whole body and to each member. It is the body of

---

[11] See R. Banks, *God the Worker: Journeys into the Mind, Heart and Imagination of God.*

Christ, not the corpse of Christ nor a body of Christians. God is the ultimate equipper.[12]

Not only do these metaphors describe the vertical but also the horizontal life of the people of God. We are branches of the same vine, sheep of the same flock, brothers and sisters in the same family, stones linked in the same building and, in the most developed metaphor, members together of the same body. Paul coins a set of new words joining the prefix *syn* (together) with other words to describe the interdependence of the members of the people of God with Christ and one another, words which in the original are one word. There are no individual Christians.[13]

Add to this the great theological themes of the people of God in the New Testament, especially the new humanity. In Ephesians 2 Paul speaks of both an abolition and a creation.[14] What was abolished was 'the law with its commandments and regulations' – the use of law to obtain acceptance with God and as a way of marking exclusionary membership in Israel. This was abolished in the flesh of Christ on the cross thereby destroying the 'dividing wall of hostility' (2:14) that separates Jews and Gentiles, men and women, free people and slaves.[15] What was created was a new humanity (2:15) that transcends distinctions but does not obliterate them. 'For through [Christ] we both have access to the Father by one Spirit' (2:18). If Christ has broken down the dividing wall between Jew and Gentile (surely an awesome miracle, 3:4–6) then it would be anathema to erect again a wall between one part of the body and

---

[12] See R. Paul Stevens, *Liberating the Laity*, 36.

[13] We are 'made . . . alive with Christ' (Eph. 2:5), 'seated . . . with him in the heavenly realms' (2:6), 'fellow citizens with God's people' (2:19), 'joined together' (2:21), 'being built together' (2:22), 'heirs together', 'members together', sharers together' (3:6), and, reaching a climax, 'joined and held together by every supporting ligament' (4:16).

[14] Stott, *One People*, 24.

[15] The work of Christ and the Spirit has several dimensions: bringing near (separated people, Eph. 2:13), making the two one (2:14), destroying the barrier (2:14), abolishing the legal/performance way of righteousness (2:15), creating a new humanity (2:15), preaching and making peace (2:15,17), reconciling both to God (2:16), putting hostility to death (2:16), giving mutual access to the Father (2:18).

another. Yet this, as we have seen in Chapter 2, is what has happened.

Getting behind the division

The apostle Paul was faced in his own day with something roughly parallel to clericalism, namely performance of the law as a means of gaining righteousness and defining membership. Paul's approach to the problem gives us an important clue. Paul went behind discussions of the law to rediscover something that *preceded* the law and gave it meaning – namely the promise (Gal. 3:15–18). In a biblical theology of the laity we must get behind the clergy–lay problem that has plagued the church since the third century and find out what God originally intended for his people.[16] Only in this way can we avoid a compensatory theology and transcend, rather than merely oppose, clericalism. To do this we must explore, first, the meaning of the Trinity and, second (in the next chapter), the original vocational intention of God for his creatures on earth. We will take up each of these matters in turn.

2. One God – Three Persons

A fully trinitarian approach is needed since the identity and ministry of the *laos* is shaped by the God whose people we are.[17] God has called out 'a *laos* for himself' (Acts 15:14) or as the KJV puts it, 'a people for his name'. The identity of the *laos* comes from the Trinity – a people in communion with God – and the vocation of the *laos* also comes from communion with God. In this way both the being and the doing, both the identity and the vocation of the *laos* will be considered.

Trinitarian identity and vocation

The ministry of the *laos* is not generated exclusively by the people, whether from duty or gratitude. All ministry is God's ministry and

[16] Some of this discussion I owe to a conversation with Ray S. Anderson of Fuller Theological Seminary.
[17] Much of the following was first published in *Crux* 31.2 (June 1995), 5–14.

God continues his own ministry through his people.[18] This ministry begins not when we 'join the church' to help God do his work but when we join God (Jn. 1:12) and have 'fellowship with the Father and with his Son' (1 Jn. 1:3). *Laos* ministry is participation in the 'in-going' ministry of God (relationally among God the Father, Son and Holy Spirit), and simultaneously participation in the 'out-going' (sending) ministry of God. On this latter point Jesus prayed in the high priestly prayer, 'As you sent me into the world, I have sent them into the world' (Jn. 17:18). On the first (the in-going) God is 'lover, the beloved and the love itself', as Jürgen Moltmann puts it, reflecting on a phrase from Augustine.[19] On the second, God is sender, sent and the sending.

So there was ministry before there was a world, that ministry taking place within God himself (Jn. 17:5,24). This pre-creation ministry was neither curative nor redemptive. There was nothing broken nor fallen to restore, even though 'the lamb that was slain from the creation of the world' (Rev. 13:8) is an evocative hint of God's redemptive willingness. God's ministry is creative and unitive (Jn. 17:21–3) and not only curative and redemptive, thus constituting a broader definition of service and relationship than is normally ascribed to the term 'ministry'. Like their God the people of God have ministry that is both creative (making) and restorative (mending); ministry is both unitive (connecting) and curative (correcting) – thus challenging the common evangelical preoccupation with the Great Commission (Mt. 28:19–20) as the exclusive definition of ministry, as important as that mandate is.

To this rich understanding of peoplehood and ministry each of the three persons of the Godhead contributes. The Father creates, providentially sustains, and forms a covenantal framework for all existence. The Son incarnates, mediates, transfigures and redeems. The Spirit empowers and fills with God's own presence. But each shares in the others – coinheres, interpenetrates, co-operates – so that it is theologically inappropriate to stereotype the ministry of any one. But that is exactly what is done.

---

[18] This is implied in Acts 1:1. See R.D. Bell, 'A Theology of Ministry', (unpublished manuscript, Carey Theological College, Vancouver, 1984), 12.

[19] Moltmann, *The Trinity and the Kingdom*, 32.

Playing favourites

Christians tend to 'play favourites' when it comes to describing peoplehood and ministry.[20] For order, providence, and sustaining the structures of society we appeal to the Father. The Son is associated with redemption and winning the lost. The Holy Spirit is the favourite of those seeking renewal, empowering charisms and direct religious experience. Churches and denominations tend to form around one of the three: Father-denominations emphasize reverent worship and stewardship. Son-denominations stress discipleship and evangelism thus furthering the work of the Kingdom of God. Spirit-denominations promote gifts and graces. The implications of this specialist approach for peoplehood, vocation and leadership in the church can be expressed in the following chart:

	PEOPLEHOOD	VOCATION	LEADERSHIP
FATHER	Covenant Community	Creational Stewardship	Hierarchical
SON	Kingdom Community	Christocratic Service (continuing works of Jesus)	Servant
SPIRIT	Charismatic Community	Exercising Gifts Empowerment	Charismatic

A rich and full doctrine of the Trinity avoids such stereotypical designations. God is more than the sum of the three. God is not God apart from the way the Father, Son and Holy Spirit give and receive from each other what they essentially are.

'One God' (the primary confession of Islam) is ironically the Christian's deepest praise. We affirm that God is more one *because* he is three, not in spite of his threeness. Within the limitations of rational discourse, and recognizing that if we could fit God into our

---

[20] For example, as I have already mentioned, Kraemer reduces the church to a Christocratic community, thus neglecting the full participation of Father and Son.

puny minds he would be too small a God to worship, we respectfully confess that the unity of the Holy Trinity is neither a homogenized unity that blurs the distinctions, nor a collective. As is often noted in the history of theological reflection the Orthodox Church started with the diversity and made the unity of God a matter of doxology, while the Western Church started with an abstract notion of unity and struggled to grasp rationally the possibility of diversity. The net result of this latter effort is that God appears to be one *in spite of* being Father, Son and Holy Spirit. A biblical approach reverently affirms the opposite. God is one *because* he is three.

The various images and metaphors of the people of God, explored earlier (the people, the body, the household, the Israel of God), show that the people of God are unified into 'God in ministry'.[21] One insight in particular is illuminating.

Perichoresis

The fourth-century Cappadocian fathers (Basil, Gregory of Nyssa, and Gregory of Nazianzus) taught that the essence of God is relational, that God exists in a plurality of distinct persons united in communion. They avoided the twin dangers of collectivism and individualism by speaking of perichoresis (reciprocity, interchange, giving and receiving without blurring). Perichoresis involves a relatedness that is both static and dynamic. As Edwin Hui notes, 'The three persons of the Trinity [are] "being in one another" – drawn to the other, contained in the other, interpenetrating each other by drawing life from and pouring life to each other – as the communion of love.'[22]

Colin Gunton speaks of 'reciprocity, interpenetration and *interanimation*' since he finds the Latin derivative 'coinherence' less

---

[21] See Collins and Stevens, *The Equipping Pastor*, ch. 6, 92–107. See also R. Paul Stevens, ' "Analogy or Homology", An Investigation of the Congruency of Systems Theory and Biblical Theology in Pastoral Leadership', in *Journal of Psychology and Theology* 22.3 (1994), 173–81.

[22] Edwin Hui, notes from unpublished lecture, 'Perichoresis, Communion, and Interpenetration of the Three Divine Persons', 'The Trinity and the Christian Life' course, Regent College, Vancouver, 1994, 1.

satisfactory suggesting as it does a more static conception.[23] The heart of the matter is the sociality of the Triune God, an elegant truth sometimes expressed through the metaphor of family: three persons, one family.[24] The net effect of this recovery of perichoretic reflection is doxological reflection on the Triune God under the category of community rather than individuality. Commenting on John Damascene's doctrine of perichoresis Jürgen Moltmann put the matter this way: 'The doctrine of the perichoresis links together in a brilliant way the threeness and the unity, without reducing the threeness to the unity, or dissolving the unity in the threeness.'[25]

3. Communion or Union?

The implications of this for peoplehood are substantial. Being *laos* means that members of the people of God have communion with God and with one another without being merged with God or one another. The apostle Paul witnessed to this participatory and personal communion with God through Christ in his celebrated and repeated confessions, 'I in Christ', and 'Christ in me'. Paul was apprehended by Christ (Phil. 3:12) but not absorbed.[26] In the same

---

[23] C. Gunton, *The One, the Three and the Many: God, Creation and the Culture of Modernity* (Cambridge: Cambridge University Press, 1993), 163 (emphasis mine).

[24] J. Moltmann (*The Trinity and the Kingdom*, 199) suggests that the analogy is not arbitrary since the divine image is person with person – which is exactly what family is about. Indeed Gregory of Nazianzus saw Adam, Eve and Seth as an earthly parable because they were consubstantial persons.

[25] Ibid., 175.

[26] A classic work by Adolf Deissmann expresses what is called 'Christ-mysticism'. 'The aim of mysticism is either *unio* or *communio*; either oneness with God, or fellowship with God; either loss of the human personality in God or sanctification of the personality through the presence of God; either transformation into the deity, or conformation of the human towards the divine; either participation in the deity or prostration before the deity. In fact ego-centric mysticism or Theo-centric mysticism! Mysticism of aesthetic intoxication or mysticism of ethical enthusiasm! Mysticism that denies personality, or mysticism that affirms

way the people of God is animated and energized by Christ but it is not lost in Christ. We are in Christ; Christ is in us, but we are not Christ. The church is the body of Christ but not Christ. Further, the members of the body are in communion with one another but are not unified (in the sense of mutual absorption). We are 'in' one another but we are not each other.

Unity through diversity

In the same way Paul affirmed that diversity and unity thrive together in the people who bear God's name. In 1 Corinthians 12 Paul contradicted the Corinthian preoccupation with one Spirit manifestation – tongues – as the litmus test of true spirituality. Instead Paul affirmed that diversity is what the body is about.[27] The *laos* does not have a 'mashed potato' unity as is sometimes alleged but a rich social unity in which each member becomes more himself or herself through experiencing an out-of-oneself (ek-static) community life. Unity is not the means to the end – a practical necessity to get the church's work done. Unity is the end, the goal, the ministry itself.[28]

To be *laos* then is not merely to be a bouquet of Christians or a cluster of individual saints. The term 'saints' in Scripture is always a corporate term.[29] To be *laos* means simultaneously to be communal

---

[26] *(continued)* personality! . . . In communion with Christ [Paul] found communion with God; Christ-intimacy was experience and confirmation of God-intimacy. He was not deified nor was he transformed into spirit by this communion, nor did he become Christ. He was not like some who at a later day imagined themselves Christ . . . he was one whom Christ possessed and a Christ-bearer . . . Paul himself subordinated ecstasy to ethos' (*Paul: A Study in Social and Religious History*, trans. W.E. Wilson [New York: George H. Duran, 1926], 150–56).

[27] See G.D. Fee, *The First Epistle to the Corinthians* (Grand Rapids: Eerdmans, 1987), 569–625.

[28] Eph. 1:10; 4:13; Jn. 17:22; Col. 1:17,20.

[29] E.g. Eph. 3:18. My colleague Stan Grenz makes the community of God the starting point for his biblical and systematic theology. See S. Grenz, 'The Community of God: A Vision of the Church in the Postmodern Age', *Crux* 28.2 (June 1992), 19–26; ' "Community" as a Theological Motif for the Western Church in an Era of Globalization', *Crux* 28.3 (September 1992), 10–19.

and personal. God who is community of Father, Son and Spirit has
created a community that expresses God's love life on earth. In
the long history of trinitarian reflection this supreme idea of the
personal and interpersonal within God forms the true basis for
the identity and vocation of the God–imaging people.

Being *laos* means that members of Christ coinhere,
interanimate, and pour life into one another without coalescence
or merger. It means belonging communally without being com-
munistic or being a collective. Moreover, and pertinent to the
clergy–lay dilemma, being a perichoretic people means being a
community without hierarchy, though it is a community with
roles. The community of Father, Son and Holy Spirit finds its
earthly reflection as Moltmann says, 'not in the autocracy of a single ruler but in the democratic community of free people, not in
the lordship of man over the woman but in their equal mutuality,
not in an ecclesiastical hierarchy but in a fellowship church'.[30]

Indeed when trinitarian theology was adopted without
perichoresis, as came to be the case even in the Eastern Church
(though less markedly so), there developed a thoroughly hierarchical approach to church life. A perichoretic community can have
leadership and rich diversity without hierarchy;[31] it can be a
community without superiors and subordinates; it can be a church
without laity or clergy – in the usual sense of these terms. Three
conclusions may be drawn from this.

---

[30] *The Trinity and the Kingdom*, viii. Moltmann's use of 'democratic' is
probably an unfortunate injection of a modern and Western perspective.
The communal principle, however, stands without needing to affirm an
egalitarian perspective.

[31] Perichoresis means that the submission of the Son to the Father is not
subordination but the quality of the way the Son relates to the Father. No
hierarchy is implied. In line with Athanasius we affirm the monarchy is *in*
God and not just the Father, and that *archē* in the Father does not mean
hierarchy. Hui, 'perichoresis', in 'Perichoresis, Communion, and
Interpenetration of the Three Divine Persons', 6. This has been recently
challenged by Simon Chan in *Spiritual Theology: A Systematic Study of the
Christian Life* (Downers Grove: InterVarsity Press, 1998), 43–55.

The perichoretic church

First, there is no such thing as an individual member. If, as I have proposed above, we live out the Christian life interdependently, 'the individual Christian' is an oxymoron. Consistent with the Old Testament, the 'saints' in Paul's letters is really a unit. As Ernest Best says, 'it is this unit which is just as much in Christ as the individual believer'.[32] Believers are held together in what can be conceived as a corporate, inclusive personality. It is biblically and theologically inconceivable for a person to be a believer in Christ and not a member of his community.[33] So for Paul 'there is no such thing as a solitary Christian' and 'it is impossible to conceive of a Christian who is not a member of the Church, which is related to Christ as in him and as his body . . . Individual Christians consequently do not exist.'[34] This is remarkably in harmony with the message given to John Wesley by a 'serious man' before Wesley was converted to Christ: 'Sir, you wish to serve God and go to heaven? Remember that you cannot serve him alone. You must therefore find companions or make them; the Bible knows nothing of solitary religion.'[35] The believer's identity is corporate as well as individual. In Christ we can say, 'I am us!' Within the granular individualism of Western Culture, the basic unit of the church is the individual member. But for Paul the basic unit of the church is the church!

Second, there is no hierarchy of ministries. In his seminal work on the theology of the laity Hendrik Kraemer says, 'All members of the *ekklēsia* have in principle the same calling, responsibility and dignity, have their part in the apostolic and ministerial nature and calling of the church.'[36] Incarnating our loving submission to Christ's lordship in every arena of life precludes saying that certain tasks are in themselves holy and others are secular. William

---

[32] E. Best, *One Body in Christ: A Study in the Relationship of the Church to Christ in the Epistles of the Apostle Paul*, 25.

[33] Ibid., 113.

[34] Ibid., 190, 193.

[35] Quoted in H.A. Snyder, *The Radical Wesley and Patterns for Church Renewal* (Downers Grove: InterVarsity Press, 1980), 148.

[36] Kraemer, *A Theology of the Laity*, 160.

Tyndale, the English Reformer, was considered heretical and executed for teaching, among other things, that 'there is no work better
than another to please God: to pour water, to wash dishes, to be a
souter [cobbler], or an apostle, all are one; to wash dishes and
to preach are all one, as touching the deed, to please God'.[37]

Third, all members of the laos *of God belong to one another, minister to
one another, need one another and contribute to the rich unity and ministry
of the whole.* The church is not composed of those who minister and
those who are ministered 'unto'. Even Paul wrote to the Romans
that he was coming that he and they 'may be mutually encouraged
by each other's faith' (Rom. 1:12). To speak of one person, or one
group in the church as 'the' minister is a tragic denial of the new creation crafted in Christ. Sometimes the question is asked, 'Who is
ministering to the pastor?' The answer should be, 'The rest of the
people.'

'Only a layperson' is a phrase that must never be found on our lips.
It is irreverent and demeaning. It denies that God has adopted, called,
empowered, and gifted us to receive the incredible privilege of being
co-lovers of God, lovers of one another and those who share God's
love for the world. This is our identity – a molecular social identity.
The Duke of Windsor, recalling his upbringing in the royal house of
King George V, claimed that every day his father would say, 'Never
forget who you are.' Better yet, is never to forget *whose* we are. We
are not *laikoi* or *idiōtai*. We are *laos* and *klēros*. Laity, in the popular
sense no longer exists in Christ. It is useless to mount a conspiracy
against it by promoting professionalism in ministry.

It is equally ludicrous to liberate such a laity. Why try to liberate
what is no longer alive? That people – segmented into higher and
lower, subject and object of ministry, ministers and 'their' people –
no longer exists except as a tragic anachronism. Instead, there is the
laos of the Triune God. We get our identity and our vocation from
being the people of the Triune God. And the ministry of that people

---

[37] William Tyndale, 'A Parable of the Wicked Mammon' (1527), in
Henry Walker (ed.), *Doctrinal Treatises and Introductions to Different Portions of the Holy Scriptures*, Henry Walter (ed.) Vol. 42 (1848), range pp.
45–126, quotation from p. 102, in *Publications of the Parker Society*, Henry
Gough (Gen. ed.) 55 vols (Cambridge: Cambridge University Press,
1843–1855).

is to love and be loved. It is so sublimely simple that we could miss its reverent beauty and its life-giving potential. That potential must be seen in the vocation, the work and the ministry of the whole people of God in church and world, matters to which we now turn.

For further study/discussion

1. Read and discuss the following case, which will conclude this first
    part and introduce the next chapter. Use the notes following:[38]

    Case Study: Dream Job. Jim Thompson walked out of his apartment
    into the cool night air. In less than forty-eight hours he was booked to
    take a night train from Cambridge to Edinburgh where he would
    undergo a day-long interview for a junior post in theology. At the end
    of the day he would probably be offered the job (since his mentors in
    the postdoctoral programme assured him he was the top candidate);
    he would need to respond immediately – that same day! It was his
    dream job. Jim and his wife Cheryl had lived in Edinburgh for three
    years while he did his PhD. He loved the country. He also had no
    desire to return to his United States college from which he was on
    leave and which was embroiled in political issues which Jim thought
    might do him in if he returned. But it was not an easy decision for
    Cheryl.

    Cheryl had been trying for months to secure a British nurses'
    licence. She had her RN in the United States but discovered that she
    could not transfer this credential to the United Kingdom without
    a full year of experience in the hospital. She would have to do a
    three-year programme in England or, as an alternative, return to the
    United States for a year to gain the necessary transferable experience.

    Jim made it clear that neither of these options fitted his interview
    plans. Complicating matters was Cheryl's inability to have children
    after seven years of marriage. Jim could not imagine adopting a child.
    So Cheryl made it clear that, if she could not raise a family, her calling
    (every bit as legitimate as teaching theology) was to be a nurse.

    Jim had not previously faced such a crisis in his marriage. When
    they first started courting he held the traditional view that the husband
    was called to make the major decisions and wives were called to

---

[38] Note: This case is adapted from one published in *Case Studies*,
published in *Journal for Case Teaching* 5 (autumn 1993), 67–8 (67–70) (permission received). The 'Dream Job' case study was written by Craig C.
Blomberg © The Case Study Institute. All names have been disguised to
protect the privacy of the individuals involved.

follow. But in more recent years they had a more egalitarian approach, emphasizing calm conversation and mutual give and take. What should he do – now that Cheryl was resisting Jim's personal vision and dream, especially when this new assignment would allow him to be an evangelistic voice in a pluralistic university setting.

Their parents said they would be supportive whatever they decided. John Gordon, a trusted friend in Cambridge, articulated what Cheryl would have said years ago but no longer believed: 'God calls the husband to be the head of the family; if he is obedient to God's call, his wife will be edified.' But Rita Mussett, another local Christian friend took a different approach: 'God never calls husband and wife in opposite directions. If you pray together, talk together and are both obediently seeking God's will, you *will* come to an agreement. Until that happens it would be a grave mistake to take any action.'

But for Jim time was running out. If only he could have a clear sign from God! 'God why are you doing this to me?' he asked. But the silence was deafening.

Discussion guide for using 'Dream Job' in a small group:

a. Introduction: What feelings have you had when your desire to do something vocationally ran counter to the desires of someone close to you (family, parents or spouse)?
b. Read the case.
c. Vote in the group to see which way Jim should go.
d. Role-play in small groups of seven:
   • one person to role-play Jim Thompson meeting with small group in his church
   • three people to be members of the small group
   • one person to reflect on the marriage issues
   • one person to reflect on the view of ministry and vocation which each of the following had: Jim Thompson, Cheryl, parents, John Gordon, Rita Mussett
   • one person to reflect on the biblical resources (texts, theological principles) available to help Jim make a decision
e. Feedback of the two designated persons to 'reflect' to larger group.
f. Share learnings.

2. Discuss the following quote from Yves Congar in the light of one people.

> At a time when the active role of the laity is being found again, it is not without significance that the relationship of clergy and laity is often expressed by the word 'couple.' We hold, then, that there is an analogy between what the Bible shows to be the law of God's work and what the Bible also shows to be the Church's concrete regime. Hierarchy and people are like husband and wife (or the children) in a family. 'The head of the woman is the man . . . he is the image and glory of God: but the woman is the glory of man' (1 Corinthians xi,3,7); but the woman too sways the man and takes in his decisions in her own way . . .'[39]

---

[39] Congar, *Lay People in the Church*, 284.

PART II

SUMMONED AND EQUIPPED BY GOD

Chapter 4

Calling in a Post-vocational Age

My father is a seller of fish. We children know the business too having worked from childhood in the Great South Bay Fish Market, Patchoque, Long Island, New York, helping our father like a quiver full of arrows. It is a small store and it smells like fish. I remember a Thursday afternoon long ago when my dad was selling a large carp to a prosperous woman and it was a battle to convince her. 'Is it fresh?' It fairly bristled with freshness, had just come in, but the game was part of the sale. They had gone over it anatomically together: the eyes were bright, the gills were in good colour, the flesh was firm, the belly was even spare and solid, the tail showed not much waste, the price was right . . . Finally my dad held up the fish behind the counter, 'Beautiful, beautiful! Shall I clean it up?' And as she grudgingly assented, ruefully admiring the way the bargain had been struck, she said, 'My, you certainly didn't miss your calling.'

Unwittingly she spoke the truth. My father is in full-time service for the Lord, prophet, priest and king in the fish business . . . When I watch my dad's hands – big beefy hands with broad stubby fingers, each twice the thickness of mine, they could never play a piano – when I watch those hands delicately split the back of a mackerel . . . when I know those hands peddled fish from the handlebars of a bicycle in the grim 1930s . . . twinkling at work without complaint, past temptations, always in faith consecratedly cutting up fish before the face of the Lord – when I see that I know God's grace can come down to a man's hand and the flash of a scabby fish knife.[1]

---

[1] C. Seerveld, *Christian Workers, Unite!* (Toronto: Christian Labour Association of Canada [90 Hadrian Drive, Rexdale, Ontario], 1964), 7–8. Quoted with permission.

Calvin Seerveld's moving story contains a deep Christian truth. Our ordinary occupations find their true meaning in something larger than personal fulfilment. They are *callings* taken up in what the apostle Paul calls 'my purpose' (2 Tim. 3:10). But the story, taken by itself, contains a dangerous half-truth: the idea that vocation equals occupation. As we shall see, the Christian doctrine of vocation – so central to the theology of the whole people of God – starts with being called to *Someone* before we are called to do *something*. And it is not something we choose, like a career. We are chosen. The Latin roots of the word 'vocation', *vocatio* and *voco*, mean simply to be called or to have a calling. We might do well to eliminate the word 'vocation' for a while and substitute 'calling', which invites the question, '*Who* called?' The loss of vocation in the modern and postmodern world is further indicated by the fact that almost the only people who speak of being 'called of God' are 'full-time' missionaries and pastors.

We live in a post-vocational age.[2] Without any theology of vocation we lapse into debilitating alternatives: fatalism (doing what is required by 'the forces' and 'the powers'); luck (which denies purposefulness in life and reduces our life to a bundle of accidents); karma (which ties performance to future rewards); nihilism (which denies that there is any good end to which the travail of history might lead); and, the most common alternative today, self-actualization (in which we invent the meaning and purpose of our lives, making us magicians). In contrast the biblical doctrine of vocation proposes that the whole of our lives finds meaning in relation to the sweet summons of a good God. In this chapter we will explore the personal, the Christian and the human vocation.

1. Personal Vocation

My late colleague, Klaus Bockmuehl, offered a useful metaphor to show the relationship of the human, Christian and personal

---

[2] See L.T. Almen, 'Vocation in a Post-Vocational Age', in *Word and World* 4.2 (spring 1984), 131–40. Almen develops some of the factors affecting this loss of vocation: unemployment, consumption, creative leisure and worker alienation. He does not explicitly mention secularism.

vocations. A wedding cake has a large base (the human vocation), a smaller layer built upon it (the Christian vocation) and a still smaller layer at the top (the personal vocation). They are interrelated, each building on the other. The Christian is not exempt from the human vocation (including earth-keeping) but there is another dimension of the call of God as shown in 'call' language in both testaments. And finally each of us is a called person. But that call is some combination of the human and Christian vocations that is unique to our own person and life path.

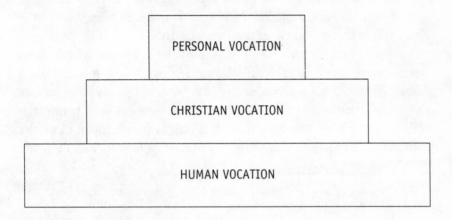

PERSONAL VOCATION

CHRISTIAN VOCATION

HUMAN VOCATION

Personal vocation in Scripture

In one place it seems that Paul uses call language for the 'place in life' or 'station' we occupy (slave, free, married, single, etc.). This is the text the Reformers, and particularly the Puritans made much of, too much in fact. 'Nevertheless, each one should retain the place in life that the Lord assigned to him *and to which God has called him [or her]*' (1 Cor. 7:17, emphasis mine). Luther translated *klēsis* as *Beruf* (meaning 'station') and from this, along with Calvin, developed the idea of a 'worldly calling'.

An accurate exegesis of Paul's statement in 1 Corinthians 7:17 must take into account the context: issues of bond, free, married, single, circumcised, uncircumcised. Further one must consider the over-realized eschatology at work in Corinth, namely that in this age of end-times Spirit, tongues, 'the language of heaven' was the ultimate spiritual gift. Earthly realities like marriage no longer mattered. In the Corinthian church people were leaving their life situation (even their marriages) as though this change had religious significance. Paul's word in 7:17 and 7:24 that they are to abide in the situation '*to* which they were called' and in 7:20 that 'each one should remain in the situation which he [or she] was in *when God called him [or her]*' (emphasis mine, but note the change) was addressed to this situation. Paul argues that though such life situations get taken up in God's call (1 Cor. 7:17,24) and are transformed by it, the call of God comes to us *in* these situations (1 Cor. 7:20) and is much more than occupation, marital status or social position.

Paul Marshall is right in saying that unless Paul has coined a new word he is here using *klēsis* in a way found nowhere else in the New Testament. 'This means that the Bible does not contain a notion of vocation or calling in one of the senses in which these terms were used in Reformation theology.'[3] At most, calling means that God is providentially involved in our lives so we are not a collection of accidents. The situation gets taken up into the calling and is sanctified by it, but calling is much more than our situation.[4] Unfortunately, the reduction of calling to station in life

---

[3] P. Marshall, *A Kind of Life Imposed on Man: Vocation and Social Order from Tyndale to Locke*, 14.

[4] In his commentary on 1 Cor. 7, Fee presses the following interpretation: The concept of call is a way of describing Christian conversion. That call comes to a person in a given social setting. This is the clear emphasis of all the verbs in the passage, especially as it is associated with various social options (vv. 18,21,22). These two realities are pressed theologically in various ways by Paul: (1) God's call to Christ that comes in Christ renders the settings themselves irrelevant (vv. 18–19,22). (2) Because of this, change is not necessary; indeed one may live out the Christian life in whatever setting that call took place. (3) On the other hand, precisely because these settings are irrelevant, if change does take place, that too is irrelevant. One is not to seek change as though it had religious significance, which it does not. (4) Although he comes very close to seeing the setting in which one is called as 'calling' itself, he never quite makes that jump. At most 'calling' refers to the circumstances in which the calling took place. This does not mean that a person is locked forever in a particular situation. 'Rather, Paul means that by calling a person within a given situation, that situation itself is taken up in the call and thus sanctified to him or her' (G.D. Fee, *First Corinthians* [New International Commentary on the New Testament; Grand Rapids: Eerdmans, 1987], 309–10).

as promoted by the Reformers eventually had the spiritual effect of inhibiting spiritual mobility and reducing the willingness of people to be sent in cross-cultural missionary service, a factor still at work in many mainline churches.

The magisterial Reformers

It is crucial to realize that the Reformers were developing a theology of calling against the backdrop of medieval monasticism through which persons elected a superior way. They were striving for a perfection beyond the Ten Commandments and so chose to obey the 'evangelical counsels' of poverty, chastity and obedience. They did not speak of the monastic life as 'vocation' because this was not the summons of God but the self-chosen election of certain Christians. To this both Luther and Calvin reacted vigorously, even to the extent of saying that the one place one could not live the Christian life was in the monastery.

Luther was eloquent on the tragic results of this two-level view of vocation: 'Monastic vows rest on the false assumption that there is a special calling, a vocation, to which superior Christians are invited to observe the counsels of perfection while ordinary Christians fulfil only the commands; but there simply is no special religious vocation since the call of God comes to each at the common tasks.'[5]

Luther railed against the attempt of people to find a superior way beyond keeping the Ten Commandments and, along with others, Luther kept pointing to the apocryphal book Ecclesiasticus: 'Search not for things beyond your ability, but the things that God has commanded you. For you have already been commanded more than you can manage' (3:21ff.). Christian perfection is to be found in normal daily tasks.

> How is it possible that you are not called? You have always been in some state or station; you have always been a husband or wife, or boy or girl, or servant. Picture before you the humblest estate . . . Yea, if you had five heads and ten hands, even then you would be too weak

---

[5] Quoted in R. Bainton, *Here I Stand: A Life of Martin Luther* (Nashville: Abingdon Press, 1978), 156.

for your task, so that you would never dare think of making a pilgrimage or doing any kind of saintly work.[6]

What is obvious from this is that for Luther one's call is not a specific trade or occupation but that person's position in society, one's 'station in life'. If you were born a woman that determined your calling as a housewife and mother. Even the shepherds, after they worshipped the Christ child, returned to their flocks because that was the shepherd's station. Anna the widow in the temple was also doing what widows should do. To leave your station would turn society upside down like 'walking on one's ears, veiling one's feet, [and] putting shoes on one's head'.[7] Calvin took a similar view in the *Institutes* adding the additional emphasis on predestination, that God has sovereignly assigned these places.[8]

At the same time as Luther and Calvin were railing against monks and monasteries, they were fighting on another front: the Anabaptists, among whom were found the early Swiss Brethren and the Mennonites. The Reformers saw these movements as otherworldly – Christians huddling together in groups of believers and forming a new monasticism. These groups downplayed the civic vocation and the Ten Commandments. They stressed the Sermon on the Mount and the supernatural guidance of the Holy Spirit. Calvin charged them with inventing 'secret revelations of the Spirit for themselves'[9] instead of relying exclusively on the exposition of Scripture. So both Luther and Calvin emphasized this-worldliness in vocation, but it is not hard to see how this

---

[6] J.N. Lenker (ed. and trans.), *Sermons of Martin Luther* (8 vols.; Grand Rapids: Baker Book House, 1983), I, 242.

[7] *Luther's Works*, LII, 124.

[8] 'The Lord bids each one of us in all life's actions to look to his calling . . . [He] has appointed duties to every man in his particular way of life. And that no one may thoughtlessly transgress the limits, he has named these various kinds of living "callings"' (*Institutes of the Christian Religion* [Philadelphia: Westminster Press, 1960], III.10.6).

[9] John Calvin, *Commentaries on the Epistles of Paul to the Galatians and Ephesians*, trans. William Pringle (Grand Rapids: Eerdmans, 1948), 4.12, quoted in Bochmuehl, 'Recovering Vocation Today', 32.

began the slippery slide towards the secularization of callings.
Luther said:

> The idea that the service to God should have only to do with a church
> altar, singing, reading, sacrifice, and the like is without doubt but the
> worst trick of the devil. How could the devil have led us more effec-
> tively astray than by the narrow conception that service to God takes
> place only in church and by works done therein . . . The whole world
> could abound with services to the Lord, *Gottesdienste* – not only in
> churches but also in the home, kitchen, workshop, field.[10]

Secularization of the particular call

The Puritans (sixteenth and seventeenth century) were the first to
develop systematically the distinction between the 'general call' (by
which we are called effectually to become Christians) and the
'particular call' (by which we take up a sphere of service in direct
response to the summons of God).[11] The 'particular call' is that to
which the woman in Calvin Seerveld's story was alluding: 'My, you
certainly didn't miss your calling!' But is this biblical?

The Puritans stressed that Christianity proposed a definite
emphasis on work in this world. This was not merely a chosen
activity but the summons of God – a calling. Callings or vocations
were part of God's order, a means of serving God and sustaining
God's world through supporting oneself, family and commonwealth. William Perkins taught that as soon as one discovered faith
in Christ a person should be taught to discover his calling. He notes

---

[10] Quoted in O.E. Feucht, *Everyone a Minister* (St Louis: Concordia,
1979), 80.

[11] 'The Puritans were the link between the Reformation and the modern
world' (Os Guiness, 'The Recovery of Vocation for Our Time' [unpub-
lished audiotape]). Basil Hall described the Puritans as people who were
'restlessly critical and occasionally rebellious members of the Church of
England who desired some modifications in Church government and
worship, but not . . . those who removed themselves from that Church'
(Basil Hall, 'Puritanism: The Problem of Definition', in G.J. Cuming
[ed.], *Studies in Church History* [London: Nelson, 1965], II, 283–6, quoted
in Marshall, *A Kind of Life*, 38).

that 'Adam as soon as he was created, even in his integrity, has a personal calling assigned to him by God, which was to dress and keep the garden . . . And therefore all who descend from Adam must needs have some calling to walk in, either public, or private, whether it be in the church, or commonwealth, or family.'[12]

There was some ambiguity among the Puritans, however, as to the exact meaning of the particular calling, with one or another of the following historical trends being emphasized, a process masterfully traced by Paul Marshall in *A Kind of Life Imposed on Man*. First, as we have seen, there was in the New Testament no specific doctrine of calling to a particular task. But soon, drawing on Greek dualism, the church fathers developed a doctrine of two ways, the higher (like Mary) and the lower (like Martha). Augustine used the terms *vita contemplativa* (contemplative life) and *vita activa* (active life) for these. By the medieval period calling for the common people simply equalled station in life.

> The rich man in his castle,
> The poor man at his gate,
> He made them high and lowly,
> And ordered their estate.[13]

But those who were truly called elected to go into the monastery or priesthood, which holy purpose the rest of the saints worked to support.

Then came Luther and his bold innovative translation of 1 Corinthians 7:17 as *Beruf*, a word normally used to describe the calling of someone to the clerical state. Luther took this word and applied it to all worthy occupations, extending calling to the whole people of God and focusing it in terms of estate, so fusing estate, office and duty.[14] 'What you do in your house is worth as much as if you did

---

[12] *The Workes of That Famous and Worthy Minister of Christ in the University of Cambridge, Mr. William Perkins* (London: John Legett, 1626), I, 755C. A modern abridged version is found in W. Perkins, *The Work of William Perkins* (Appleford, UK: The Sutton Courtenay Press, 1969).

[13] Quoted in P. Helm, *The Callings: The Gospel in the World* (Edinburgh: Banner of Truth Trust, 1987), 47.

[14] Marshall, *A Kind of Life*, 23.

it up in heaven for our Lord God . . . We should accustom ourselves to think of our position and work as sacred and well-pleasing to God, not on account of the position and work, but on account of the word and faith from which the obedience and the work flow.'[15]

In fact Luther did distinguish between calling and situation by emphasizing that calling was the duty of serving God by faith (a work of faith)[16] and according to the Word *in* one's situation.[17] This is apparent in the following quotation:

> Now you tell me, when a father goes ahead and washes diapers or performs some other mean task for his child, and someone ridicules him as an effeminate fool – though that father is acting in the spirit just described and in Christian faith – my dear fellow you tell me, which of the two is most keenly ridiculing the other? God, with all his angels and creatures, is smiling – not because that father is washing diapers, but because he is doing so in Christian faith.[18]

Calvin, in contrast to Luther, used 'calling' mainly to describe the call to salvation or the call into the ministry. But he also used 'calling' to describe the work itself that one does (and not merely the faith called forth in the work, as with Luther). Unlike Luther Calvin considered that a Christian might change a calling with proper reason.[19]

Building on Calvin, Perkins emphasized calling as *the particular duties which God requires of us in our estates* – a state of life or lifestyle, though Perkins himself often spoke of callings as though they were simply occupations, some of which were not lawful callings. It seems Perkins fused the two ideas of duties and occupations.[20] In

---

[15] Quoted in W.R. Forrester, *Christian Vocation: Studies in Faith and Work* (London: Lutterworth Press, 1951), 147–8.

[16] See Martin Luther, 'Treatise on Good Works', in J. Atkinson (ed.) and W.A. Lambert (trans.), *Luther's Works*, XLIV 15–114.

[17] This is carefully exegeted in M. Kolden, 'Luther on Vocation', *Word and World* 3.4 (autumn 1983), 382–90.

[18] Martin Luther, 'The Estate of Marriage', in Walther I. Brandt (trans. and ed.), *Luther's Works*, XLV, 40. This and other quotations from *Luther's Works* are used with the permission of the publishers, Concordia Publishing House and Augsburg Fortress Press.

[19] Marshall, *A Kind of Life*, 25.

[20] Ibid., 41.

time the Puritan movement lost the synthesis achieved by Perkins,[21] a synthesis that reflects the biblical balance of calling to salvation. The only way one could escape his or her cast-iron 'calling' (enshrined in the family names 'miller' or 'carpenter') was to seek a vocational call into the church.

Is there a personal call to everyone?

While the New Testament does not give formal evidence for the particular calling so avidly promoted by the Puritans, it does give us several theological perspectives.

First, there is *the effectual call of Christ to become a disciple*. This is the primary way in which all believers experience calling. For some, as for the apostle Paul, this is instantly transformative; for others it is a long process. One person wakes in the morning to see that the sun has risen; another waits through dusk and dawn to see its gradual emergence.

Second, there is *the providential call*. As Paul Helm says, 'It was no accident that Lydia was a seller of purple cloth, or that Aquila and Priscilla were tentmakers, or that Paul himself was a learned Pharisee.'[22] Our lives are not a bundle of accidents. So Scripture describes many people being drawn by God into a particular form of service without a supernatural call: Joseph, Esther, Bezalel and Ohaliab, Aquila and Priscilla, being examples. Discerning the providential hand of God in our lives, birth, family, education, personality, opportunities, is part of discovering our personal vocation.

---

[21] Marshall summarizes, 'It appears that the Puritans were drawing unconsciously on several different sources as they tried to relate to changing social orderings. They drew on an earlier English view of callings as God-given estates which were sites for duty, and also on the Lutheran view of calling as a manner of life to be lived in such estates. They took the traditional view of abiding in one's station, but they also sought to help those who could choose employments and not just accept a given status. They saw all calling as equal in the sight of God, but also thought that, as social roles, some callings were better than others . . . They took the Calvinist notion of effectual calling and then hinted at it also as a duty to God' (ibid., 45).

[22] Helm, *The Callings*, 49.

Third, there is *the charismatic call*. I am using charisma here in the sense of gifts and graces provided by God through the Spirit. Klaus Bockmuehl suggests a fully trinitarian approach to callings. The Father gives us the cultural mandate to subdue and develop the earth. The Son calls us to discipleship and summons us with the Great Commission. The Spirit equips us for a task: 'Now to each one the manifestation of the Spirit is given for the common good' (1 Cor. 12:7).[23] While Spirit gifts[24] are primarily given to build up and edify the body of Christ it seems that the hard and fast distinction between 'natural (though God-given) talents' and so-called 'spiritual gifts' is really untenable, especially in the light of Romans 12 where Paul alludes to an 'extra' anointing provided by the Spirit: 'if it is in contributing to the needs of others, let him give generously' (Rom. 12:6–8). Talents too are gifts of God for which we are accountable (Mt. 25:14–30).[25] Elizabeth O'Connor says, 'We ask to know the will of God without guessing that his will is written into our very beings.'[26] So Frederick Buechner advises: 'Listen to your life. See it for the fathomless mystery that it is. In the boredom and pain of it no less than in the excitement and gladness; touch, taste, smell your way to the holy and hidden heart of it because in the last analysis all moments are kept moments, and life itself is a grace.'[27] But there is more to living as called people than expressing our giftedness and talents within the divinely ordained circumstances of our lives.

Fourth, there is *the heart call*. The Spirit not only equips but constrains. The Spirit not only provides the ability but creates a desire for a particular service.[28] While it is extraordinary for people to have a direct, verbal 'call' (as in Acts 16:9–10), it is entirely ordinary for

---

[23] Bockmuehl, 'Recovering Vocation Today', 28.

[24] See G.D. Fee and R. Paul Stevens, 'Spiritual Gifts', in Banks and Stevens, *The Complete Book*, 943–9.

[25] Calvin radically reinterpreted this parable. Before his time the talents of gold were spiritual gifts and graces bestowed on Christians. But Calvin took a revolutionary approach by interpreting the parable in terms of one's calling and helped shape the modern meaning of talents (Marshall, *A Kind of Life*, 25).

[26] E. O'Connor, *The Eighth Day of Creation: Gifts and Creativity*, 14–15.

[27] F. Buechner, *Now and Then* (San Francisco: Harper & Row, 1983), 87.

[28] M. Volf counters the Reformation idea of work as vocation with this emphasis in *Work in the Spirit: Toward a Theology of Work*.

God to create a desire in our hearts to do the very thing needed, whether in the church or the world. Business people are called in this sense, as are engineers, homemakers, craftspersons, pastors and missionaries. Greg Ogden outlines three dimensions of the individual experience of the call: (1) we experience an inner oughtness; (2) it is bigger than ourselves; (3) it brings great satisfaction and joy.[29] Gordon Cosby would add the sense 'that you were born to this'.[30] Again, Buechner states it beautifully: 'Neither the hair shirt nor the soft berth will do. The place God calls you to is the place where your deep gladness and the world's deep hunger meet.'[31]

Within evangelical Christianity there is a 'guidance-mania' – the fear of not being 'in the centre of God's will'. With a poor sense of God's purpose and a low sense of the civil vocation Christians today tend to focus on personal ministry and evangelism as the only true expressions of the called life. At least the Puritans extended the call of God to all believers.

There is no need to be 'called' through an existential compelling experience to an occupation in society.[32] God gives motivation and gift. God guides. Work, family, civil vocation and neighbouring are encompassed in our total response to God's saving and transforming call in Jesus. Misunderstanding on this point has been promoted by the overemphasis of the Puritans on 1 Corinthians 7:17.[33] So vocational guidance is not discerning our 'call' but, in the context of our call to discipleship, holiness and service (now to be considered),

---

[29] Ogden, *The New Reformation*, 209.

[30] G. Cosby, *Handbook for Mission Groups*.

[31] F. Buechner, *Wishful Thinking: A Theological ABC* (New York: Harper & Row, 1973), 95.

[32] The question of whether there is a special call to the professional ministry will be considered in Chapter 6.

[33] The later Puritan interpretation (especially those who came after Perkins) has the advantage of *universalizing* vocation among the people of God but it (1) minimizes the corporate, people of God, aspect of vocation, (2) makes too much of the specific place one occupies in society as though the place itself were the calling, and (3) focuses on task/doing to the exclusion of being. Nevertheless one should regard the various contexts of life – marriage/singleness, workplace, neighbourhood, society – as taken up into the call of God and therefore expressed in terms of holiness and service rather than arenas chosen for personal self-fulfilment.

discerning the guidance of God in our lives and learning how to live in every dimension to please him.[34]

2. Christian Vocation

We turn now to the explore more fully 'the effectual call' to become a disciple mentioned above. The call of God in Christ, as we shall see, is not only personal and individual but corporate. The people of God (*laos*) is a called people (Acts 15:14).[35]

'Call' in the Old Testament[36]

The word *qara* means 'call out', a summons that implies sovereignty through naming. Naming, however, in Hebrew was not merely attaching 'a verbal handle', but 'to be called something was to *be* something'.[37] When God called Israel, they *became* his people. Tragically Israel was called but sometimes did not respond

---

[34] See Stevens, 'Vocational Guidance', in Banks and Stevens, *The Complete Book*, 1078–85.

[35] K.L. Schmidt, '*ekklēsia*' in Gerhard Kittel and Gerhard Friedrich (eds.), *Theological Dictionary of the New Testament*, trans. Geoffrey W. Bromiley (10 vols.; Grand Rapids: Eerdmans, 1964–76), III, 487–91. This concept of 'calling' is the root meaning of the word used most frequently for 'church', *ekklēsia*. This word is derived from *klēsis* (calling) and means 'an assembly duly summoned'. In the same way that *laos* is usually found with the genitive, 'the people of God' (*tou theou*), *ekklēsia* is found with a defining modifier, 'the church or churches of God'. 'The church of God' can be used for a single congregation or for several, for the church at large or even the church expressed in a house fellowship. But the emphasis is always on the gathering by the initiative of God. Even in Mt. 18:20, 'where two or three come together in my name, there am I with them', the emphasis is not on a self-chosen fellowship but a summoned congregation. So the whole church is a people with a calling and all of the members of the *ekklēsia* have a calling both corporately and individually.

[36] See, Schmidt, '*kaleō–klēsis*' in Kittel and Friedrich, *Theological Dictionary of the New Testament*, 491–501. Some of the following is adapted from Stevens, 'Calling', in Banks and Stevens, *The Complete Book*, 97–102.

[37] Marshall, *A Kind of Life*, 12.

(Is. 65:12). In the last days God will even summon pagan nations (Is. 55:5).

The 'call' is an inviting summons, as in the case of Moses (Ex. 3:4) and Israel: 'When Israel was a child I loved him and out of Egypt I called my son' (Hos. 11:1). In the later chapters of Isaiah 'call' language is used in its highest sense for the Servant whom God calls in righteousness (Is. 42:6) *for service* as a type of those called from the beginning of humanity (Is. 41:2,4). 'I, the Lord, have called you in righteousness; I will take hold of your hand. I will keep you and make you to be a covenant for the people and a light for the Gentiles' (42:6). The use of 'call' language for the commissioning of patriarchs (Moses, Abraham), judges (Gideon), and prophets (Isaiah, Jeremiah, Ezekiel, Amos) is worthy of detailed study.[38] Such research reveals that in each case God's call was to a function, a specified task, rather than to an office.

Most people in the Old Testament who find their way into a position of service (e.g. Joseph) where they are fulfilling God's purposes are not 'called' in the dramatic sense. They were certainly guided by God, though often this was only seen in hindsight (Gen. 45:8). So people are drawn into God's work differently. Perhaps prophets and religious leaders were given dramatic and compelling 'calls' because their main purpose was to call others. In this way the means matches the purpose.

In summary, 'call' language in the Old Testament is used primarily for the people of God who are summoned to participate in God's grand purpose for the world. It is a call to salvation, a call to holiness and a call to service. When applied to individuals 'call' language relates to that salvation purpose rather than being the means of identifying and giving credentials to leaders. This use of 'call' extends into the Greek (LXX) translation of the Old Testament.[39] Within Judaism, however, 'only the men of Qumran seem to have had a special sense of call'.[40] So, as we enter the New Testament, we

---

[38] See D.J. Falk, 'A New Testament Theology of Calling with Reference to the "Call to the Ministry"' (MCS thesis submitted to Regent College, Vancouver, May 1990), 30–64.

[39] Falk, 'A New Testament Theology', 71.

[40] L. Coenen, 'Call', in Colin Brown (ed.), *New International Dictionary of New Testament Theology*, 4 vols. (Zondervan: Grand Rapids/Carlisle, UK: Paternoster Press, 1975), I, 273 (271–6).

encounter a new thing: not only is the people as a whole called but each and every believer is called.

'Call' in the New Testament

The Greek words *kaleō* (to call, summon forth) and *klēsis* (calling, vocation) are used prolifically in the New Testament. This is in sharp contrast to the surrounding culture where in classical Greek *kaleō* and *klēsis* are only seldom used of divine call, usually in conjunction with the mystery religions.[41]

In the Gospels, Jesus used 'call' to describe his invitation to repent, turn to him, and live for the Kingdom of God: 'For I have not come to call the righteous, but sinners' (Mt. 9:13).[42] Specifically 'call' is used for the summons Jesus issued to the Twelve to be with him and to be sent out (Mk. 3:14; Mt. 4:21; 10:1). It is easy to misunderstand these call narratives as a change in occupation similar to what may happen today when a person leaves a 'secular' occupation to go into 'the' ministry. That is not the Gospel-writers' purpose.[43] The first followers are prototype disciples. The call of the disciples, recorded thirty years after the event, was necessarily transformed into a metaphor with timeless relevance. While in one sense the discipleship of the Twelve was unique, all Christians are now called to be disciples.[44]

K.L. Schmidt notes: 'The fact that God is the *kalōn* [the one who calls] and that Christians are the *keklēmenoi* [the called ones], with no qualifying addition, makes it clear that in the New Testament *kalein* [to be called] is a technical term for the process of salvation.'[45] Thus one can distinguish between the 'external' call (which is the good news announced) and the 'internal' call (the effectual call which secures a response).[46] This appears to be part of the meaning of

---

[41] Coenen, 'Call', 271.

[42] Mk. 2:17; Lk. 5:32.

[43] Falk, 'A New Testament Theology', 92.

[44] Ibid., 145.

[45] Schmidt, '*kaleō,*' in Kittel and Friedrich, *Theological Dictionary of the New Testament*, III, 489.

[46] P. Helm puts it this way: 'It is the activity of God who makes a person receptive and responsive to the truth which he hears. The inward "call" is not more information, it is the clearing and renewing of the mind of the

'many are invited [*klētoi*], but few are chosen [*eklektoi*]' (Mt. 22:14).
In the same way Peter uses 'call' to describe the initiative of God in
our salvation ('all whom the Lord our God will call', Acts 2:39). So
does Paul.

'Call' in Paul's letters

The apostle Paul uses 'call' language in an especially rich way and
has been profoundly influential in the church. He uses 'call' in four
ways: (1) salvation in Christ, (2) living in a Christian way, (3) the
interface of Christian discipleship and our life situation, and
(4) Paul's own experience of anointing as an apostle of Christ.

First, Paul uses call language to express the invitation of God to
experience salvation. In Christ all are called 'to belong to Jesus
Christ' (Rom. 1:6), 'to be saints' (1:7), 'according to his purpose'
(8:28), 'into fellowship with his son' (1 Cor. 1:9), 'to be holy' (1:2),
'heavenward' (Phil. 3:14), to salvation (2 Thess. 2:14), to eternal life
(1 Tim. 6:12), and to hope (Eph. 1:18). So we must 'live a life worthy of the calling [we] have received [literally, "to which you have
been called"]' (Eph. 4:1).

Second, Paul also uses call language to describe the summons of
God to holy corporate living. In Paul's letters the people of God is
not a self-elected community but a called people.[47] Almost all of the
statements quoted above have a corporate context rather than individual. We are 'called to live in peace' (1 Cor. 7:15; Col. 3:15),
'called to be free' (Gal. 5:13), 'called to one hope when you were
called' (Eph. 4:4), called 'to live a holy life' (1 Thess. 4:7; 2 Tim.
1:9). Western Christians read these as exhortations to individual
Christians but they were written to communities for holy corporate
living. The multiple contexts of Christian calling can be represented
in the drawing opposite.

Third, in one place, as explored above, it seems that Paul uses call
language for the 'place in life' or 'station' we occupy (slave, free,
married, single, etc.). Though such life situations get taken up in

---

[46] *(continued)* one who hears so that he understands the good news . . . it is
the renewing of the will in order that the response of faith and obedience
may be made as the good news is announced' (*The Callings*, 3–4).

[47] Rom. 8:30; 9:24; 1 Cor. 1:24,26; 1 Thess. 2:12; 5:24.

DIMENSIONS OF CHRISTIAN VOCATION

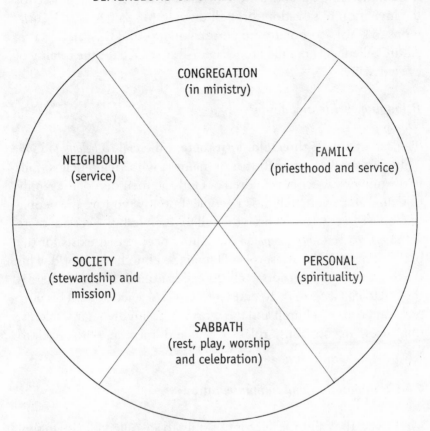

CONGREGATION
(in ministry)

NEIGHBOUR
(service)

FAMILY
(priesthood and service)

SOCIETY
(stewardship and
mission)

PERSONAL
(spirituality)

SABBATH
(rest, play, worship
and celebration)

God's call (1 Cor. 7:17,24) and are transformed by it, the call of God comes to us *in* these situations (1 Cor. 7:20) and is much more than occupation, marital status or social position.

Fourth, in other New Testament writings there is a similar use of 'call' to what we have encountered in the Gospels and the letters of Paul.[48] In two places 'call' is used for the leading of God to a specific ministry: 'Set apart for me Barnabas and Saul for the work to which I have called them' (Acts 13:2; cf. Acts 16:10). These are obviously exceptional, though God may call individuals in a direct supernatural way. It is, however, questionable whether one can make a doctrine of calling to a specific ministry from such scanty references. What can be affirmed from the New Testament is the desire of God to *lead* each believer.

---

[48] Heb. 3:1; 9:15; 1 Pet. 1:15; 2:9; 2:21; 2 Pet. 1:3; Jude 1; Rev. 19:9.

Summarizing the entire New Testament witness, 'call' is used for the invitation to salvation through discipleship to Christ, the summons to a holy corporate and personal living, and the call to serve. All are called. All are called together. All are called for the totality of everyday life.

Belonging, being and doing

The call of God is threefold. First there is the call to *belong to God*. Thus persons without identities or 'names', who are homeless waifs in the universe, become children of God and members of the family of God. 'Once you were not a people, but now you are the people of God' (1 Pet. 2:10).[49] This is the call to discipleship. Second, there is the call to *be God's people in life*, a holy people that exists for the praise of his glory in all aspects of life in the church and world. This is expressed in sanctification; it is the call to holiness.[50] Third, there is the call to *do God's work*, to enter into God's service to fulfil his purposes in both the church and the world. This involves gifts, talents, ministries, occupations, roles, work and mission – the call to service.[51]

Christian vocation and human vocation

Moreover, the call to service is not only to so-called Christian service in terms of evangelism and edification. The Christian vocation summons us to take up the human vocation in its totality. We are not redeemed by Christ to become angels preparing for an immaterial heaven, but saved to become fully human beings serving God and God's purposes in the world through the church. So it is crucial to understand that for which we were originally formed and called by God.

---

[49] Hos. 11:1–2, 17; Mt. 9:13; Mk. 2:17; Lk. 5:32; Acts 2:39; Rom. 1:6,7; 8:28; 9:24; 1 Cor. 1:24,26; 7:17,20; Eph. 1:18; 4:1; Phil. 3:14; 1 Thess. 2:12; 5:24; 1 Tim. 6:12.
[50] 1 Cor. 1:8–9; 7:15; Gal. 5:13; Eph. 4:4; Col. 3:15; 1 Thess. 4:7; 2 Tim. 1:9.
[51] Ex. 19:6; Is. 41:2,4; 42:6; Mt. 4:21; Mk. 3:14; Eph. 4:1; 1 Pet. 2:9–10. For a development of these three dimensions see Bockmuehl, 'Recovering Vocation Today', 25–35.

3. Human Vocation

In most discussions of vocation two biblical mandates are cited: the Creation Mandate and the Great Commission.

Two mandates or one?

The Creation Mandate (Gen. 1:27–30), sometimes called the Cultural Mandate, means we are called to have dominion over the earth as expressed in our civic responsibilities like earthkeeping and engineering.[52] The Great Commission (Mt. 28:19–20), sometimes called the New Creation Mandate, means that Christians are called to witness to Christ to the ends of the earth. One concerns creation, the other salvation. Denominations line up in their preference for one or the other with mainline denominations and European churches, by and large,[53] stressing the former and evangelical churches emphasizing the latter. Separating these two mandates has been tragic. When so separated mission becomes disconnected from life and becomes a 'discretionary-time' activity. Further, social action and evangelism become separated and prioritized.[54] The Christian life is essentially unbalanced and fragmented when God intends it to be unified.[55] A better way involves viewing the human

---

[52] See P. Marshall, *Thine is the Kingdom: A Biblical Perspective on the Nature of Government and Politics Today* (Basingstoke, UK: Marshalls, 1984), 20–38. In this brilliant and comprehensive exposition of the creation mandate Marshall shows how Christian service is as wide as creation itself. He proposes that 'we must see these two mandates [the creation and the gospel] as essentially two aspects of the same thing – that we are servants and followers of God through Jesus Christ in whatever we think or feel or do in any and every area of God's creation' (20).

[53] See K. Bochmuehl's comparison of European and North American churches in this context, in 'Recovering Vocation Today', *Crux* 24.3 (September 1988), 32–3 (25–35).

[54] See G.E. Ladd on righteousness and justification in *A Theology of the New Testament* (Grand Rapids: Eerdmans, 1993), 480–90. The record of the church's service in the world is truly inspiring. See E.H. Oliver, *The Social Achievements of the Christian Church*.

[55] See C.R. Klein, 'The Lay Vocation: At the Altar in the World', in R.J. Neuhaus and G. Weigel (eds.), *Being Christian Today* (Washington, DC: Ethics and Public Policy Center, 1976), 197–210.

vocation in terms of a covenant encompassing creation, redemption and final consummation.[56] Salvation is both a rescue operation (recovering our lost vocation in Eden) and a completion project (preparing for the final renewal of creation at the second coming of Jesus). Eschatology (the end times) is critical to understanding our vocation as Christians in this world.

The last thing we do is the first thing we think about. If we want to have a party with a cake, we first think about the party, then the cake. Then we obtain the ingredients and turn the oven up. We do not first turn on the oven, go out to buy ingredients, and then plan a party.[57] God envisioned the final party – the wedding supper of the Lamb (Rev. 19–22) – and then 'thought up' creation. The whole of

---

[56] Elsewhere I have developed some of the dimensions of covenant theology as it applies to marriage, but here in relation to the vocation of humankind. See my *Married for Good* (Downers Grove: InterVarsity Press, 1986), 15–53. The essence of the covenant is contained in the two-pronged formula 'You will be my people and I will be your God' (Jer. 30:22; Deut. 10:12–22; Ezek. 11:20). They are a marriage pair. The Hebrew word for covenant, *berîth*, is also used for the constitution or agreement between the monarch and the people (2 Sam. 3:21; 5:3; 1 Chron. 11:3). It states not only a relationship but the performance expectations implicit in the treaty or agreement. It provided what amounted to a limited constitutional monarchy, making Israel unique in the ancient world. David Atkinson defines covenant as an 'agreement between two parties based on promise, which includes these four elements: first, an undertaking of committed faithfulness made by one part to the other (or by each to the other); secondly, the acceptance of that undertaking by the other party; thirdly, public knowledge of such undertaking and its acceptance; and fourthly, the growth of a personal relationship based on and expressive of such a commitment' (D. Atkinson, *To Have and to Hold: The Marriage Covenant and the Discipline of Divorce* [Grand Rapids: Eerdmans, 1979], 70). The most comprehensive treatment of this is found in Walther Eichrodt, *Theology of the Old Testament*, I, trans. J.A. Baker (Philadelphia: Westminster Press, 1961). Into this ancient idea God breathed the inspiration of his own word to express his relationship with his people and creation. For some pastoral implications of covenant theology see W. Brueggemann, 'Covenanting as Human Vocation: A Discussion of the Relation of the Bible and Pastoral Care', *Interpretation* 33.2 (April 1979), 115–29.

[57] I am indebted to Ray S. Anderson for this analogy.

our human existence makes sense in the light of the *eschaton*, the end.

Covenant mandate

Living under covenant is larger than simply saying that the purpose of the gospel of Jesus is to restore us to the creation mandate. It is that, but much more.[58] Exploring the relationship of covenant and creation in Genesis 6:18 and 9:8–17 William J. Dumbrell concludes that there is only one divine covenant which starts with Genesis 1:1 and ends with the renewal of all things in Revelation 21:5: 'the very fact of creation involved God's entering into relationships with the world . . . The world and man are part of one total divine construct and we cannot entertain the salvation of man in isolation from the world which he has affected'.[59]

The first two chapters of Genesis are foundational for our understanding of the human vocation, as are the last few chapters of Revelation.

Communion with God

The first work of Adam and Eve is described rather than pre-scribed. Implicit in their humanity is the commission to dwell in communion with God. The man and the woman experienced the uninterrupted presence of God in a relationship of loving awe.

---

[58] Theologically the covenant God made with his creation and people had (1) a relational foundation, encompassed by the formula 'you are my people; I am your God'; (2) obligations which were twofold: blessing God and living faithfully the lifestyle of God's covenant people as prescribed in the Ten Commandments; and (3) the blessing of the covenant (the family, the land and the blessing of the nations). While the blessings were condi-tional on obedience, the covenant itself was essentially unconditional. In this chapter we are exploring the obligations of the covenant in a threefold way. For a consideration of the conditionality of the covenant see Jungwoo Kim, 'Psalm 89: Its Biblical-Theological Contribution to the Presence of Law within the Unconditional Covenant' (Doctoral thesis submitted to the faculty of Westminster Theological Seminary, 1989).

[59] W.J. Dumbrell, *Covenant and Creation: An Old Testament Covenantal Theology* (Nashville: Thomas Nelson, 1984), 41.

The text suggests that the garden was not raw wilderness but a sanctuary-garden, a place of real meeting with God.[60] No activity was intended to take them away from their centre, though like all relationships there were seasons of special intimacy, as suggested by God's walking in the garden in the cool of the day looking for his creatures' fellowship (Gen. 3:8). The high point of the creation story is the sabbath, which is delight in God, one another and creation (Gen. 2:3). The practice of the presence of God is not the exclusive vocation of professional ministers and cloistered monks. Nor is it a sacred interlude but woven into the warp and woof of everyday life. It is part of our calling.

This is the *personal* covenant with God. What is missing in the simple proposition that the gospel restores human beings to the creation mandate is the fact that God has made us for himself, to enjoy the loving communion of the triune God. It is this communion that is restored by the gracious work of Christ so that John can write, 'Our fellowship is with the Father and with his Son, Jesus Christ' (1 Jn. 1:3). The human vocation is perichoretic – it is an abiding in God and having God abide in us. Corporate worship is critical to sustaining a sense of peoplehood as it constantly reminds us who we are and Whose we are. Abraham Heschel has beautifully asserted that the practice of surrendered gratitude as expressed in the doxology is the last full measure of humanness in which the creature of God is turned fully towards the Creator: 'The secret of spiritual living is the power to praise. Praise is the harvest of love. Praise precedes faith. First we sing, then we believe.'[61]

As an alternative to communion, the Enemy invited Adam and Eve to doubt the goodness of God (Gen. 3:1), to cease practising continuous thanksgiving (Rom. 1:21–3) and to turn their attention

---

[60] Dumbrell, *Covenant and Creation*, 38. See also W.J. Dumbrell, *The Search for Order: Biblical Eschatology in Focus* (Grand Rapids: Baker Book House, 1994), 22.

[61] A.J. Heschel, *Who Is Man?* (Stanford: Stanford University Press, 1965), 116. 'The biblical words about the genesis of heaven and earth are not words of information but words of appreciation. The story of creation is not a description of how the world came into being but a song about the Lord's glory of the world's having come into being. "And God saw that it was good" (Genesis 1:25)' (ibid., 115).

away from God. When he succeeded, Adam and Eve disobeyed their Creator, rejected their creatureliness, and sought what William Dumbrell calls 'absolute moral autonomy, a prerogative which the Bible reserves for God alone'.[62] God continues to seek the presence of man and woman (Gen. 3:9) but they play hide-and-seek until God graciously finds them (ultimately in Christ) and restores communion.

Revealed in the entire Bible is the wonderful truth that God wants communion with humankind and continuously calls people into communion. In Leviticus 26:11–12 God says, 'I will put my dwelling place among you . . . I will walk among you and be your God, and you will be my people' (thus repeating the covenant 'formula' – your God, my people). The covenant is essentially a relational agreement, not a performance contract. The essence of our experience of the New Covenant through the blood of Christ (Mt. 26:28) is not a service contract, but belonging: you are my people – I am your God (Rev. 21:3). The New Testament images of temple, people, body, bride, household, colony of heaven confirm that dwelling with God in persistent gratitude, and knowing ourselves to be known by God (Ps. 139; Gal. 4:9) is the heart of it.

The Bible ends with a glorious vision of perfect communion. Central to the vision of Revelation 21–2 is simply that 'I shall know fully . . . as I am fully known' (1 Cor. 13:12). Our primary 'work' in the new heaven and earth will be worship, the grateful appreciation of God himself (Rev. 4–5), thus fulfilling the personal dimension of God's covenant. There will be no temple 'because the Lord God Almighty and the Lamb are its temple' (Rev. 21:22). The consummation of this divine–human marriage is summarized by the announcement, 'Now the dwelling of God is with men, and he will live with them.' Then, fulfilling the communion dimension of the covenant, John repeats the covenant formula, 'They will be his people, and God himself will be with them and be their God' (Rev. 21:3). Our Christian experience now as we look towards this consummation is not *marriage* to Christ (Rev. 19:7), as some Christian mystics have suggested, but betrothal, the Jewish form of presexual marriage (2 Cor. 11:2).

---

[62] Dumbrell, *Creation and Covenant*, 38.

Community building

If the call to communion has been neglected through a narrow emphasis on the Creation Mandate, so has the call to build the human community on earth. This is the *social* covenant. God's first negative statement in the Bible is that 'it is not good for the man to be alone' (Gen. 2:18). God judges man's solitariness. So God makes a 'helper suitable for him' (2:18). God makes humankind innately social and inevitably sexual. The image of God is essentially relational and procreational.

> So God created man in his own image,
>   in the image of God he created him;
>   male and female he created them.
> God blessed them and said to them,
> 'Be fruitful and increase in number; fill the earth and subdue it'
>   (Gen. 1:27–8).

Adam and Eve were called to live in grateful awareness of the cohumanity of life, male and female being the image of God together and not alone (Gen. 1:26–8), each sex evoking the other's sexuality, and together enabling humanity to be a mysterious expression of God's own love (Eph. 5:32). As designed by God, male and female are equal partners and heirs of the grace of life, complementary and side by side, rather than senior and assistant.

The family becomes God's prototype community on earth and is part of every person's vocational calling, whether one remains single or gets married. People-making (Gen. 1:28) gives Adam and Eve the further privilege of making people in their own likeness (Gen. 5:3) as God made them in his. With the birth of Seth and Seth's son, people 'began to call on the name of the Lord' (Gen. 4:26) thus becoming truly the people of God. Single people, while not creating a new generation, are included in the call to cohumanity and can express fecundity in other ways (Is. 56:4–7).

So humankind's duty and destiny is to build community, to express neighbourliness, to celebrate cohumanity – in a word, to love. We dare not relegate this to discretionary time activities. For example, it would be dangerous for me to think of myself as a part-time husband or a part-time grandfather. Some will earn their salary in community-building by being town-planners or family counsellors, just as others will earn it by evangelism or carpentry. The way one earns one's living turns out to be incidental. The truth is that vocation demands our all. The call of God that comes to every believer (Eph. 4:1) embraces all of life: work, family, neighbourhood, politics, congregation and sabbath.

The whole story of salvation in the Bible is presented to us in the grammar of covenant: mutual belonging. The individual is not lost in this but rather found in community. Persons such as Adam, Abraham, Isaac and Jacob are 'presented as already sharing in the experience of their descendants; their life is like a resume of that of their posterity' and their death is a return to their fathers.[63] Six of the Ten Commandments deal with communal relationships.[64] Jesus summarized the law in terms of loving God *and neighbour*. Western 'individualized' Christians have much to learn from Asian brothers and sisters in achieving a balance between the individual and the community.[65] It is, once again, perichoretic; we have our being in communion. As we will see in the chapter on mission, our calling is to build both the human community on earth (the matter under consideration here) and to build the community of faith (which we have considered under the Christian Vocation).

Sin shattered the social aspect of the covenant. The relationship of Adam and Eve became politicized. The 'curse' (Gen. 3:16) means the man will 'rule' the woman and the woman will desire to overmaster the man (the word for 'desire' in 3:16 is the desire to 'overpower' as is found in the use of 'desire' in Gen. 4:7). Tragically some Christians think that rule and revolt between the sexes is God's ultimate design.[66]

---

[63] A. Gelin, *The Concept of Man in the Bible*, trans. David Murphy, (London: Geoffrey Chapman, 1968), 63.

[64] K. Bockmuehl, 'The Ten Commandments: Are They Still Valid?' *Crux* 15.4 (December 1979), 20–25.

[65] See P.C. Vitz, 'A Covenant Theory of Personality: A Theoretical Introduction', in L. Morris (ed.), *The Christian Vision: Man in Society* (Michigan: Hillsgate College Press, 1984), 75–99.

[66] In fact, the modification of nature, resistant land, and political relations between the sexes is the divinely proscribed 'groaning' for full redemption (Rom. 8:22). The issue is whether one looks to fallen life in the garden or eschatologically to the ultimate fulfilment of God's purposes as

Instead of family there is social alienation and individualism. Self-consciousness was born in sin. Their 'selves' were naked and they felt shame (Gen. 3:7). The first spiritual death in the human family (death to God) was socially experienced (death to true self and the other). Instead of co-creating life, human beings now take life and, tragically, the first physical death in the human family was a murder (Gen. 4:8).

Only in Christ does the curse get reversed. Instead of rule and revolt between the sexes there is mutual submission (Eph. 5:21,22,25,33). Instead of social alienation there is call to build community in two senses, first to be neighbourly (Lk. 10:25–37), and second, to build the true family of God in the church (Mk. 3:33–5).[67]

The ultimate hope contained in the last book of the Bible is a new heaven and new earth, combining both perfect city, the New Jerusalem, and a restored earth – the perfect garden, in which the people of God dwell. Heaven is a great interracial, international, intercultural community composed of people from 'every nation, tribe, people and language' (Rev. 7:9). Even the powers will be restored.[68] All dimensions of social unity will be restored according to God's design, including the 'principalities and powers' that provide structure to communal life, is suggested by statements like Rev. 21:24: 'The nations will walk by [the light of the Lamb], and the kings of the earth will bring their splendour into [the city].' We live somewhere between Eden and the New Jerusalem but we live in hope (Rom. 8:24–5).

---

[66] *(continued)* our model for the relationship of the sexes, indeed for the human (and therefore Christian) vocation in full. The outpouring of the Spirit on the church at Pentecost convinced the first Christians that the last days were upon them (Acts 2:17) and they became convinced that they should order their lives not around the beginning but the end. For us such living with heavenly-mindedness makes for intensely practical living here and now.

[67] Gal. 6:10; Eph. 2:19; 4:11–16.

[68] See Chapter 9.

Co-Creativity[69]

The third part of the covenant mandate is commonly called the Creation Mandate. The call to have 'dominion' or 'rule' (Gen. 1:28–30) is the *creational* vocation of humankind. We are using the term co-creativity[70] to describe this because, as Loren Wilkinson

---

[69] I leave aside the consideration of whether 'co-creativity' is an appropriate term to describe the participation of humankind in God's ongoing care and development of his own creation. Lines of inquiry include considering the commonality of words used both for God's and humankind's work (with the exception of *bara* as indicated by T.E. McComsky, '*Bara*', in R.L. Harris, G.L. Archer. B.K. Waltke (eds.), *Theological Wordbook of the Old Testament* (2 vols.; Chicago: Moody Press, 1980), I, 127 (127–8); See also P. Parker, 'The Active Life: A Spirituality of Work, Creativity and Caring', *Review and Expositor* 91 (winter 1994): 118–9; D.L. Sayers, *Christian Letters to a Post-Christian World* (Grand Rapids: Eerdmans, 1969), 77–9; 'Towards a Christian Aesthetic', in Nathan A. Scott (ed.), *The New Orpheus* (New York: Sheed & Ward, 1964); *The Mind of the Maker* (San Francisco: Harper, 1987); J. Holland, *Creative Communion: Toward a Spirituality of Work* (New York: Paulist Press, 1989), 36, 58. An alternative viewpoint critiquing 'co-creativity' is expressed in N. Wolterstorff, *Art in Action* (Grand Rapids: Eerdmans/ Carlisle: Paternoster, 1980). See also W.J. Bouwsma, 'The Renaissance discovery of human creativity', in J. O'Malley, et al., *Humanity and Divinity in the Renaissance and Reformation* (Leiden: E.J. Brill, 1993), 17–34. Surveying the diverse Christian approaches to the artist as creator, W.D.O. Taylor ('Co-Creativity: The Artist in the Eighth Day of Creation' [unpublished paper, Regent College, Vancouver 1996]) proposes the following: Dorothy Sayers – artist as co-creator; Calvin Seerveld – artist as co-cultivator; Nicholas Wolterstorff – artist as responsible steward; Matthew Fox – artist as reverent mediator (Taylor notes that Fox puts humankind too close to the level of God thereby making co-creativity the co-operation of like creatures); Jeremy Begbie – artist as priest of creation. The term 'subcreativity' probably captures the biblical balance best.

[70] Dorothy L. Sayers's use of the word 'create' for human action based on the doctrine of the image of God has dangers of human arrogance and indispensability, dangers which she acknowledges in her play 'The Zeal of Thy House', in Peter Smith (ed.), *Religious Drama 1* (New York: Meridian Books, 1957), see esp. 69–70.

says, 'God invites [us] to participate with him in shaping the world.'[71] In doing this we become co-creators or subcreators as we make discoveries and inventions 'following the clues left by God'.[72] This includes not only creating new things but the art and craft of sustaining the world and providing for others, thereby embracing both God's providence as well as God's ongoing creation. Another term to describe our unique relation to creation is 'regents', earthly rulers representing a heavenly King. The regency of humankind includes the full range of creational tasks and all kinds of 'world-making': cultural, material, political, aesthetic, artistic, musical, technical, and relational.

They were to 'take care of' creation (Gen. 2:15) as God 'keeps us'.[73] This is one important way of understanding the 'image of God' (Gen. 1:27). 'Image' probably refers to the whole person in his or her function in the world. As Dumbrell says, 'By creation, man is then the visible representative in the created world of the invisible God.'[74] Unfortunately this 'dominion' is, as proponents of the New Story of creation charge – all too easily marked by oppressive rule. But, as Loren Wilkinson argues, 'the deepest truth of the Old Story of Christian orthodoxy is that the divine nature is most fully seen not in lordly transcendence, but in the agony of incarnation and

---

[71] L. Wilkinson, 'Art as Creation or Art as Work', in Donald M. Lewis (ed.), *With Heart, Mind and Strength: The Best of Crux 1979–1989* (Langley, BC: Credo), 298 (289–99).

[72] M. Novak, 'The Lay Task of Co-Creation', in M.L. Stackhouse, D.P. McCann, S.J. Roels, P.N. Williams (eds.), *On Moral Business: Classical and Contemporary Resources for Ethics in Economic Life* (Grand Rapids: Eerdmans, 1995), 903 (903–8). See also the Roman Catholic encyclical of John Paul II, 'Laborem Exercens', in M. Walsh and B. Davies (eds.), *Proclaiming Justice and Peace: Documents from John XXIII–John Paul II* (Mystic, CT: Twenty-Third Publications, 1984), 271–311. In the context of a philosophy of science see J. Polkinghorne, 'Creation Continua and Divine Action', *Science and Christian Belief* 7.1 (October 1995), 101–8.

[73] Loren Wilkinson notes that this is the same Hebrew word as is found in the Aaronic blessing: 'May the Lord bless you and keep you . . .' ('The New Story of Creation: A Trinitarian Perspective', *Crux* 30.4 (December 1994), 34 (26–36).

[74] Dumbrell, *Covenant and Creation*, 34.

crucifixion'.[75] Like God, like people. The triune God is essentially 'being in communion'. Contrary to the charge of advocates of the New Story of Creation who critique the Old Story of orthodoxy, God is not a distant patriarchal engineer but, as Loren Wilkinson says, an immanent-and-transcendent triune God that is 'a passionately involved personal being . . . [who] upholds each thing in its distinctness – but things have their distinctness only through their relationships'.[76] So to be in the image of God means that humankind is not to be a cold and distant lord over creation but an involved and relational participating steward.[77]

Where sin entered, the man and woman lost their stewardship. Instead of being regents of the creation that bears God's signature, the man and woman begin to manipulate their environment to satisfy their own greed, or contrarily, to worship the created order (Rom. 1:25). Pollution, sinful distributions of the world's resources, evil social systems, perverse art and aesthetics deepen the alienation, symbolized by the building of a fallen city (Gen. 4:17), a symbol of human arrogance. The *imago dei* (image of God) is severely distorted, broken, mangled.

All human effort is tainted. Creativity is paralysed. Work is cursed, not merely the tilling of the soil which now will be by the sweat of the brow (Gen. 3:17), but also community building, justice work, love-work, peacemaking and even so-called Christian work or ministry. Human beings try to find their identity in themselves, in their community, or in their own efforts, rather than in relation to God.

By restoring us to himself through the New Covenant, Christ not only restores communion and community building but co-creativity. The 'painful toil' of work (Gen. 3:17) may be substantially though not completely undone. Through their various civil occupations men and women make God's world work (Gen.

---

[75] Wilkinson, 'The New Story of Creation', 35. See also John D. Zizioulas, 'Preserving God's Creation: Three Lectures on Theology and Ecology', *Kings Theological Review* 12.1–5 (spring 1989), 41–5; 13.1–5 (spring 1990).

[76] Wilkinson, 'The New Story of Creation', 34.

[77] In Chapter 7 we will explore more completely what it means to be kings and queens under God.

2:5,15) and address the problems of pollution, food distribution, injustice, disease, and the proliferation of violence and weaponry. In so doing they are fulfilling their calling, even their Christian calling! In the short run this work may seem unsuccessful, but in the long run this work will be gloriously enduring as the believer co-operates with what Christ wants to do in renewing all creation.

The prophetic literature of the Old Testament indicates that the new heavens and the new earth, when they are consummated, will include work:

> They will build houses and dwell in them;
>   they will plant vineyards and eat their fruit . . .
> my chosen ones will long enjoy the works of their hands (Is. 65:21–2).

Paul Marshall notes that the evocative image of beating their 'swords into ploughshares and their spears into pruning hooks' (Mic. 4:3) suggests not only the destruction of implements of war but the creation of new tools for work.[78]

The drama, music, beauty, movement, orderliness, sounds and sights of the New Jerusalem are powerful hints that heaven will mean not only a restored creation, but restored creativity. The bride of Christ is an adorned bride (Rev. 21:2). The tree of life, once graciously barricaded, is now the centre of true re-creation: 'On each side of the river stood the tree of life, bearing twelve crops of fruit, yielding its fruit every month. And the leaves of the tree are for the healing of the nations. No longer will there be any curse' (Rev. 22:2–3).

At the End the cosmos will be both the result of human activity as well as something new that God will do – a cosmic Easter for the universe. As Ted Peters says, 'The New Testament promises us that God will yet do something new for the cosmos on the model of what God has already done for Jesus on Easter, namely, establish a new creation.'[79] The scientific debate between creation out of

---

[78] Marshall, *A Kind of Life*, 15–16.

[79] T. Peters, 'On Creating the Cosmos', in R.J. Russell, W.R. Stoeger, SJ, and G.V. Coyne, SJ (eds.), *Physics, Philosophy and Theology: A Common Quest for Understanding* (Vatican City State: Vatican Observatory, 1988), 292 (270–96). In the second-century *Epistle of Barnabas,* a phrase is used

nothing (*creatio ex nihilo*) versus continuing creation (*creatio continua*) needs to be resolved by holding both. God has done and will do a new thing. At the same time God allows us to continue to function as co-creators in an unfolding creation until he will, once again, do that new thing.

Taken as a whole the covenant mandate gives us a comprehensive vision for the human vocation as expressed in the following chart.

THE COVENANT MANDATE

	CREATION ONE		CREATION TWO	
	Design	**The Fall**	**Substantial Salvation**	**Final Salvation**
Communion With God	grateful awareness	bitterness alienation	access adoption	full communion
Community-building	relationality holy sexuality family	homicide broken sexuality alienation	neighbouring church redeemed sexuality	garden city bride of Christ
Co-creativity	world-making stewardship	earth-raping manipulation	redeemed work subcreativity	beauty fulfilled creativity work and sabbath
	Gen. 1–2	Gen. 3	Eph. 2–3	Rev. 21–2

---

[79] *(continued)* that suggests an ultimate sabbath. Speaking for God, Barnabas says, 'The present sabbaths are not acceptable to me, but that which I have made, in which I will give rest to all things and make *the beginning of an eighth day, that is the beginning of another world*. Wherefore we also celebrate with gladness the eighth day in which Jesus also rose from the dead, and was made manifest and ascended into heaven' (*Barnabas* 15:8–9, in K. Lake [trans.], *The Apostolic Fathers* [2 vols.; Cambridge, MA: Harvard University Press, 1975], I, 395–7 [emphasis mine]).

The new heaven and the new earth, presented prophetically as God's ultimate sabbath rest (Heb. 4:1–11) is communion, community and co-creativity – full and final salvation. Significantly the Lord Jesus said, 'Come to me . . . and I will give you rest . . . for I am gentle and humble in heart . . . and you will find rest for your souls' (Mt. 11:28–9). But the rest Jesus brings is not only personal peace but complete *shalôm* for the universe. Sabbath rest is the threefold rest of God, humankind and creation. This is the ultimate goal of God's saving and consummating work and therefore our true destiny.[80]

All human beings are called to the human vocation. Christians have heard the call of Christ and taken up their vocation of being fully human (life in the church being an outcropping of the Kingdom and a sign of the age to come), and their vocation of humanizing the earth for God's glory.

So the call to *belong* to God restores communion. The call to *be God's people* restores community building, though now with a double focus: the human community (family, neighbourhood, city and nation), and also the community of faith (the church). And the call to *do God's work* recovers co-creativity, though now (again) with a double focus: making God's world work in all the ways we serve as regents on earth, and, in addition, to witness to the gospel since the goal of the Christian vocation is that people will have fellowship with God through Jesus Christ.[81] All of this is encompassed in the vocation to love, making amateurs out of all of us.

Meditations on the triune God take us inevitably to the profound revelation of John 17. In that chapter Christ reflects on the love the Father had for him even before the creation of the world (17:24) and prays that the Father's love may be in the disciples (17:26) while disciples and Master, disciple and disciple, and Son and Father all mutually indwell one another (17:22–3,26). This

---

[80] For an exposition of sabbath see A.J. Heschel, *The Earth is the Lord's and The Sabbath* (New York: Harper & Row, 1951); J. Moltmann, *God in Creation: An Ecological Doctrine of Creation*, trans. M. Kohl (London: SCM Press, 1985); L. Wilkinson, 'Garden-City-Sabbath: Hints Toward a Theology of Culture' (unpublished, Regent College, Vancouver, 1989).
[81] Barth, 'The Doctrine of Reconciliation', *Church Dogmatics*, IV.3.11, 554ff.

gives new and deeper meaning to the well-worn text, 'God is love' (1 Jn. 4:16). Love is not merely an attribute of God but love is who God is and what God does. That is what was affirmed by Jürgen Moltmann's reflection on a line by Augustine in the words quoted above, proclaiming that God is 'lover, the beloved and the love itself'.[82] This was also expressed by the trinitarian theologian John Duns Scotus (c. 1265–1308) when he affirmed that creation and redemption flow out of the love within God himself. The world was made by love, runs on love and will end with a glorious eternal love-in. In the same way love is the being and the doing of the *laos*.

We should recover the amateur status of the Christian in terms of the three full-time love-works of God's people. What Christ produces by his glorious redemption is not a new generation of angels but truly human beings and the beginnings of a renewed creation. In other words, the dignity of being *laos* is nothing more or less than becoming as substantially as possible in this life the people God originally intended his first human family to be. Adam and Eve[83] are the prototype amateurs – those who work and serve for love. They are also the prototype Christians. But the ultimate vocation, as we have seen, is not merely restorative of Eden but anticipatory of the new heaven and the new earth.

Co-lovers

Communion, community building and co-creativity – this expresses the vocation and ministry of the *laos* of God. How is our sense of vocation enriched by a trinitarian understanding of God? First, we experience *communion* by becoming co-lovers of God. By

---

[82] Moltmann (*The Trinity and the Kingdom*, 58) quotes these words from Augustine:

Thou seest the Trinity
  when Thou seest love . . .
For the lover, the beloved and the love
  are three.

[83] Not surprisingly the trinitarian theologian Gregory of Nazianzus viewed Adam, Eve and Seth (the first to call on the name of the Lord) as the earthly parable of the divine Trinity (Moltmann, *The Trinity and the Kingdom*, 199).

the miracle of adoption we are drawn into the love life within God himself. This is the heart of 'loving God' and the essence of spiritu- ality. Second, through *community building* we become lovers of one another. To live perichoretically means to reject individualism and to live with a molecular identity – loving neighbour, family and friend. Many do not think of this as 'ministry', 'service' or 'priest- hood' but it is. It is holy ministry to play with one's children or to listen to a friend. Indeed a theology of the whole people of God must inform us of the theology and spirituality of our everyday rela- tionships.[84] Third, *co-creativity* draws us into God's love for the world (Jn. 3:16). The purpose of creation is the glorification of God.[85] Creation is expressive of God's character, an overflow of the love within God himself. The world was 'created to be transfigured and glorified through the Spirit at the end'.[86] Incarnation is the highest expression of nature and not only what God did to redeem the world. So a biblical theology of the whole people of God is not only a rescue effort but is a realignment with God's ultimate purpose for the world: a transfigured creation. What is truly astounding is that humankind has, through the Spirit's irruption in our lives, the privi- lege of participating in the creative work of God. We do this, as we shall now see, partly in the context of daily work.

---

[84] Moltmann expresses this beautifully: '[The unity of the triune God] only corresponds to a human fellowship of people without privileges and without subordinances. The perichoretic at-one-ness of the triune God corresponds to the experience of the community of Christ, the commu- nity which the Spirit unites through respect, affection and love . . .' (*The Trinity and the Kingdom*, 157–8).

[85] See ibid., 209.

[86] Edwin Hui, 'Trinity and Creation', unpublished lecture in 'The Trinity and the Christian Life', Regent College, Vancouver, 1994.

For further study / discussion

1. Consider the opening story from Calvin Seerveld in the light of the biblical teaching on calling. What feelings did the story awaken? What questions? How does Scripture speak to these?

2. Revisit the 'Dream Job' case study at the end of Chapter 3. What do you now understand to be the vocational issues being faced by Jim and Cheryl? How can the biblical doctrine of vocation help them practically to find a way through their dilemma?

3. Compare, contrast and critique biblically two perspectives on co-creativity in humankind: Dorothy L. Sayers, *The Mind of the Maker* (San Francisco: Harper & Row, 1987); and Nicholas Wolterstorff, *Art in Action* (Grand Rapids: Eerdmans, 1980; Carlisle: Paternoster, 1997).

4. Explore the balance of individual and community in contemporary culture in the light of biblical truth.

Chapter 5

Doing the Lord's Work

We must deplore and protest against the secularization of the biblical conception of vocation in our modern usage; we cannot with propriety speak of God's calling a man to be an engineer or a doctor or a schoolmaster. God calls doctors and engineers and schoolmasters to be prophets, evangelists, pastors and teachers as laymen in his Church, just as he calls bricklayers, engine-drivers and machine-minders.

Alan Richardson[1]

Most of us, like the assembly line worker, have jobs that are too small for our spirit. Jobs are not big enough for people.

Nora Watson quoted by Studs Terkel[2]

In the Western world and in most of the newly industrialized countries, work remains the defining experience of a person's identity. But work itself is hard to define.

If one restricts oneself to remunerated employment then homemakers and hospital volunteers are not working. John Stott defines work as 'the expenditure of energy (manual, mental or both) in the service of others, which brings fulfilment to the worker, benefit to the community and glory to God'.[3] But that means that people manufacturing cigarettes or missiles are not working. In this chapter

---

[1] A. Richardson, *The Biblical Doctrine of Work* (London: SCM Press, 1952), 36.

[2] S. Terkel, *Working* (New York: Ballantine, 1972), xix.

[3] J. Stott, *Issues Facing Christians Today* (Basingstoke, UK: Marshalls, 1984), 162.

'work' is defined as purposeful activity involving mental, emotional or physical energy, or all three, whether remunerated or not.

1. Changes in Work

A *Time* article on 'Jobs in an Age of Insecurity' proclaims, 'What you have seen is the end of work as marriage.'[4] In the West many are experiencing the demise of careers or 'dejobbing'. People now are forced to sell their services as value-added to companies and customers rather hope to secure a 'position with advancement'. Except for a few professionals, most people will have several careers in their lifetime. Formerly a curriculum vitae with thirty years of service with one firm was an asset, a sign of loyalty and dependability; now it is seen as a liability (Does this person have initiative and creativity?). Adaptability has become one of the most important qualities for survival in the workplace.

There have been huge changes in the nature of work: from making products to offering a service, from generalist work to specialist, from repetitive tasks to interventions, from tenure to scramble. The workplace has changed from large corporations to smaller, from strata-department to team. Most people today are working with intangibles rather than tangibles. The information industry is one of the largest. Of great significance is the shift from hard work to stressful work.

While much of the world still works to survive, people in the Western world and the newly industrialized countries are looking for new psychological/spiritual satisfactions from work: meaning, relationships, expression of gifts, and sufficient time (the new currency) for leisure – a perspective nurtured by postmodernity. We have moved from a survival culture to an identity culture. Now, to survive, one must know who he or she is. And work is one of the primary ways of establishing this (so it is thought).

Changes in the workplace

The workplace has been globalized. Except in a few monolithic cultures, Asians and Caucasians, and Christians and New Agers work

---

[4] Cone Bending in George J. Church, *Time* (23 November 1993), 24–8.

side by side. In the global marketplace of goods, ideas and professional services, it is more urgent than ever to understand why people
are working, why they work as they do and what work means to
them. We especially need to understand the Asian work ethic.[5]

Not only has the workplace been globalized but it is radically
changing as a *place*.[6] With telecommuting, mobile phones,
modems and faxes it may not be a place at all but rather a network
of connections experienced 'on the move' or based in one's home
office. This may unwittingly contribute to workaholism as people
take their computers on vacations and remain 'in touch' even
when having an intimate conversation with their spouse over
dinner. Work has become totally intrusive, all-encompassing, a
defining environment.

Ironically much of the world wants this. Rural people in the
developing world flood into urban slums looking for work as
the world becomes progressively urbanized and technologized.[7]
The transition from agricultural to industrial and then to the information age, a process that took several generations in Europe and
North America, is happening in parts of Asia, South America and
Africa in a single generation. The rate of change itself is
delibilitating.

Structural unemployment presents a new challenge, not fully
envisioned in biblical revelation.[8] While it is still true that
workaholism and laziness are expressions of moral sloth, it is simply
not true that everyone unemployed is lazy. Remunerated work is
not now an autonomous activity but is structured within the

---

[5] Compare a Western approach in Robert Banks, 'Work Ethic,
Protestant', in Banks and Stevens, *The Complete Book*, 1129–35, with
three Asian perspectives: K. Siemens, 'The Confucian Work Ethic',
Vocatio 1.1 (February 1998), 11–14; E. Wan, 'Confucian Ethic and Atti-
tudes Toward Work', *Crux* 24.3 (September 1988), 2–6; S. Ling,
'Chinese Attitudes Towards Work and Vocation: A North American
Perspective', *Crux* 24.3 (September 1988), 7–13.

[6] See R. Banks, 'Workplace', in Banks and Stevens, *The Complete Book*,
1132–5.

[7] On the influence of technology on work see G. Preece, *Changing Work
Values: A Christian Response*, 13–112.

[8] 2 Thess. 3:6–15 deals with people who will not work, not with those
who cannot.

principalities and powers in this complex information society (the subject of chapter 9 and indicated in the case at the end of this chapter). So a theology of work must consider how one grapples with structures and the demonic.[9] Retirement,[10] forced or elected, too presents new challenges. Does retirement signal the end of work and the introduction to an orgy of leisure, or should it be a transition from remunerated work to voluntary work (or possibly work in a non-job setting)?

Issues facing Christians

Christians are not, of course, immune to these great trends but they have some special problems, problems related to the subject of this book. Their commitment to serve and love their neighbour leads church people to exalt those professions that have an obvious direct impact for the kingdom of God. As we have seen, the missionary is at the top of the list. In most circles, the missionary is roughly equivalent to the martyr in the second century. Next to the missionary is the pastor. Then down it goes in descending order of 'Christian' value: people-helping work, intellectual work, creative work, physical work, political work. The trades are not highly esteemed but they offer 'clean' work. Then comes business, which involves getting one's hands 'dirty' even though business is probably the best hope of the poor of the world.[11] This is followed by the questionable occupations: law, stockbrokering, sales, advertising, the military. Even though the New Testament does not list unacceptable occupations for Christians (except prostitution and extortion) every generation has its 'list'. The Puritan William Perkins excluded those in the fashion industry; Luther excluded monks, and on it goes. But why this prioritization of work? Why is rubbish collecting more dignified to Christians than advertising a new cosmetic?

---

[9] See R. Luecke, 'Faith, Work, and Economic Structures', *Word and World* 4.2 (spring 1984), 141–50.

[10] See S.B. Babbage, 'Retirement', in Banks and Stevens, *The Complete Book*, 855–9.

[11] See M. Novak, *Business as a Calling* (New York: Simon & Schuster, 1996).

2. Work Yesterday and Today

In reality the theology of work held by most Christians comes from a variety of sources often unconsciously absorbed from the great history of ideas that has shaped our world-view.

The ancient world

While there was no uniformity in the ancient Greek world in its view of work, the classical period generally held work in disdain, especially the philosophers. Work was a curse, unmitigated evil; and to be out of work was a piece of singularly good fortune.[12] Unemployment allowed one to participate in the political domain and to enjoy the contemplative life. The whole of society was organized so that a few could actualize the highest human potential. Not surprisingly, 80 per cent of the Greek city-states were comprised of slaves, which Aristotle defined as instruments endowed with life.[13] Work was called 'unleisure'.

Since the Greeks had no sense of vocation they described an individual's activity in society as *ergon* or *ponos*, a burden and toil. Sparta forbade its citizen-soldiers to engage in manual labour, and, during the fifth century before Christ, the government of Thebes issued a decree prohibiting its citizens from engaging in work! One has to think of Christian slaves in Greek households being told by Paul to serve their masters as though they were working for Jesus![14] Probably Christ's labouring status was part of the 'foolishness' that scandalized the Greeks.[15]

---

[12] See *Aristotle's Politics*, trans. B. Jowett (Oxford: Clarendon Press, 1908), 1.10.2.1–4.44–6; *The Nicomachean Ethics of Aristotle*, trans. D.P. Chase (London: J.M. Dent, 1915), 10.7.249–52.

[13] Aristotle, *Politics* 1.4.2–3.31.

[14] Not all city-states were opposed to labour, and in Corinth, for example, the merchants and artisans were more favourably treated. In Athens, the working-class freemen who owned no land, were allowed to participate in the political process. Plato wrote that the workers were the most influential class in a democracy (see Plato, *Republic* 8.565).

[15] S. Griffin, 'Toward a New Testament Understanding of Work' (MCS thesis, Regent College, Vancouver, 1993), 21.

Later developments

A Christianized form of the Greek view found its way into medieval church life. Thus productive work that met the needs of the temporal body had no lasting significance. In contrast, the *vita contemplativa* was building for eternity and was fulfilled in the monastic life. The spiritual life and the worldly life were related as upper and lower, hierarchically organized.[16]

In the fifteenth century came the Renaissance, with the rediscovery of Greek philosophy. There was a reversal on the contemplation theme: the true contemplation of God, the master Artist and Architect, was now expressed in creative activity in the world. The ultimate worker was the artist.

As noted in the last chapter, the Protestant Reformation left a profound legacy. 'You certainly haven't missed your calling!' means that work in one's station in life sovereignly established by God himself is where one fulfils one's Christian calling and duty. As previously noted, this was formed largely *in reaction to medieval monasticism* (with its two-level spirituality).

Modern and postmodern world

The Industrial Revolution changed much of this. While preindustrial life involved the integration of work, home and church, the Industrial Revolution brought about disintegration. It institutionalized the job – work for pay. Work became subdivided, simplified, routinized, and distanced from the results, so much so, that Jacques Ellul concluded that now 'work has no meaning in modern society'.[17]

---

[16] Thomas Aquinas said, 'It is impossible for one to be busy with external action and at the same time give oneself to divine contemplation' (Aquinas [ST, II–II, Q. 182, see also Q. 179, A.2]). In contrast, the word used for 'work' in Gen. 2:15 is later used for 'worship', although one does not find in Scripture a complete identification of work and worship as is proposed in Thomas Carlyle's famous adaptation of the monastic rule *ora et labora* (pray and work) into *laborare est orare* (working is praying), *Past and Present* (London: Dent, 1960), 193.

[17] J. Ellul, *The Ethics of Freedom* (Grand Rapids: Eerdmans, 1976), 461.

Two influential modern thinkers, Marx and Freud, each in a different way, presented work as the autonomous activity of persons. As an alternative to contemplating God, Karl Marx proposed that we should find fulfilment in contemplating ourselves through the work of our own hands.[18] Freud saw work as a tragic necessity since we are primarily pleasure-seeking organisms.[19] These two towering figures have done much to shape the post-vocational culture in which twentieth-century people try to find meaning in work.[20]

The enveloping culture of postmodernity is characterized by high tech and high touch. Meaning is now at the surface in a new way. John Naisbitt argues that the introduction of high technology requires a 'balancing human response' – the personal. But now there are new forms of inequality, especially in relation to the ubiquitous service jobs. It is noted that 'McDonalds now employs more people than the entire US steel industry, but pays less than the wages of agricultural workers.'[21]

It is not hard to see the connection between these historical trends[22] and contemporary attitudes that Christians hold concerning their work. Work in society, so it is thought, has no intrinsic value; the work of ministry lasts forever (Greek dualism). Full-time pastoral or missionary service is the vocation of vocations (medieval monasticism). Physical and manual labour is less worthy than 'creative' and religious work (Renaissance). One ought to be able to find personal fulfilment in one's daily work (Marx, the Renaissance autonomy of the person, the individualism and privatism of postmodern man). So this is the world of work. But, to obtain a theology of work we must also listen to the timeless Word of God.

---

[18] See L. Hardy, *Fabric of This World*, 30.

[19] Ibid., 38–40.

[20] See C. Redekop and U.A. Bender, *Who Am I? What Am I?: Searching for Meaning in Your Work* (Grand Rapids: Zondervan, 1988).

[21] Preece, *Changing Work Values*, 27.

[22] Lee Hardy is especially helpful on the history of work attitudes.

3. Work in Scripture

The range of literature in the Bible gives us a rich comprehensive vision for human work.[23]

God the worker

The Bible opens with God working – speaking, fashioning, designing, crafting, sculpting. God makes light, matter, space, time, sea and land, and most beautiful of all – human beings.

The Old Testament is rich in metaphors to describe God as worker (Gen. 1–2; Job 10:3–12; Ps. 139:13–16) as builder/architect (Prov. 8:27–31), teacher (Mt. 7:28–9), composer and performer (Deut. 31:19), metalworker (Is. 1:24–6), garment maker and dresser (Job 29:14), potter (Is. 31:9), farmer (Hos. 10:11), shepherd (Ps. 23:1–4), tentmaker and camper (Job 9:8).[24] These metaphors, while limited, offer a correspondence of meanings between the work of God and the work of humankind. They suggest that our work is a point of real connection with God and therefore a source of meaning and spirituality.

Human work as blessing and curse

The Bible also commences with a parallel vision. Human beings are made in God's image and are commissioned to 'work [the garden] and take care of it' (Gen. 2:15). The first description of someone actually working is the picture of Adam naming the animals.[25] Contrary to what most people think, the world was not made for human beings; human beings were made for the world. We take care of the world in spectacular ways (town planning, serving in parliament or congress, sending a rocket into space, and

---

[23] I acknowledge my indebtedness for some of this section to Alan Richardson, *The Biblical Doctrine of Work*.

[24] See R. Banks, *God the Worker: Journeys into the Mind, Heart and Imagination of God*.

[25] My colleague Donald Anderson remarks that the first-mentioned work is taxonomy, a scientific work honoured by God!

splicing a gene) as well as the most mundane (collecting the rubbish, keeping financial accounts, putting a meal on the table and selling paint). All of it 'keeps stable the fabric of the world' (Ecclus. 38:25–32,34 RSV). To dream of a workless paradise is to seek something other than the purpose and plan of God.[26] Work is good – good for creation, good for our neighbour, good for us. But work is limited. Humankind was also created like God to rest (Gen. 2:2). Work is not everything.[27]

When we turn to Genesis 3 we discover that work has been cursed through human sin. Now there is sweat, toil, drudgery, futility, meaninglessness and injustice. Fallen powers and structures render some work dehumanizing, create structural unemployment or demand a workaholic lifestyle. Redemption in Christ brings substantial healing to our work through the power to invest meaning in ordinary work by viewing that work in relation to God (Col. 3:22–4:1). But there is also substantial healing because the powers have been disarmed by Christ's death, thereby making it possible to be 'overcomers' in the workplace (Col. 2:15), not victimized by the system. Nonetheless complete healing will not take place until the second coming of the Lord (Rom. 8:19–21). We will struggle with work until the end, even when we engage in so-called Christian work.

Work of all kinds

The first extended description of someone actually working is found in the story of Jacob (Gen. 29–31). In this penetrating narrative we get inside how Jacob works as a slave, how he suffers injustice in the workplace and how love redeems his work (Gen. 29:20) though Jacob himself becomes exploitive. While Jacob is the first extended treatment of someone at work, elsewhere in the Old Testament there are significant vignettes such as the picture of Saul working with his hands behind the plough even while he was king (1 Sam. 11:5). There are vivid descriptions of people doing leadership work, like the military work of Gideon; royal work, such as that done by David; and prophetic work, as in the leadership of Jeremiah. There is

---

[26] Richardson, *The Biblical Doctrine of Work*, 27.
[27] Ibid., 55.

no depreciation of manual labour in the Bible, no exalting of 'creative work' over manual labour. Alan Richardson notes that the depreciation of manual work found in the intertestamental Ben Sira (Ecclus. 38:24–34) 'is unparalleled in the Bible'.[28]

Work with and without God

In the Proverbs there are repeated warnings against idleness (Prov. 6:6); and in Amos (and the prophets) warnings against the idle rich (Amos 6:3–6). In the Psalms 'man goes out to his work, to his labour until evening' (Ps. 104:23), but always in the context of the need for our work to be blessed by God (Ps. 128:2). Indeed work that is not blessed by God is vain, empty and futile (Is. 62:8; 65:23).

God gives wisdom for our work (Is. 28:23–9). Ecclesiastes offers a reflection on the futility of work 'under the sun' (2:17–23), pushing the ambiguous nature of work to its limit as the Professor does first-hand research on the nature of work, separated from the wisdom and strength to work that comes from God. In the Bible as a whole there is no exaltation of the work of man's hands, this exaltation often being associated with the making of idols (Ps. 115:4; Is. 40:18ff.; 44:9ff.). Indeed labour that is not blessed by the Lord ('the bread of anxious toil') is fruitless even though it keeps the worker brooding over the work when he should be sleeping (Ps. 127:1–2).

Jesus as worker

The New Testament does not, by itself, deal comprehensively with human work. There are two reasons. First, it assumes the Old Testament and cannot be understood without it. Second, the primary purpose of the apostles was to witness to the birth, death and resurrection of Jesus – gospel work. So there are sparse references to work in the usual sense of energy expended. It does, however, start with the illuminating truth that Jesus was an artisan – either a carpenter or a mason, since *tektōn* can be translated in more than one way. Jesus might have made houses, boats, cradles or ox-yokes. As Alan Richardson notes aptly: 'A workman's jacket was a fitting

---

[28] Ibid., 18.

garment for the God whom the biblical revelation had all along represented as himself a worker.'[29]

Many of the references to work and workers are illustrations, as is the case in the parables. Their purpose is not to teach us about work, or fair pay (especially, e.g., Mt. 20:1–16), but to illuminate the kingdom of God. But the main use of 'work' in the New Testament is metaphorical. 'Work' in the New Testament is kingdom ministry.

The believer's work

The believer's work is to participate in God's work through faith: 'The work of God is this: to believe in the one he has sent' (Jn. 6:29: see Phil. 2:13; 2 Thess. 1:11). In this way we are fellow-workers or co-workers with God (1 Cor. 3:9; Mk. 16:20). Christ's work is not primarily to make ox-yokes but to redeem: 'My food is to do the will of him who sent me and to finish his work' (Jn. 4:34; 5:17; 6:28; 9:3). This work was fulfilled on the cross from which Jesus could say, 'It is finished' (Jn. 19:30).

But kingdom work does not exempt Christians from significant daily work. So the so-called housetables in the letters[30] focus mainly on the relationship of slaves to masters, rather than on what kinds of work are appropriate for Christians. There is no list of prohibited or commended occupations in the Bible such as was promulgated at various periods of church history. When John the Baptist was asked by various people what they should do to 'produce fruit in keeping with repentance' (Lk. 3:8) he told people with two tunics to share with those who had none; tax collectors not to collect more than their due and soldiers not to extort money (3:11–14).[31]

Master and slave

One theme that is developed rather fully in the New Testament is the master–slave relationship: in Greek, *kyrios–doulos*. In the ancient Greek world slaves were sometimes like tenured employees. They

---

[29] Ibid., 48.
[30] Eph. 6:5–9; Col. 3:22–4:1; 1 Tim. 6:1; Tit. 2:9; 1 Pet. 2:18–25.
[31] Being an extortioner, or work that involves swindling, is clearly excluded in 1 Cor. 5:11; 6:10.

were treated with respect and included as members of the family – *oiketai* (1 Pet. 2:18), Joseph in Potiphar's house being an Old Testament example. Thus many of the New Testament exhortations have to do with the reciprocal duties of masters and slaves. In both cases they are serving Christ (Col. 3:24; 4:1). Therefore the emphasis is not on their rights but their duties. But the *kyrios–doulos* theme is also used metaphorically.

In Paul's letters Christ took the form of a worker (literally a *doulos*, Phil. 2:7). Paradoxically, this great condescension leads to his being confessed as *kyrios* ('lord', 2:11). These two words – lord and slave/servant – are the chosen way to describe the relationship of Christ to believers. Christians are wageless *douloi* who are not working for their reward of acceptance with God. They are justified through grace by faith (this is evidently the meaning of Lk. 17:7–10 and Mt. 20:1–16). So work is much more than a necessity for survival or a means of self-fulfilment; it accomplishes a spiritual good, serving kingdom purposes and drawing us to God.

In the New Testament there are difficulties in the workplace. But injustices, perhaps especially these, can become, according to 1 Peter 2:21–4, an imitation of Christ if we bear the suffering patiently. Indeed, it is a fundamental theme of the New Testament that our daily work has significance not in the world today (pay, prestige and personal fulfilment) but in the world to come (Mt. 25:14–46). It is then that we will be wonderfully rewarded (note Col. 3:24). So, in a sense, it is impossible for a Christian to be underpaid! The resurrection of Christ is proof positive that work in this world is not resultless (1 Cor. 15:58).

Eschatological perspective

This eschatological (end times) perspective is not easily held. With the Lord's coming just around the corner some of the Thessalonians thought ordinary work was unnecessary. So they sponged on others (2 Thess. 3:6–13). In dealing with this tendency for 'a fully realized' eschatology Paul deliberately worked with his hands 'night and day . . . so [he] would not be a burden to any of [them]' (3:8). Ultimately, in the new heaven and new earth there will not only be a reward-inheritance but more work! – as is powerfully suggested by the kings of the earth bringing their splendour, along with the glory and honour of the nations, into the holy city (Rev. 21:24,26).[32]

The theological approach we have been taking thus far needs to be synchronized with a deductive approach. This is so that we can think simultaneously from the text of Scripture to the realities of our postmodern information society.[33] Here we will explore godly work in relation to the nature and activity of God, and in particular the trinitarian understanding of God.

4. God's Work

When people speak of 'doing the Lord's work' they normally refer to doing witnessing, preaching and caring for souls. Only this work, so it is thought, lasts. The old poem says it well:

> Only one life,
>   'twill soon be past;
> Only what's done for Jesus
>   Will last.

As we will see, the poem while intending to encourage 'saving souls' is ironically and profoundly true: only what's done for Jesus will last. But the biblical answer to the question 'What is the work of God?' is much more inclusive:

> making, adorning, separating, organizing, cultivating, beautifying, improving, fixing, redeeming, renovating, informing, announcing, revealing outcomes, healing breaches, making peace, helping, sustaining, being with, communicating worth, celebrating, expressing joy, making beautiful things, imagining, dealing with evil, designing, planning, enlisting, empowering, consummating, entertaining, welcoming, providing a context, showing hospitality, serving, and bringing to a conclusion.

---

[32] See R.J. Mouw, *When the Kings Come Marching In: Isaiah and the New Jerusalem.*

[33] See Volf, *Work in the Spirit*, 77–8.

The great themes of the Bible are evocative of the work of God. God the *creator* forms, fabricates, maintains and finishes.[34] God the *lover* does relational work, bringing dignity, health and meaning.[35] God the *saviour* does redemptive work, mending, uniting, and saving.[36] God the *leader* does community-building work and brings things to consummation.[37] Every legitimate human occupation (paid or unpaid) is some dimension of God's own work: making, designing, doing chores, beautifying, organizing, helping, bringing dignity, and leading. Here a trinitarian perspective is illuminating.[38] Believers are drawn into the work of God in its fullness.

---

[34] Samples of verbs used for God's work as creator in the law, prophets, gospels, and apocalypse include the following: God creates (Gen. 1:1), separates (1:4), finishes (2:2), does a new thing (Is. 42:9), fixes limits (Job 38:10), clothes the fields (Lk. 12:28), makes everything new (Rev. 21:5).

[35] Samples of verbs describing God's relational work as lover include the following: God blesses (Gen. 1:22, 28; 9:1), listens to (30:17), takes away disgrace (30:23), loves (Is. 43:4), carries, sustains, rescues (46:4), calls back as if you were a wife deserted and distressed in spirit (54:6), takes delight in you (62:4), gives rest (63:14) and esteem (66:2), dwells in the heart (Eph. 3:17), feeds and cares for his body (5:29), loves and rebukes the churches (Rev. 3:19), wipes away tears (7:17; 21:4).

[36] Examples of God's saving work include the following: God chooses (Gen. 18:19), makes a covenant (15:18), helps (49:25), reveals glory (Is. 40:5), rules (40:22), sweeps away offences (44:22), raises up (45:13), restores (49:6), extends mercy (Lk. 1:50), brings down rulers (1:52), casts out demons (4:35), forgives sins (5:20), confers a kingdom (22:29), intercedes (23:34), lavishes grace (Eph. 1:7–8), includes (1:13), gives the Spirit (1:17), reconciles (2:16), reigns (Rev. 11:15), hurls down the dragon (12:9), makes everything new (21:5).

[37] God negotiates (Gen. 18:22–3), reassures (26:24), tends his flock (Is. 40:11), gently leads (40:11), gives strength (40:29), refines (48:10), comforts (51:3), takes delight in (62:4), gives authority (Lk. 10:19), joins and makes his building rise (Eph. 2:21), makes us a kingdom and priests to serve our God (Rev. 1:6), dwells with (21:3).

[38] The trinitarian approach has several advantages: (1) it firmly connects human work with its source, inspiration and creator: God; (2) it allows for a more comprehensive understanding of God-imaging work by not limiting human work to the work of one of Father, Son or Spirit in isolation;

Father work – stewardship

As we have already seen Adam and Eve were set in a sanctuary garden and told to 'work it' and 'take care of it' (Gen. 2:15), to 'be fruitful and increase in number; fill the earth and subdue it; rule . . .' (1:28). The verbs, be fruitful (flourish), increase, fill, and subdue, suggest more than simple dominance. Humankind was designed to thrive and to make the whole of creation flourish. It is seldom noticed that this is the blessing of God. 'God blessed them and said . . .' (1:28). God communicates his good will and empowers his creature to do this godlike work of cultivating and enculturating creation, including everything from animal husbandry to nuclear physics, from homemaking to accounting – all the ways we make God's world flourish.

Son work – Kingdom ministry

The proper work of Christians is the furtherance of the gospel and serving God's kingdom purposes in the world (1 Cor. 3:6–9; Jn. 4:35–8; 2 Cor. 5:20–6:1). To this work all believers are called (Eph. 4:1; 1 Cor. 7:20). Some believers, notably the apostles, were called to put aside normal occupations to work for Jesus in another way (Mk. 2:13–17; Lk. 5:1–11), though it is arguable that they took their trades with them. The privilege of being supported, which is the right of the apostles (1 Cor. 9) and preaching/teaching elders (1 Tim. 5:17), is a grace gift of the church and should come through the initiative of the church.[39] Where such support is not forthcoming the believer is clearly 'called' to support themselves with ordinary work! So Christians work in both senses, Father work in creational stewardship and Son work in furthering the gospel.

---

[38] *(continued)* (3) it finds in the relationality of God and God's creation the absolute centre for work motivation and purpose: love; (4) it expands the concept of work as ministry beyond the merely religious or ecclesiastical to the domestic, creational, aesthetic and creational expressions of godlikeness.

[39] See Stevens 'Financial Support', in Banks and Stevens, *The Complete Book*, 419–22.

There is not a single instance in the New Testament of a person being called to be a religious professional. The 'work' of the ministry is essentially voluntary, an amateur 'for-love' activity. In the same way there is not a single instance in the New Testament of a person being called to a societal occupation,[40] though all worthy occupations, paid and unpaid, become a means of service in and to the Kingdom of God (Acts 18:3).

Kingdom work, however, does not provide an alternative to humane work (as Karl Barth calls it) – all the ways we care for God's earth and for our neighbour. Kingdom work makes humane work possible and sensible. But for this we need the Holy Spirit as God's empowering presence. If Father-work (taken by itself) gets reduced to vocation and creational stewardship, and Son-work is understood primarily to be gospel ministry and furthering the kingdom of God, there is need for what Miroslav Volf calls 'work in the Spirit'.[41]

Spirit work – giftedness and empowerment

Earlier we have noted that Luther attempted to overcome the medieval hierarchy in which the *vita contemplativa* was superior to the *vita activa*. He did this by secularizing all the callings. But there is a problem with this. Volf critiques this strictly vocational approach to work and proposes a charismatic approach based on the work of the Spirit.[42] Volf argues that human work is co-operation with God. The Spirit of the resurrected Christ works through us. As the gift of the Spirit is the guarantee (2 Cor. 1:22; Rom. 8:23) of the ultimate

---

[40] Richardson, *The Biblical Doctrine of Work*, 36–7.

[41] Volf, *Work in the Spirit*.

[42] Volf's critique proceeds along these lines: (1) Luther's understanding of work was indifferent toward alienation in work; (2) there was a dangerous ambiguity between the spiritual calling and external (station in life) calling so that eventually, with the consecration of occupation as vocation (Volf here quotes Moltmann), 'Vocation began to gain the upper hand over the call; the Word of God on the right (gospel) was absorbed by the Word of God on the left (law)'; (3) Luther's view was misused ideologically so that even dehumanizing work was ennobled; (4) it assumed a stable society in which a person could undertake one occupation for a lifetime; (5) as work changed over the years vocation became reduced to gainful employment (Volf, *Work in the Spirit*, 107–9).

realization of the new creation, 'cooperation with God in work is proleptic cooperation with God in God's eschatological *transformatio mundi* [transformation of the world]'.[43]

Volf further asserts that charisms (Spirit gifts) include more than ecclesiastical activities. He notes the gift of evangelist (Eph. 4:11) and contributing to the needs of the destitute as two clear examples in the ad hoc gift lists in Paul's letters.[44] The theological basis of Volf's argument is the charismatic nature of all Christian activity. We are in the age of the eschatological Spirit. What occasionally was experienced in the Old Testament as Spirit-inundation for skilful work, as in the cases of Bezalel and David (Ex. 31:2–3; 1 Chron. 28:11–12), is now the inheritance of all believers. As mentioned in the New Testament survey above, the significance of our work on earth lies not only in this world but in the world to come (Mt. 25:14–46). This ultimate direction is brought by the Holy Spirit. The gift of the Holy Spirit is indeed the tangible deposit/seal and pledge of the age to come.[45]

The implications of living in the age of the Spirit may, however, be taken a step further, if not because of the gifts of the Spirit certainly for the fruit of the Spirit (Gal. 5:22–3). One can easily consider in Paul's letters the contrast of flesh work and Spirit work (Gal. 5:19–26) and apply Paul's exhortation to 'walk in the Spirit', 'keep in step with the Spirit', and 'live with the Spirit' to work, as Paul clearly intended this for daily life and not mere 'spirituality'. The lists of the 'works of the flesh' and 'the fruit of the Spirit' provide a clear contrast of two ways of working. The first is arrogant, autonomous, self-seeking and destructive. The second is upbuilding,

---

[43] Ibid., 115.

[44] Volf notes that this secular explanation of gifts is also found in Michael Harper's *Let My People Go*, 100 (quoted in *Work in the Spirit*, 111).

[45] The problem with Volf's thesis, however, is not substantially different from that which Luther faced. When one secularizes spiritual gifts into all possible human occupations the line between gospel work and creation work will be blurred once again. More than likely, gospel work will be subsumed and secularized. Further, it is questionable whether there is any significant biblical evidence that Spirit-gifts are given for societal good rather than for building up the body of Christ. See Gordon Fee and Paul Stevens, 'Spiritual Gifts', in Banks and Stevens, *The Complete Book*, 943–9.

covenantal and loving. It is the clear teaching of the New Testament that the Spirit is poured out on the entire people of God for ethical living and neighbourly service, not primarily for ecstatic experiences. It is the Spirit that enables, equips and empowers. Otherwise our work would be duty-bound, a human effort to please God in our work unaided by God.

One further implication of Spirit work has to do with sanctification. Unfortunately this was the almost exclusive interest of the early church fathers and so the doctrine of sanctification provided the theological context for considering work. Thus the *Epistle of Barnabas* (second century) affirms 'working with thine hands for the ransom of thy sins';[46] and in the monastic tradition work was regarded as a spiritual exercise and a penitential discipline. The doctrine of sanctification provides as legitimate if not crucial a perspective on work.[47]

Father work, Son work and Spirit work. Each person of the Trinity provides an important perspective on human work. Together, we are invited to find communion with God in God's work.

What is the work of God? God's work includes fabricating work, maintaining work, love work, restorative work, gospel work and leading work. *Who does God's work?* All the people of God (the *laos*), and, without their knowing it, most not-yet-believers. *Where is God's work done?* In the church and world including the physical creation, the home, society and community, politics, culture, education and finance realms, all the 'worlds' which we are making and mending. *Why should we work?* The Bible's answer is that God invites us to have communion with him as co-workers while God brings the world to its consummation in the new heaven and new earth. Human work is a duty and a godlike activity.

---

[46] *Barnabas* 9.10, quoted in Volf, *Work in the Spirit*, 72.

[47] For Luther there is a cross in the workplace. *One's daily work is the situation in which the Christian's sinful self must be put to death* within and by the demands of daily life in vocation. Luther said: 'I ask you where our suffering is to be found. I shall tell you: Run through all the stations of life from the lowest to the highest, and you will find what you are looking for . . . therefore do not worry where you can find suffering' (*Werke*, 404). See also T. Green, *Darkness in the Marketplace: The Christian at Prayer in the World* (Notre Dame: Ave Maria Press, 1981).

5. Good Work

When God finished making the world and the first couple he said, 'it is very good' (Gen. 1:31). Work has *extrinsic* value: it is good for what it produces (money, provision for one's family, etc.). Work also has *intrinsic* value: it is good in itself. Mostly, pastoral ministry and people-helping professions are seen as having both intrinsic and extrinsic value while business and the trades are deemed to have only extrinsic value. Are ordinary occupations intrinsically valuable? Making electronic toys, driving a bus, designing a piece of clothing, flying an aeroplane? Teaching in a preschool? Working as a hospital nurse?

Certainly those engaged in providing goods or services that *seem* to have less intrinsic value and durability will require an occupational conversion to view their work as holy, pleasing to God and worthy of God's 'it is good'. This, of course, is precisely what a good theology of work must do. Where society does not invest meaning in a task, does not socially reinforce it, we must regard this task as God does – as part of making God's world work. Intrinsically work is good for us, good for the world and good for God. This is one of the most crucial and most neglected equipping tasks of the church.[48]

Good for the world

All kinds of making are included in the original mandate (Gen. 1:26–8): garden-making, city-making, family-making, beauty-making, tool-making, data-making, word-making, design-making, dress-making, machine-making, program-making, order-making, relation-making. It does not matter whether or not we earn our living by it – it is good for the world.

---

[48] See 'Redirecting Sunday Toward Monday', in G. Preece, 'Work', in Banks and Stevens, *The Complete Book*, 1123–9. See also 'The Ministry of Work', in Stevens, *Liberating the Laity*, 77–91, and Stevens, *The Equippers Guide to Every Member Ministry* (Downers Grove: InterVarsity Press, 1992, 91–111.

Good for the neighbour

Work enables us to provide for ourselves and our loved ones (2 Thess. 3:7–10). It equips us to help the poor and needy by sharing our excess, paying taxes and being stewards (Eph. 4:28). It is a practical way of showing neighbour love. It makes cities thrive, keeps the streets clean, makes the soil productive, keeps dinner on the table and clothes clean, makes people attractive, heals through medicine, instructs people in schools, makes the stock market (and thus our economy) work, gets papers delivered to our door, puts data into the right data banks, and connects people through phone, fax, modem and e-mail.

Gospel work restores people to God and brings peace, meaning, forgiveness and hope. Some of this work is an obvious ministry – counselling, pastoring, teaching and healing. Most of it is hidden, behind the scenes, but just as important in God's eyes – intrinsically good (and not merely a means of making money to support the real 'ministers').

Good for us

Bonhoeffer has a brilliant section on the therapeutic value of work:

> Work plunges men into the world of things. The Christian steps out of the world of brotherly encounter into the world of impersonal things, the 'it'; and this new encounter frees him [or her] for objectivity; for the 'it'-world is only an instrument in the hand of God for the purification of Christians from all self-centredness and self-seeking. The work of the world can be done only where a person forgets himself [or herself], where he loses himself in a cause, in reality, the task, the 'it'. In work the Christian learns to allow himself to be limited by the task, and thus for him the work becomes a remedy against the indolence and sloth of the flesh. The passions of the flesh die in the world of things. But this can happen only where the Christian breaks through the 'it' to the 'Thou', which is God, who bids him work and makes that work a means of liberation from himself.[49]

---

[49] D. Bonhoeffer, *Life Together*, trans. J.W. Doberstein (New York: Harper & Row, 1954), 70.

In this life work is a wonderful way of getting out of ourselves. Even (perhaps especially) retired people, unemployed people, handicapped people and underemployed people need to work – whether paid or not. Sometimes it is the means of a deep healing.[50] It is good for us, good for the world, good for others and even good for God. We get our final pay on the Last Day when Christ comes again and ushers us into our final workplace – the new heaven and the new earth where (guess what?) we will work forever and bring the best we can make into the Holy City to bring glory to God. If God says of work 'it is good', why shouldn't we?

---

[50] See J.M. Blomquist, 'Discovering Our Deep Gladness: The Healing Power of Work', *Weavings* 8.2 (January/February 1993), 20–26.

For further study / discussion

Case Study: The Pullover Factory. The offer of a promotion that came to Roberta after two years of service would normally be uncomplicated except for the unique role she played as manager of one production department in a pullover factory in Manila. It employed 400 workers. Since orders were booked seasonally and varied from year to year, the company would accept orders that required extensive overtime hours for workers. For five months each year the production schedule would involve work from Monday to Sunday eight to thirteen hours a day. Salaries were paid on a piece-rate basis. During the lean periods, workers were forced to take vacation leaves of two to four weeks. Some workers were laid off but hired again the following year during the busy months. Elseleina, the general manager and owner said, 'Roberta, I like your work. You are completely dependable. And I want you to become my personal assistant. I also think it will be better for you not to be so close to the women in the factory.'

In her present job Roberta already worked in the office and had the privilege of a regular monthly salary irrespective of the seasonal workload and better working conditions. An air-conditioned office was a pleasant contrast to the sweatshop out back. She was seldom required to work more than eight hours. However, during the busy months, Roberta stayed longer working alongside the factory workers in menial tasks though she was not involved in the production end of things.

Sometimes she would help the women fill the cartons with pullovers, enjoying conversation with them as they worked together. Roberta was very bothered by the disproportionality of workload and benefits. The owner and general manager drove a Mercedes and owned a fabulous wardrobe to entertain international buyers. The proposed new position for Roberta would involve hosting buyers from all over the world and being of direct assistance to the general manager in planning production and overseeing staff. Roberta could not help comparing the affluence of the office with the grinding poverty of the women who worked out back. She wondered if the company was exploiting the workers and whether she was indirectly participating in the exploitation. But there was another kind of exploitation that bothered Roberta even more.

Almost all of the workers in the factory were women. Most were away from their home and family for long periods of time. Lesbian relationships developed among the workers living in the factory dorms. Some of Roberta's supervisors gave extra work and therefore more income to the women with whom they had relationships. Suzanna, one of the supervisors, explained it this way, 'Everything in this world is based on give and take. I get benefits from some of the women and they get employment benefits from me. That is how the world runs.' The offer of advancement meant that Roberta would not be directly responsible for the oversight of the supervisors or have regular contact with the women in the factory. Roberta felt a mixture of relief and sadness as she considered a 'move up'.

1. Reflect on the pullover factory case study in the introduction as a small group:

   a. Read the Case (5 minutes).
   b. Assign and appoint the following small-group roles:
      • Elect one person as chairperson (this person must move the group along to its various learning and theological reflecting experiences).
      • One person to role-play Roberta as she meets with her small group in the church to share her dilemma (can be a man or woman).
      • Two people to function as 'issues identifiers' – these people will not speak in the discussion but will observe the discussion and identify the issues involved in the case.
      • Two people to be 'theological reflection persons' – these people will identify biblical themes, specific texts, and theological principles involved. They will observe and listen but not participate in the discussion.
      • The rest will function as a small support group for Roberta:
         i. Role-play and small-group discussion (20 minutes).
         ii. Feedback from 'issues identifiers' (5 minutes). Write these down.
         iii. Feedback from 'theological reflection persons' (5 minutes). Write these down.
         iv. Vote on whether Roberta should take the promotion and then ask why.
         v. Share learnings (5 minutes)

2. The pullover factory case can be used individually or as a group for theological reflection of a situation using the following outline:

   a. Identifying the issues:
      • injustice, exploited workers financially and sexually
      • multiple but mutually exclusive possibilities of influence
      • homosexuality
      • personal gifting – desire to be close to the women
      • poverty

   b. Identifying the heart of the matter:
      • cannot be both for the poor (the women out back) and the rich (the owner) at the same time, and yet gospel-living brings about their reconciliation

   c. Exploring the discrepancy or tension between our experience and our faith:
      • fabulous wealth and grinding poverty: God's preference for the poor
      • the possibility of influencing 'the system' at the apparent price of becoming captive to its values and standards

   d. Identifying specific Scriptural insights, perspectives, descriptions or prescriptions (concordance, theological dictionaries, word studies):
      • labour worthy of pay
      • homosexuality
      • living graciously – extra mile
      • poverty

   e. Drawing on the great biblical theological themes to bring perspective:
      • the justice of God
      • God's preferential love for the poor
      • God's identification in Christ with the least, last and lost
      • grace and the freedom of living within the gospel – the possibility of working in morally ambiguous situations because our salvation is by grace not by works
      • grappling with the powers

   f. Sharing the process with the community of faith (prayer group, small group, church).

   g. Praying for wisdom.

   h. The spirituality of decision-making:

- deciding eschatologically – having in view the now and yet coming Kingdom
- deciding with gospel confidence
- deciding in view of the providence of God (even mistakes can be redeemed and woven into God's purpose Gen. 45:8; 50:19–20).
- not looking back but learning through the experience.

3. Discuss this statement by Thomas Aquinas: 'It is impossible for one to be busy with external action and at the same time give oneself to Divine contemplation.'

4. In the light of Scripture, critique Alan Richardson's comment quoted at the beginning of the chapter.

Chapter 6

Ministry – Transcending Clericalism

None are so unholy as those whose hands are cauterised with holy things; sacred things may become profane by becoming matter of the job. You now want spiritual truth for her own sake; how will it be when the same truth is needed also for an effective footnote for your thesis . . . I've always been glad myself that 'theology' is not the thing I earn my living by. On the whole, I'd advise you to get on with your tentmaking. The performance of a duty will probably teach quite as much about God as academic Theology would do.

Letter by C.S. Lewis to Vanauken shortly after his conversion.[1]

For centuries the clerical state was exalted as virtually a 'supernatural' one, and there is a slight connotation of mystical awe when a man says: 'People should respect the clergy.' And if someday a science which has long been overdue – pastoral pathology – is taught in the seminaries, its first discovery might be that some 'clerical vocations' are in fact rooted in the morbid desire for that 'supernatural respect,' especially when the chances of a 'natural' one are slim. Our secular world 'respects' clergy as it 'respects' cemeteries: both are needed, both are sacred, both are out of life. But what both clericalism and secularism – the former being, in fact, the natural father of the latter – have made us forget is that to be a *priest* is from a profound point of view the most natural thing in the world. Man was created priest of the world, the one who offers the world to God in a sacrifice of love and praise and who, through the eternal eucharist, bestows the divine love upon the world.

Alexander Schmemann[2]

---

[1] Quoted in James Houston, 'The Amateur Status of the Christian Life' (unpublished, Regent College, Vancouver, 1989), 1.

[2] A. Schmemann, *For the Life of the World: Sacraments and Orthodoxy*, 92.

How confusing this subject is. Christians are told that ministry is something everyone in the church does, that some people do it more than others, that not everything is ministry, that ministry may relate to certain functions more than others, but may 'happen' in almost any context, is done by some full time and by others part time, yet ministry *par excellence* is what the pastor does. No wonder good Christians are mixed up. And no wonder when good pastors hear of someone's call into 'the' ministry, they think instinctively of preaching and sacramental ministry.

1. Ministry Today

Unfortunately, most people define ministry by what they see 'the' minister doing – preaching, administering the sacraments, caring for the spiritual needs of people. If ministry is evangelizing the lost and edifying the found, then only a small minority of the church can do ministry continuously, at most 1 per cent that can be supported financially for 'full-time' ministry. For the rest of the people of God ministry is a discretionary time activity – something done with the few hours that can be squeezed out of the week's schedule after working, sleeping, homemaking, neighbouring, washing and doing the chores.

Contemporary criteria

Ministry is an 'accordion' word that has come to mean whatever air we put into it! Sometimes ministry is defined by (1) *place* (i.e. work in the church rather than the marketplace and home), (2) *function* (i.e. done on behalf of the whole, such as priestly ministration), (3) *need* (i.e. meeting 'spiritual' needs rather than secular needs such as preparing a meal for a family), (4) *title* (i.e. 'Reverend'), and, following a category suggested by Yves Congar, (5) *designation*, with overt reference to Christ, so that service is rendered to others in the name of Christ and because of Christ.[3]

_____

[3] Y. Congar uses the following designations: (1) general/universal ministry – any service to another human being in need – a universal call rooted in our vocation of being a human being; (2) general/specific ministry –

Books on the theology of ministry invariably deal with the theology of the ordained clergy.[4] For example, Michael Lawler defines ministry as 'action done in public on behalf of the church, as a result of a charism of service, proclaimed, made explicit and celebrated in the church in sacrament, to incarnate in symbol the presence of Christ and of the God whose kingdom he reveals'.[5]

2. Ministry in Scripture

The Bible addresses this massive confusion with a liberating perspective: ministry is defined by Who is served (the interior form) rather than the shape and location of the deeds done (the exterior form). Ministry is *service to God and on behalf of God in the church and the world*. Ministers are people who put themselves *at the disposal of God* for the benefit of others and God's world. It is not limited by the place where the service is rendered, the function, the need met, by the title of the person or even by the overt reference to Christ.[6] As we will see, the Greek word for ministry (*diakonia*) is

---

[3] *(continued)* any special service rendered by those called to serve in the helping professions (nursing, etc.); (3) Christian/universal ministry – any service rendered to others in Christ and because of Christ, a ministry rooted in baptism; (4) Christian/specific ministry – a service rendered to others in Christ and because of Christ for the sake of helping the Church fulfil its mission – something Congar calls 'designated' ministry. Congar's definition presupposes one to view the Christian/specific ministry as a superior form of Christian/universal ministry, and tends to minimize the human vocation (Y. Congar, 'My Pathfindings in the Theology of the Laity and Ministries', *Jurist* 2 [1972], 190).

[4] Even N. Pittenger's book *The Ministry of All Christians: A Theology of Lay Ministry*, written from an Anglican perspective, tries to expound simultaneously the general ministry of all believers and the special ministry of bishops, priests and deacons, but focuses exclusively on various in-house church functions: celebrating, preaching, teaching and shepherding.

[5] M. Lawler, *A Theology of Ministry* (Kansas City: Sheed & Ward, 1990), 28.

[6] Note in Mt. 25:31–46 the surprise of the righteous that what had been done gratuitously was actually done for Christ, and the concern of the unrighteous that if they had known it was Jesus they were serving, they would gladly have done it.

simply the word 'service'. They are totally interchangeable ways of speaking of the same reality. It might be a good thing if we could permanently substitute the word 'servant' wherever we now use the word 'ministry'. Imagine someone saying, 'I have been called into service in the church.' This approach to ministry transcends clericalism.[7]

'Ābad

One of the most common Old Testament words for service is *'ābad*. *'Ābad* combines the meaning of 'to work or to make' and in later usage 'to worship'. In other words, it is service that is directed towards things, people or God. Commenting on Genesis 2, William Dumbrell shows that Adam and Eve are depicted as kings-priests offering their worship to God through their work in the sanctuary-garden which is the centre of the world. 'Paradoxically,' he notes,

> man exercises dominion over his world by service and worship in the divine presence. His service in the garden is denoted by the verb *'ābad* (used 290 times in the Old Testament with the basic meaning of 'work' or 'serve') . . . but the use of the word in the later Old Testament as the customary verb for 'worship' imports into the Genesis 2 context the further nature of man's response in what is clearly a sanctuary presence . . .[8]

---

[7] Prophets, priests and kings will be considered in the next chapter. Congar enumerates some of the Old Testament references for such anointing: For the priests, cf. Ex. 30:30; Lev. 8:2–12; 10:7. For the kings, 1 Sam. 9:16; 10:1,6,10; 16:11–12; 3 Kgs. [1 Chron.] 1:34–9; 19:15–16; 4 Kgs. [2 Chron.] 9:1–6; 11:12. For the prophets only 3 Kgs. [1 Chron.] 19:16, but see also Lk. 4:18 (Is. 61:1), where the Spirit anoints a man and finally Jesus himself as a prophet. See Congar, *Lay People in the Church*, 61.

This Old Testament anointing is developed theologically in T.F. Torrance, 'The Ordering and Equipping of the Church for Ministry', in Anderson, *Theological Foundations for Ministry*, 410–12.

[8] W. Dumbrell, 'Creation, Covenant and Work', *Crux* 24.3 (September 1988), 19 (14–24). Dumbrell argues that the idea that the garden in Gen. 2 is a shrine comes not only from ch. 2, but markedly from the manner in which Ezek. 28:11–19 describes Eden, the cosmic forces in the world in the alternate terms of garden/holy mountain of God (cf. vv. 13,14).

Adam and Eve's service is divine service which shows itself first in submission to the Creator in what is required.[9]

Šarat

The second word, *šārat*, also falls into two categories: personal service rendered to an important personage, such as a ruler (Gen. 39:4), and the ministry of worship on the part of those who stand in a special relationship to God, such as priests (Ex. 28:35).[10] Claus Westermann notes how *ʿābad* and *šārat* are sometimes distinguished. Jacob's service to Laban was *ʿābad* (work) while Joseph's service to the important prisoners in Egypt was *šārat* (personal service).[11]

The servant of the Lord

Hendrik Kraemer is, I think, correct in critiquing Congar for dwelling exclusively on prophet, priest and king to exegete a theology of the laity, when *ʿebed* (servant) in the Old Testament and *diakonia* (service) in the New Testament provide a more foundational textual basis for understanding the ministry of the whole people of God. When modified by 'of the Lord' *ʿēbed* (servant) shows us that the minister is someone who serves God. That is the sense in which God calls the Israelites to be his servants in Leviticus 25:55: 'the Israelites belong to me as servants. They are my servants . . .' Matching God's choice of a servant is the servant's choice of God, thus completing the covenant relationship, as in Joshua 24: 'as for me and my household, we will serve the Lord' (14–15). In each of the Servant Songs of Isaiah 42:1–7; 49:1–9; 50:4–10; 52:13–53:12 the servant or minister is addressed as the 'servant of the Lord' or (by God) as 'my servant'.

This concept of the servant of the Lord is radically different from the contemporary view of ministry which boils down to being

---

[9] Ibid., 13–14.

[10] H.J. Austel, 'Šārat', in Harris, Archer and Waltke, *Theological Wordbook of the Old Testament*, II, 858.

[11] C. Westermann, 'Šrt', in Ernst Jenni and Claus Westermann (eds.), *Theological Lexicon of the Old Testament*, trans. Mark E. Biddle (3 vols.; Peabody, MA: Hendrickson, 1997), III, 1406 (1405–7).

servants of people or the church for God's sake rather than serving God for the benefit of people and God's world. The difference is subtle and sublime. The essence of ministry/service is being put at the disposal of God. The need is not the call to service. The call comes from God – from the most comprehensive service of Adam and Eve in Eden to the work of an evangelist. The servant passages in Isaiah make this point explicitly: the servant is God's servant, pure and simple.

Serving the Lord is serving in an enduring way with one's whole existence.[12] There is no room for 'spiritualization' or compartmentalization. 'And now, O Israel, what does the Lord your God ask of you but . . . to serve the Lord your God with all your heart and with all your soul . . .' (Deut. 10:12).

Remarkably, in the prophetic critique of Israel's cultic hypocrisy in Isaiah 43:22–4, God says that Israel has not served the Lord with offerings but rather has made God serve because of their sins.[13] This takes the mutuality of covenant a step farther. Normally God cannot be an *ʿebed*. Yet this is exactly what happens in the epicentre of servant vision of Isaiah. God becomes a servant! This is the extraordinary messianic hint in the Servant Songs of Isaiah.

In the last twenty-seven chapters of Isaiah the term occurs twenty times in the singular (chs. 39–53) and eleven times in the plural (chs. 54–66). As Walter C. Kaiser notes, 'in twelve of the twenty examples in the singular[14] and in all eleven in the plural,[15] the servant is the nation Israel. But there are passages in which the servant is differentiated from Israel as a whole and in these the servant has a mission to Israel.[16] Ultimately a single individual was

---

[12] See L. Newbigin's critique and exposition of the Western division of theory and practice in *Proper Confidence*, 1–15. Further study of the comprehensive unity of the person will be found in Hans Walter Wolff, *Anthropology of the Old Testament*, trans. M. Kohl (Philadelphia: Fortress Press, 1964).

[13] See C. Westermann, '*Ebed*/Servant', in Jenni and Westermann, *Theological Lexicon of the Old Testament*, II, 831 (819–32).

[14] Is. 41:8–10; 42:18–19; 43:9–10; 44:1–3,21; 45:4; 48:20; and perhaps 49:3.

[15] Is. 54:17; 56:6; 63:17; 65:8–9,13–15; 66:14.

[16] Harris, Archer and Waltke, *Theological Wordbook of the Old Testament*, II, 639.

envisioned, an individual who would gather up all the service expected of Israel in his own person, who would undertake a mission to Israel and through Israel to the world.

While some of the references to the servant are reminiscent of Jeremiah's prophetic service, the suffering of this servant sets him apart. In Isaiah 52:13–53:12 the servant suffers representatively, redemptively and with divine approval, this reference surpassing anything previously said in the Old Testament about a servant in the Lord's service.[17] But even more paradoxically, in this messianic vision of the servant, God becomes his own servant, a vision wonderfully fulfilled in Jesus the Servant (Acts 3:13; Phil. 2:5–11).

An hourglass[18] emerges: national Israel at the top (possibly suggested by Is. 42:19), spiritual Israel (41:8–10) in the narrow portion, Messiah in the neck, as the culmination of the servant-motif (52:13–53:12), and in Christ (as the hourglass now widens) all those who find their service to God in fellowship with Jesus the Servant.[19]

OLD AND NEW COVENANT MINISTRY

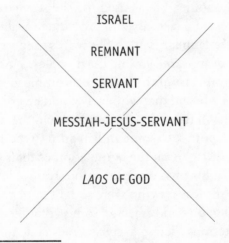

ISRAEL

REMNANT

SERVANT

MESSIAH-JESUS-SERVANT

LAOS OF GOD

[17] Westermann, '*Ebed*/Servant', 819–32.

[18] This image is a combination of one suggested by Delitsch, quoted in W.C. Kaiser, '*ebed*', in Harris, Archer and Waltke, *Theological Wordbook of the Old Testament*, II, 640 (639–41), with a pyramid leading to the Messiah, and two triangles joined at the apex, an idea suggested by George Adam Smith.

[19] O. Cullmann, *The Christology of the New Testament* (London: SCM Press, 1977), 51–82.

Once again, ministry was intended to be the service of the whole people of Israel. That service was fulfilled in Christ the Messiah-Servant, not merely the prophets, priests and kings. New Testament apostles, prophets, evangelists and pastor-teachers are not the culmination of their Old Testament counterparts. That is the fatal equation that leads to exclusively male pastors and priests in the church. Jesus himself fulfils all Old Testament leadership and service. And in Christ the people *as a whole* become the servant of the Lord. Baptism is the universal ordination of people into the universal ministry of the people of God: 'we were all baptized by one Spirit into one body . . . Now the body is not made up of one part but of many' (1 Cor. 12:13–14).[20] Leaders are merely people who serve other servants in a particular way.

Service in the New Testament

The word for ministry in the New Testament, *diakonia*, is simply the word for service, a term that originally means anything done in the 'employ' of another but is used for the service of the Word, practical love, apostolic activity and providing meals.[21] We may be inoculated by overfamiliarity with the words used to describe Jesus as a servant. Christ appeared among the disciples as 'one who serves' (Lk. 22:27), thus reversing the usual relationship between serving and being served. He said that whoever would be great 'must be . . . servant' (Mt. 20:26), thus turning upside down the usual standards of leadership. In contrast to some Indian gurus, who have their feet washed by their disciples on the completion of their training, Jesus washed the feet of his own disciples as the shadow of the cross fell. Unlike the rabbinic leaders who were sought out by disciples, Jesus chose his own disciples and rejected some volunteers.

Though the term is used sparsely as a messianic title in the New Testament, Jesus is called the Servant in Peter's sermon in Acts 3:13,

---

[20] Significant Roman Catholic documents take up the same perspective with a retrieval of 'baptismal consciousness' and a 'revivifying of the sense of mission' by the whole people of God. See Gerard Austin, OP, 'Baptism as the Matrix of Ministry', *Louvain* 23 (1998), 101–13.

[21] H.W. Beyer, '*diakoneō*', in Kittel and Friedrich, *Theological Dictionary of the New Testament*, IV, 84 (81–93).

fulfilling the enigmatic prophecy in the four poems in Isaiah 42–53 and showing – marvellously – that service is at the heart of God's being. When the people did not fulfil God's intent to have a servant on earth, God became his own servant – the very thing Paul expounds in Philippians 2. *Diakonia* is from God, to God and in God.

The church is ministry

So those who follow Jesus and are incorporated into the family of God are servants. The decisive thing about being a disciple of Jesus is *diakonia*, offering one's life in the 'employ' of the Lord even unto death. Christians are people who put themselves at the disposal of God. 'The man who loves his life will lose it, while the man who hates his life in this world will keep it for eternal life. Whoever serves me must follow me; and where I am, my servant also will be' (Jn. 12:25–6). Ministry is not an exceptional optional activity for the people of God but rather part of its essence. The church does not have a ministry (or a minister); it is ministry. But it is not mere activity, energy expended in waiting on tables or in religious activity, matters about which we might take pride. It is service arising from life in the Servant, which takes us into the life of the Father, through the Spirit (as is apparent from Mt. 25:42–4). As Hermann Beyer says, 'Here it is plain that *diakonein* is one of those words which presuppose a Thou, and not a Thou towards whom I may order my relationship as I please, but a Thou under whom I have placed myself as a *diakonēn*.'[22] If vocation implies both a callee and a caller, service implies both a servant and a master. That is the point made in Mark 10:43–5.

To emphasize the derivative nature of service Paul chooses the Greek word for slave/servant (*doulos*) to describe his own function (Rom. 1:1; Gal. 1:10; Col. 4:12), pointing out that the Christian servant is first and finally a servant of God, not of people, and a servant of people because he or she is a servant of God. Paul nicely defines this in 2 Corinthians 4:5: 'For we do not preach ourselves, but Jesus Christ as Lord, and ourselves as your servants for Jesus' sake' (here using *doulos*). Paul continues to use *doulos* when he

---

22 Beyer, '*diakoneo*', 85.

speaks about Christian leaders in 2 Timothy 2:24: 'The Lord's servant must not quarrel; instead he must be kind to everyone, able to
teach, not resentful.'

So it is significant that many of the Greek words available to distinguish an official ministry from ordinary *diakonia* were not used by
the inspired New Testament authors: *telos* (office), *time* (task,
emphasizing the dignity), *archē* (magistry) and *leitourgia* (public service or priestly cultic service). With the exception of *telos*, when
these words are found in the New Testament they refer to Jewish
priests, to Moses, to pagan civil officers and sometimes to Jesus, but
not to church leaders. When Paul does use a priestly word, as he
does in Romans 15:16, it is the priestly duty of proclaiming the gospel, not ministering at the altar, a priestly ministry that all believers
share. John A.T. Robinson makes the insightful remark, 'The
unpriestly character of early Christianity must surely have been one
of the things to strike an outsider, whether he was Jewish or
pagan.'[23]

There is a consistent refusal to use words that would make a
distinction between selected official ministers and the ministry of
ordinary believers.[24] All are servants; all are able to minister. The
reason for this refusal to make distinctions of rank for certain official
servants is profoundly theological, and crucial to developing a
theology of ministry for the whole people of God. Biblically we
must start with the whole people in Christ, the servant people in the
Servant, not the special role of the pastor. To fully grasp this, we
must take a trinitarian approach.

3. Trinitarian Service

As we have seen before without a trinitarian basis, ministry is usually
defined in terms of one member of the Godhead. What is needed is

[23] J.A.T. Robinson, 'Christianity's "No" to Priesthood', in N. Nash and
J. Rhymer (eds.), *The Christian Priesthood*, quoted in Lawler, *A Theology of
Ministry*, 54.
[24] See R.E. Schweizer, 'Ministry in the Early Church', in David Noel
Freedman (ed.), *The Anchor Bible Dictionary* (6 vols.; New York:
Doubleday, 1992), IV, 836 (836–42).

not one, not even the sum of the three, but the whole who is more than the sum of the parts! And the reason is sublime.

There is ministry in God; God is ministry

There was ministry before there was a world, ministry in the being of God. This mutual interanimation, interpentration, indwelling, covenantal loyalty and othering – what the Cappadocian fathers in the fourth and fifth centuries called 'perichoresis' – is the mutual service rendered within God.[25] Ministry is not a mere human activity engaged in because of duty or admiration for the example of Jesus. It is something that takes us to the heart of God. Ministry is of God not merely for God. As we have seen in Chapter 3, the ministry of the triune God is relational, characterized by love. It is both unitive and creative, as well as redemptive and curative.

God's ministry is invested in the whole people of God

Jesus' high priestly prayer (Jn. 17) was that 'they may be one as we are one . . . to be with me where I am' (17:22,24), dwelling in the Trinity, with all the resources of the Holy Trinity, participating in the 'family' life of God. It is the people, the *laos tou theou*, that become the servant of the Lord in the Servant Jesus.

Ministry is Christ-ian in precisely this sense: it is through Christ in the Spirit that the *laos* of God participates in the love life of God and undertakes God's service on earth. Christ is himself, as Torrance says, 'the outgoing of the innermost Being of God toward men in active sympathy and compassion, the boundless mercy of

---

[25] As mentioned earlier, Simon Chan in *Spiritual Theology: A Systematic Study of the Christian Life* critiques what he calls the 'social analogy of the Trinity' as derived from and relevant to Western socio-political contexts and not appropriate to the Eastern hierarchical and ordered society. While not fully persuaded by this critique, I affirm his recalling the church to the mystery of immanence and transcendence in the triune God and to the continuing relevance of Augustine's psychological analogy of one God and three persons. All models will be less than God and were we able to fit God into our puny minds God would be too small to worship. See 40–55.

God at work in human existence'.[26] We may carefully speak of the
laos of God not so much as a Christocratic community, as Kraemer
does, but a 'Christodiakonic' community (if I may be allowed to
coin a word). It is the people through whom God continues to serve
through Christ in the power and presence of the Spirit.[27] It is both
kenotic (self-emptying) and ek-static (taking one outside of self). It
is ministry by God, for God and to God.[28] Such a ministry under the
New Covenant makes the whole people of God the true
ministerium. Roy Bell says, 'The ministry is of the entire community without class distinction.'[29] It cannot be delegated to the
clergy.[30] Who is the minister of the church? Jesus, in the Father,
through the Spirit! Who is the minister in the world? God through
God's people as a whole.[31]

---

[26] T.F. Torrance, 'Service in Jesus Christ', in Anderson, *Theological
Foundations for Ministry*, 718.

[27] Torrance says: 'Christ was Himself the *diakonos par excellence* whose
office it was not only to prompt the people of God in their response to the
divine mercy and to be merciful themselves, not only to stand out as
the perfect model or example of compassionate service to the needy and
distressed, but to provide in Himself and in His own deeds of mercy the
creative ground and source of all such *diakonia*' ('Service', 718).

[28] John D. Zizioulas notes how the ministry of the church can be
identified with that of Christ only if we see 'the mystery of Christ as being
initiated by the Father who actually sends the Son in order to fulfil and realize the eternal design of the Holy Trinity to draw men and creation to
participation in God's very life' *Being as Communion* (Crestwood, NY: St
Vladimir's Seminary Press, 1993), 210–11.

[29] Bell, 'A Theology of Ministry', 12.

[30] Zizioulas argues for the hierarchical nature of the church's life and
ministry because the Holy Trinity is hierarchical by reason of 'specificity
of relationship'. Quoting Gregory of Nazianzus, 'the Son has everything
in common with the Father and the Spirit except being Father or Spirit
and the Spirit possesses everything the Father and the Son possess except
being Father or Son' (*Being as Communion*, 223). But I have argued elsewhere that monarchy resides in the Trinity, as Athanasius affirmed, not
the Father, notwithstanding the specificity of relationships. See
Moltmann, *Trinity and the Kingdom*, viii.

[31] To this point Zizioulas notes 'the expression "the ministry *of* the
Church" is not to be understood as a possessive genitive. The being of
the Church does not precede her actions or ministries. Charismatic life

Ministry is characterized by love

Ministry is God's ministry, arising from the communal life of God, the Father, Son and Spirit ministering in love to one another even before there was a world to save (Jn. 17:24). Ministry for the people of God is not a delegated activity but derived, participatory and perichoretic. Ministry is God continuing his own loving service in and through his own people 'incorporating our servant-existence in Himself and incarnating among us the self-giving of God in sheer love and compassion to mankind' (Torrance).[32]

So in the Servant Songs of Isaiah, the Servant will not break a bruised reed nor snuff out a dimly burning wick (42:3), so profound is his respect for human personality especially among the marginalized and broken. So identified is Jesus with his creatures that on the last day when our final examination is given in terms of relationships, he will say, 'I was hungry and you gave me something to eat . . . a stranger and you invited me in' (Mt. 25:31–46). The Christian person has essentially an amateur status – serving for the love of it, out of being loved, and in love.

Ministry seeks the blessing of creation through incarnation

The ministry of God the Father and Spirit through Jesus is not merely illustrative; it is normative. Those who are in God because they are in Christ through the Spirit must participate in the world

---

[31] *(continued)* (i.e. concrete ministries) is constitutive of and not derivative from the Church's being' (*Being as Communion*, 217). Speaking to this from a Roman Catholic perspective in the wake of Vatican II Maxwell E. Johnson writes, 'The recovery of a baptismal spirituality invites us to a renewed sense of both the lay and ordained ministry in the life of the Church. By water and the Holy Spirit *all* are, we might say, "ordained" as priests, initiated into that royal, prophetic, and communal priesthood of the baptized in which, of which, and for which the specially ordained serve as the sacramental sign not to *do* the ministry of the baptized, but to lead the baptized in their collaborative ministries of proclamation, service, prayer, and witness in the world' (quoted in Austin, 'Baptism as the Matrix of Ministry', 110).

[32] Torrance, 'Service in Jesus Christ', in Anderson, *Theological Foundations for Ministry*, 716.

that God so loves.[33] This is the ek-static (out-of-oneself) life of God through which the people of God finds its life. As Zizioulas says: 'The relational character of the ministry implies that the only acceptable method of mission for the Church is the *incarnational* one: the Church relates to the world through and in her ministry by being involved existentially in the world. The nature of mission is not found in the Church's *addressing* the world but in its being fully in *com-passion* with it.'[34]

Ministry is eschatological

A fully trinitarian doctrine of ministry affirms that ministry is charismatic; it is an active expression of the empowering presence of God through the Spirit. In this sense the end of the ages has come upon us and God has poured out his Spirit on all flesh (Joel 2:28–30; Acts 2:17–21). Therefore ministry is not merely a human activity undertaken in obligation to a command (not even the Great Commission); it is God's own continuing ministry through the Spirit. As John Zizioulas says, the 'fundamental interdependence between the ministry and the concrete community of the Church . . . is brought about by the *koinonia* [fellowship] of the Spirit'.[35] It is through the Spirit that we are incorporated into one body (1 Cor. 12:13). The definition of body-life is diverse Spirit giftedness (12:4) making a Godlike unity.

The church ministers not only in the 'now' of the Spirit but in the 'not-yet' of the full coming of the Kingdom. It looks for, lives for, longs for and serves in view of the full irruption of the Kingdom at the second coming of Jesus. As such its goal is not only souls saved for eternity but the renewal of all creation under the headship of Jesus Christ (Eph. 1:22; Col. 1:19–20).

In sum, a trinitarian theology of ministry proposes that service is the expression of the relational love life of the triune God through the whole people of God in the empowering presence of the Spirit. Trinitarian ministry expresses God's grace through the

---

[33] See Loren Wilkinson, 'Immanuel and the Purpose of Creation', in Lewis and McGrath, *Doing Theology*, 245–61.

[34] Zizioulas, *Being as Communion*, 224.

[35] Ibid., 212.

incarnational service of Jesus to create unity through diversity in the gathered life of the church, and build Kingdom community on earth. The ultimate end is the full consummation of the Kingdom and the renewal of creation in the new heaven and new earth. Such a theology of ministry as outlined above is counterpoised with several clerical alternatives: the sacramental model of priestly ordination (there are no non-ordained people in the church),[36] the 'Reformational' reduction of ministry to Word and sacraments, the professional approach of licensed and accredited experts, and the business reduction of ministry to scientific management.

In the New Testament we are introduced to a church that is ministerium (a ministering community), to flexible and changing leadership forms adapted to the situation, to a community in which men and women served together in full partnership, to a people in which all are called (Eph. 4:1), though each uniquely, to a community in which ordination as a rite or ceremony that confers power or office does not exist,[37] to a community in which leadership serves and assists all the people to fulfil their calling in the church and world. In a word, every member of God's people is a servant-minister for reasons that are theologically argued in the New Testament.

All the people of God have experienced the inbreaking of the reign and kingdom of God. All are called to service (Eph. 4:1). All are servant/ministers (Lk. 22:27; Acts 19:22). All are empowered and gifted for service by the Spirit (1 Cor. 12:7). All are included in the royal priesthood (1 Pet. 2:5–10). Clericalism is thus effectively transcended. What can we then say about the ministry of leaders?

4. Ministering Leaders

While the New Testament has no place for clergy as a separate category of believer, the Scripture has many references to leaders within God's *laos*. There is a rich diversity of leadership words in the New

---

[36] See ibid., 215–16. In spite of this statement Zizioulas, however, focuses on the ordained in-church ministry as a practical expression of trinitarian ministry, 209–46.

[37] Warkentin, *Ordination*, 187.

Testament. In Romans 12:8 the word for leadership is a verb, not a noun, *proistēmi* (the one who goes before); in 1 Corinthians 12:28 leadership is a function, *kybernēsis* (administrators); in Philippians 1:1 the word for leadership is a term for a minor responsibility, *episkopoi* (overseers; see also Acts 20:28; 1 Tim. 3:1); in 1 Timothy 3:8 the word represents a position of lower status, *diakonos* (servant); in Titus 1:5 the word is a descriptive term, *presbyteroi* (elders, or older, wiser people); and in Ephesians 4:11 the word is a metaphor, not a title, *poimēnes* (pastors or shepherds). Conspicuously missing from the list of leadership words is 'priest' (*hiereus*), a word which until the end of the second century was reserved for Christ and the whole believing community.[38]

Function or office?

As noted above, the doctrine of the Trinity is critical to our view of ministry, especially the ministering leader. God is 'imaged' in a community that is an earthly icon of trinitarian holiness and love. This means that members will serve with distinguishable and interdependent personal functions, including the leaders. Stated roles will necessarily emerge but not offices that can be filled even when there is no authentic participation in the service of God, no charismatic reality.[39] Edward Schillebeeckx describes the healthy tension between function and office: 'Ministry without charisma becomes

---

[38] Remarkably Congar notes that, with the one exception (Clement, in his letter to the Corinthians, 40.5 [c. AD 95]), philologically the Reformers were right, though he insists that the term 'priest' is simply a syncopation of the Greek *presbyteros*, elder, *Lay People*, 133.

[39] In contrast to this David L. Schindler argues that the doctrine of the Trinity yields a healthy distinction between ecclesial institution and ecclesial charism defending 'ecclesial institution as rooted in the "objectivity" of the Son and ecclesial charism as rooted in the "subjectivity" of the Spirit' ('Institution and Charism: The Missions of the Son and the Spirit in Church and World', *Communio* 25 [summer 1998], 260 [253–73]). This is based on, 'a *revealed* order within the trinitarian unity-within-distinctiveness of subjectivity and objectivity, an order indicated by the Creed's distinction between "begetting" on the one hand and "proceeding" on the other . . . The Son, as the begotten Word, is properly "objective" and hence "visible" as "form"; and the Spirit, as breath "proceeding from", is properly the "subjective" unity between the

starved and threatens to turn into a power institution; charisma without any institutionalization threatens to be volatilized into fanaticism and pure subjectivity, quickly becoming the plaything of opposing forces, to the detriment of the apostolic communities.'[40]

Nowhere is there justified what Congar calls 'two simultaneous truths, a clear inequality on account of function and a radical equality as members of one body'.[41] Rather there are multiple models of leadership for the people of God, each suited to the occasion and context, including elders, presbyters, bishops/overseers, deacons, deaconesses, evangelists, apostles, prophets and pastor-teachers.[42]

---

[39] *(continued)* Father and the Son, and as such remains "anonymous" even in his character as the "objective" fruit of that unity – anonymous, that is, by way of a presence that is precisely "excessive", lying "beyond" the visible Word. Our proposal, then, is that this (circumincessive) order of subjectivity and objectivity in the life of the Trinity provides the ultimate ground for the distinction within unity between charism and institution in the Church . . .' (260–61).

In this way Schindler proposes to counter the extremes of Joachism which emphasize one-sidedly the charismatic nature of the church, and clericalism which emphasizes one-sidedly the institutional nature of the church.

[40] E. Schillebeeckx, *Ministry: A Case for Change*, trans. John Bowden, 24. See also R.Y.K. Fung, 'Function or Office? A Survey of the New Testament Evidence', *Evangelical Review of Theology*, 18.1 (April 1984), 37–8.

[41] Congar, *Lay People*, 115.

[42] Congar argues from this diversity that it is all to be contained in the one Catholic Church rather than in the rich diversity of expressions of the people of God interculturally and in history. 'It has often been remarked (and not by Anglicans and Protestants only) that the early Church comprised a monarchical aspect, in the authority of the Apostles, of apostolic men or of bishops; an aristocratic aspect in the role of elders and of councils; and a "popular" aspect, in the part taken by all the faithful in the assemblies. To put these different aspects into opposition with one another, and even separate them, to erect one or another into the principle of the Church's constitution, as various heresies have done, bringing about episcopalianism, presbyterianism, congregationalism, this is to misunderstand the living organizational reality of the total Church. In life it is lived, the hierarchical principle (determinant for structure) combines with the communal principle (which calls for all to be associated together according to their order) for a work which is the work not of the hierarchs but of the Church' (*Lay People in the Church*, 282).

All these function in the charism of the Spirit and as servants of the whole. These servants of the *laos* are called to equip the saints (the body as a whole) for the work of the ministry (Eph. 4:11–12). They function, by and large, not in a solo nor monarchical manner but in plurality (Acts 13:1; 1 Tim. 4:14).[43] They are members and ministers of the *laos* serving the whole. They are not vicarious servants, not ontologically different; they do not perform a sacramental function in isolation (until later in history) and do not form a professional class. Congar's proposal that the New Testament 'presupposes the hierarchical priesthood'[44] is entirely unfounded; it 'reads into' the New Testament a later development.

It is frequently argued that Paul's charismatic (Spirit-filled) view of leadership yielded to fixed offices in the later Pastoral Epistles and thus provides the biblical justification for a clergy–lay split.[45] But the primary distinction between leaders in the New Testament, as Gordon Fee points out, is not between charismatic and official but between itinerant and resident leaders:

> Unless Rev. 2–3 provides an exception, there is no evidence in the New Testament of a single leader at the local level who was not at the same time an itinerant . . . Apart from the authority of the apostles over the churches they had founded, there seems to be very little interest in the question of 'authority' at the local level. To be sure, the people are directed to respect, and submit to, those who laboured among them and served them in the Lord (1 Cor. 16:16; Heb. 13:17). But the interest is not in their authority as such, but in their roles as those who care

---

[43] For a more complete examination of the theology and spirituality of leadership (from which some of these thoughts are drawn) see R.P. Stevens, 'Leadership, Church', in Banks and Stevens, *The Complete Book*, 568–75.

[44] Congar, *Lay People*, 213.

[45] In his fine article Dean Fleming counters this argument along several lines: (1) when official roles are named the charismatic character of the leadership service is never far from view (e.g. in 1 Tim. 3:5); (2) the flexibility of terminology for leaders shows that function takes precedence over office; (3) mention of overseers and deacons in the Pauline church of Philippi (Phil. 1:1) calls into question whether offices were relegated to a later post-Pauline, institutional period; (4) leadership in the New Testament is usually a collective (Fleming, 'The Clergy/Laity Dichotomy', 240–42).

for the others. The concern for governance and roles within church structures emerges at a *later* time. Nevertheless the twofold questions of laity and women in ministry are almost always tied to this question in contemporary debate. The great urgency always is, Who's in charge around here? which is precisely what puts that debate outside the New Testament concerns.[46]

Presbyters, overseers, pastors and deacons are given as Spirit gifts for empowering the whole people of God as God's royal priesthood (kingly and priestly) and God's prophetic people (prophets). Church leaders are essential for the right ordering of the community, for drawing out giftedness and nurturing people in the headship of Jesus. Leaders are needed to equip the saints, and to build up the body (Eph. 4:11–12).[47] Rather than having the church assist them to do the work of ministry, leaders are assistants to the rest of the body to empower them for their service in church and world.[48] Yet, Thomas Oden in

---

[46] Fee, 'Laos and Leadership', 10.

[47] The so-called equipping interpretation of Eph. 4:11–12, has been critiqued by T.D. Gordon, ' "Equipping" Ministry in Ephesians 4?', *Journal of the Evangelical Theological Society* 37.1 (March 1994), 69–78. Gordon brings to this exegetical exercise a 'grid' that service performed by the saints is not 'ministry' in the full sense, and that the service rendered by the gifted ones (especially pastor-teachers) is 'ministry'. This cannot be supported by a single New Testament text, though the New Testament does support, encourage and honour the specific Word ministries of apostles, evangelists, prophets and pastor-teachers. Gordon dissolves the ministry of the non-clergy *laos* into 'living Christ-like lives' (69) and acts of mercy. In the context of the entire New Testament, we must affirm that even Word ministry is now shared ('the prophethood of all believers' – Acts 2:17), without denying that some will serve the Body expressly by being devoted to the Word of God and prayer (Acts 6:4). It is an artificial distinction to say that the ministry of the rest of the saints is service while the ministry of the Word ministers (including apostolic, church-planters and missionaries, evangelists and prophetic leaders) is *really* 'ministry'. It is all service to God on behalf of the church and world to the glory of God. Every member ministry is not sustained by Eph. 4:12 alone but by extensive teachings in the New Testament: the royal priesthood, universal prophethood in this age of the Spirit, universal giftedness, universal vocation or calling.

[48] See Calvin, *Institutes*, IV.1, and comments on the use of administration in Thomas C. Oden, *Pastoral Theology: Essentials of Ministry*, 156.

his eloquent but substantially unbiblical defence of a theology of pastoral ministry, makes this comment: 'There remains a line as thin as a hair, but as hard as a diamond, between ordained ministry and the faithful layperson.'[49] That a line has been drawn is a certain fact in the history of the church.[50]

A line as hard as diamond

There are several lines of approach in the New Testament as evidenced in Matthew, John, Paul and the later epistles. In his fine survey of ministry in the early church Eduard Schweizer notes that 'N[ew] T[estament] writers consistently refused to make any distinction between an official ministry of a select person and that of any believer.'[51] At the same time we come to the end of the New Testament period with two options, the first involving the appointment of bishops, presbyters and deacons,[52] and the second, more in line with Johannine literature, responding to the movement of the Spirit especially in prophets and prophetesses.[53] There appear to be many options within the New Testament.

---

[49] Oden, *Pastoral Theology*, 88.

[50] See H.R. Niebuhr and Daniel D. Williams, *The Ministry in Historical Perspectives*.

[51] R.E. Schweizer, 'Ministry in the Early Church', in D.N. Freedman (ed.), *Anchor Bible Dictionary* (6 vols.; New York: Doubleday, 1992), IV, 836 (835–42).

[52] Schweizer notes that this would be legitimate according to New Testament standards as long as, '(1) it would not remain compulsory for all times and places but would flexibly yield to the will of God pertaining to new and different challenges and circumstances that might arise; (2) that no ministry would impart to its bearer a qualitatively different status from that of other believers (like that of the OT priest over against the laity); and (3) the free prophetic utterance of the Spirit is taken seriously, especially in the selection of the people to be ordained' (ibid., 841).

[53] Schweizer notes that this option would be feasible biblically, 'as long as (1) such a church would not exclude any kind of order to prevent it from dissolving into disorganized chaos; (2) the "charismatics" would not elevate themselves (and their gift) above other members; and (3) the authority of the basic gospel as preached from the beginning would not be disputed either by new religiously experienced revelations or by any adaptations to modern trends popular in the contemporary world' (ibid.).

Surveying the centuries that followed, the Catholic theologian Edward Schillebeeckx shows how for the first ten centuries, stated or designated ministries (leaders) within the church were essentially pneumatological and ecclesial; they were recognitions of the gifting of the Spirit and concrete expressions of relational life within a local church.[54] This means, says Schillebeeckx,

> that the modern situation in which a community might not be able to celebrate the eucharist because no priest is present is theologically inconceivable in the early church; the community chooses a president for itself and has hands laid on him so that they can also be a community that celebrates the eucharist . . . In that case the vitality of the community in terms of the gospel is the deciding factor, not the availability of a body of priestly manpower, crammed full of education in one place or another.[55]

In the second millennium the church fades into the background in the matter of stated ministries. Only an ordained priest can celebrate the eucharist and 'the ecclesial nature of ministry threatens to disappear' for reasons which are clearly nontheological.[56] In spite of great advances in liberating non-clerical ministry, *Lumen Gentium* (from Vatican II) reaffirmed that the ordained priesthood

---

[53] *(continued)* See also H. Küng, 'The Continuing Charismatic Structure', in Anderson, *Theological Foundations for Ministry*, 458–89.

[54] Schillebeeckx notes how canon 6 of the Council of Calcedon forbade the ordination of someone who was not in a concrete church. 'Only someone who has been called by a particular community (the people and its leaders) to be its pastor and leader authentically receives *ordinatio* . . . *Ordinatio* is an appointment or "incorporation" as minister to a community which calls a particular fellow-Christian and indicates him as its leader (or, above all in the earlier period, which accepts the actual charismatic emergence of one of its members and gives it official confirmation). An "absolute *ordinatio*", i.e. one in which hands are laid on someone without his being asked by a particular community to be its leader, is null and void. Here we can see an essentially ecclesial view of ministry' (Edward Schillebeeckx, *Ministry: Leadership in the Community of Jesus Christ*, trans. John Bowden, 38–9).

[55] Ibid., 41.

[56] Ibid., 54.

is 'essentially different from the priesthood of the believing people of God'.[57]

We have, until now, been considering ministering leaders in terms of giftedness as a ministry grace gift of God to the church, identified by the church for the church. We need also to consider the ministering leader in terms of vocation.

Is there a special call to the professional ministry?

Some theologians speak of a general call to all believers, and a secondary call to a few within the church who are summoned to give leadership, modelled on the example of Old Testament prophets and New Testament apostles.[58] For example Richard Niebuhr defines the call to the ministry as 'that inner persuasion or experience by which a person feels himself directly summoned or invited by God to take up the work of the ministry'.[59] Such language is very problematic.[60] That God might give an extraordinary supernatural

---

[57] Ibid., 70.

[58] Oden, *Pastoral Theology*, 18–25.

[59] H.R. Niebuhr, *The Purpose of the Church and Its Ministry*, 64. Niebuhr suggests that the call to the ministry involves, 'these four elements: (1) *the call to be a Christian* which is variously described as the call to discipleship of Jesus Christ, to hearing and doing the Word of God, to repentance and faith, et cetera; (2) *the secret call*, namely, that inner persuasion or experience whereby a person feels himself secretly summoned or invited by God to take up the work of the ministry; (3) *the providential call*, which is that invitation and command to assume the work of the ministry which comes through the equipment of a person with the talents necessary for the exercise of the office and through the divine guidance of his life by all its circumstances; (4) *the ecclesiastical call*, that is, the summons and invitation extended to a man [or woman] by some community or institution of the Church to engage in the work of the ministry' (64).

[60] In his 1912 Yale Lectures, John H. Jowett stressed that every preacher should testify to a unique divine call, 'a solemn communication of the divine will, a mysterious feeling of commission, which leaves a man no alternative, but which sets him on the road of this vocation bearing the ambassage of a servant and instrument of the eternal God' (John H. Jowett, *The Preacher: His Life and Work* [London: Hodder & Stoughton, 1912], 13). Another example is Herbert W. Chilstrom writing in a pastoral theology

summons is surely possible, and it sometimes happens. To require this as a basis of church leadership is to go beyond Scripture.[61]

As mentioned above (in Chapter 4), Paul uses 'call' to describe his own anointing as an apostle ('called to be an apostle' Rom. 1:1; 1 Cor. 1:1; Gal. 1:15). But he never offers his experience of a personal commission as a model for the general or special call to be experienced by other believers. David Falk shows that Paul's call is both conversion and commissioning.[62] The conversion 'call' he shares with all other believers through history. The commission 'call' is unrepeatable. It is not a paradigm for the 'call' of church leaders today. 'Luke's three accounts of Paul's Damascus road experience fail to ratify the ecclesiastical practice of a "call to the ministry".'[63] Even when addressing Timothy – a perfect opportunity to use 'call' language for a special call to pastoral leadership – Paul uses call language only with respect to Timothy's salvation.

The demand by ecclesiastical bodies that a potential pastor have a specific 'call to the ministry' as a prerequisite for pastoral office, while the rest of the people of God need no such call to exercise their gifts in the church, is not sustainable by the biblical witness.

---

[60] *(continued)* journal, 'We can begin with what one might call "the irresistible call to preach the Gospel." The term "irresistible" is chosen deliberately because it underscores the fact that the call to the pastoral office does not originate in us any more than does our call in baptism to be a Christian. It is a call from without, a call that comes uninvited, a call that forces itself upon us. It is not of course irresistible to the extent that we cannot turn aside from it (for God grants us freedom to do so). But it is a call which persists from the God whose Spirit not only creates faith in every believer, but also calls certain persons to the ministry of the Word and sacrament' ('The Pastoral Calling from the Perspective of a Bishop', *Word and World* 1 [1981], 331–7).

Might it not be that this divine imperative is simply the compulsion of the Spirit, now poured out on the whole people of God, to bear God's Word thus instituting the prophethood of all believers (Acts 2:17), a 'call' which comes to all but is heard uniquely by each?

[61] The qualifications for an elder, bishop, deacon or presbyter have to do with character and spiritual maturity; no mention is made of a 'call' (1 Tim. 3:1–13; Tit. 1:5–9).

[62] Falk, 'A New Testament Theology of Calling', 133.

[63] Ibid., 145.

The historical expression of the 'inner' or 'secret' call was expounded by Calvin largely because of concern for proper order in the church, to prevent 'noisy and troublesome men from rashly tak[ing] upon themselves to teach or to rule'.[64]

> I pass over that secret call, of which each minister is conscious before God, and which does not have the church as witness. But there is the witness of our heart that we receive the proferred office not with ambition or avarice, not with any other selfish desire, but with a sincere fear of God and desire to build up the church. That is indeed necessary for each one of us (as I have said) if we would have our ministry approved by God.[65]

Luther did allow for the call that came *from the church* to exercise ministry on the behalf of others through the office of pastor:

> [If the Christian] is at a place where there are no Christians he needs no other call than to be a Christian, called and anointed by God from within. Here it is his duty to preach and to teach the gospel to erring heathens or non-Christians, because of the duty of brotherly love, even though no man calls him to do so. . . . [I]f he is at a place where there are Christians who have the same power and right as he, he should not draw attention to himself. Instead, he should let himself be called and chosen to preach and to teach in the place of and by the command of the others.[66]

Elsewhere Luther makes a distinction between the immediate call directly from God (which is what the apostles experienced) and one mediated by the church (which is the normal way to become a church leader):

> God calls in two ways, either by means or without means. Today He calls all of us into the ministry of the Word by a mediated call, that is,

---

[64] *Institutes*, II.1062.

[65] Ibid., 1063.

[66] Martin Luther, 'That a Christian Assembly or Congregation has the Right and Power to Judge all Teaching and to Call, Appoint, and Dismiss Teachers Established and Proven by Scripture', *Luther's Works*, XXXIX, 310–1.

one that comes through means, namely through man. But the apostles were called immediately by Christ Himself, as the prophets in the Old Testament had been called by God Himself. Afterwards the apostles called their disciples, as Paul called Timothy, Titus, etc. These men called bishops, as in Titus 1:5ff.; and the bishops called their successors down to our own time, and so on to the end of the world. This is the mediated call since it is done by man.[67]

In twentieth-century pastoral theology, John Calvin's theology of calling has won and Luther's has lost. By and large we have missed the main thrust of the New Testament and reverted to a pre-Christian view of clergy and laity: a general call to the people and a special call to a few.

So how should people be called into leadership in the people of God? In addition to the *effectual*, *providential*, *charismatic*, and *heart* calls noted above in the section on personal vocation, there should be, in the case of church leaders, an *ecclesiastical call*.

The *ecclesiastical call* means quite simply that a person's suitability for church leadership needs to be discerned by the church in two ways, first in gifting, and second, in character (see 1 Tim. 3:1–13; Tit. 1:5–9). While a special existential 'call' may be perceived, the primary biblical bases upon which a person may enter pastoral leadership is character – a good reputation, practical ethical behaviour, and God-given gifts of leadership (1 Pet. 5:1–10). There is no ontological difference between leaders and people. The call to leadership in the church comes from the church!

It is this last call that is most conspicuously and most dangerously lacking in the church today with the result that many people head off to seminary on the basis of their *heart* call and, on graduation, offer themselves as self-appointed ministers for hire. Ordination all to easily becomes a certification process for tenured employment in the church and the means of obtaining special grace.

---

[67] *Luther's Works*, Am. Ed., op. cit., 'Lectures on Galatians, 1535, Chapters 1–4', (pp. 13–78) Vol. 26 (1963), Jaroslav Pelikan (ed.), 17.

Ordination

The practice of ordination is critical to maintaining the distinction of clergy and laity.[68] Luther understood the problem all too well and addressed it with a characteristic blast:

> Of this sacrament the church of Christ knows nothing; it is an invention of the church of the pope. Not only is there nowhere any promise of grace attached to it, but there is not a single word said about it in the whole New Testament. Now it is ridiculous to put forth as a sacrament of God something that cannot be proved to have been instituted by God. I do not hold that this rite, which has been observed for so many centuries, should be condemned; but in sacred things I am opposed to the invention of human fictions.[69]

As presently practised ordination sets apart people 'for the work of the ministry'. But what, if there is such, is the biblical basis of this act?

The first New Testament reference to laying on of hands after the ascension of Christ is in Acts 6:2 where the apostles appointed the Seven servants who were proposed by the people to care for the widows in the daily distribution of aid. Paul and Barnabas themselves were commissioned with prayer, fasting and laying on of hands in Acts 13:3 for their mission to the Gentiles. Unquestionably the New Testament exalts the charism of leadership as a gift to the church – though the terms for such leaders are mercurial and hard to pin down into a uniform 'biblical' order. Theologically and practically, commissioning to such leadership is important since, as we have seen, a Christian servant working in the church needs an ecclesial 'call'.

---

[68] See Warkentin, op. cit.; T. Nichol and M. Kolden, *Called and Ordained: Lutheran Perspectives on the Office of the Ministry* (Minneapolis: Fortress Press, 1990); Paul Beasley-Murray (ed.), *Anyone for Ordination? A Contribution to the Debate on Ordination* (Tunbridge Wells: Marc, 1993); D.J. Montgomery, 'Conductor or Virtuoso? A Historical and Theological Look at the Presbyterian Ministry of the Word and Sacrament with a View to its Implications for Lay Ministry' (unpublished paper, Regent College, Vancouver, April 1995).

[69] *Luther's Works*, XXXVI, 106–7.

It is beyond the scope of this book to elaborate on the fact that many of Paul's named co-workers were women – among them, it appears, a female apostle, Junia.[70] But there is nothing in the Bible like a hierarchical pattern of ordination, ordination for life, or ordination as a sacrament that conveys grace, ordination that leaves an indelible mark on the ordained and gives the priest the exclusive right to celebrate the eucharist. There is also nothing like ordination as practised by Protestants which gives exclusive right of the ordained, especially those in the Calvinist tradition, to preach the Word and minister the sacraments (*Institutes*, IV.3.8). In emphasizing the need for order and office in the church Calvin says: 'For neither the light of the sun, nor food and drink, are so necessary to nourish and sustain the present life as the apostolic and pastoral office is necessary to preserve the church on earth' (*Institutes*, IV.3.2).

What are we do about it? Schillebeeckx wisely proposes that the tension between an ontological sacerdotalist view of ministry on the one hand and a purely functionalist view on the other must be resolved by a theological view of the church's ministry as a charismatic office, the service of leading the community, and therefore as an ecclesial function within the community and accepted by the community. Precisely in this way it is a gift of God.[71]

In this chapter we have addressed several questions: First, what is ministry? It is putting ourselves at the disposal of God for God's purposes in the church and world. Ministry is from God, to God and of God.

Second, who are the ministers? The whole people of God as community is God's true ministerium in both its gathered life (*ekklēsia*) and dispersed life (*diaspora*). Together Christians are a royal (kingdom) priesthood and prophetic Word-bearing people (the prophethood of all believers). Sometimes even those not consciously serving God are nevertheless God's ministers (Is. 44:28; 45:1; Mt. 25:31–46).

---

[70] See R. Paul Stevens, 'Contemplative Sexuality', and 'Full Partnership in Ministry', in *Disciplines of the Hungry Heart*, 67–75, 77–87.

[71] Schillebeeckx, *Ministry: Leadership*, 70. See also Küng, 'The Continuing Charismatic Structure', in Anderson, *Theological Foundations for Ministry*, 458–89.

Third, how is ministry undertaken? What form does it take? It is in both word and deed, both overtly and covertly, to persons and to organizations, both directly and indirectly.

Fourth, where is ministry undertaken? Service from God and for God takes place in both the church and the world.

What would happen if we reinstated the ministry of the whole people of God? Morton and Gibbs, in their classic volume *God's Frozen People*, say it would be like discovering a lost continent or like finding a new element. Consider what it would mean for pastors, now liberated from the impossible task of being the comprehensive, all-encompassing ministers of the church, to be able to exercise their gifts of leadership to empower the people to grow corporately and individually into maturity. Think of a church of two hundred members ministering seven days a week in all the contexts which our sovereign God has placed those members. They do not have to be persuaded or inveigled into going into the world; they are already there. Envision the waiting world – closed countries, partially Christian countries, nominally Christian countries, post-Christian countries. We can never reach the world for Christ by sending fully supported missionaries. We must mobilize the whole people of God.

With some delicacy Thomas Gillespie considers what must happen for the reinstatement of the ministry of the whole people of God:

> It will be realized only if the 'nonclergy' are willing to move up, if the 'clergy' are willing to move over, and if all of God's people are willing to move out. For the ministry of the community is rendered first and foremost in the world and for the world. It is performed in the daily lives of its people, in their participation and involvement in the structures of a complex society, in their sacrificial obedience in 'worldly affairs,' in their mission to reclaim the world for the God who claims the world in love.[72]

---

[72] T.W. Gillespie, 'The Laity in Biblical Perspective', *Theology Today* 36.3 (October 1979), 327 (315–27).

For further study / discussion

1. Consider an experiment that has been undertaken in several churches. The culture of a local church can be partially changed in fifty-two weeks by refusing for one year to give 'air-time', speaking-time to visiting missionaries, denominational officials and professors from denominational colleges in the Sunday service. Instead each week an ordinary member should be brought forward and in five minutes interviewed along these lines: What do you do for a living? What are the issues you face in your work? What difference does your faith make to the way you address these issues? How would you like us as a church to pray for you in your ministry in the workplace? Then if you pray for that person, and do this with fifty-one others, you will have effectively ordained fifty-two people to their service, and created a church culture in which ministry is not only what the pastor does, but what the people do to serve God and God's purposes in the church and world – people putting themselves at God's disposal, as vehicles of God's own service in bringing creation to its consummation, until Christ comes and inaugurates the new heaven and the new earth.

2. Consider and critique the chapter on 'ordination' in Greg Ogden's *The New Reformation*. Do further research in the New Testament and in Marjorie Warkentin's book, *Ordination: A Biblical, Historical View*.

3. Discuss the quote by the Orthodox theologian Alexander Schmemann, in the introduction.

4. Reflect on whether, in the end, distinctions are impossible to eliminate, or whether it is even desirable so to do.

5. Evaluate the *actual* theology of ministry practised in your local church.

PART III

FOR THE LIFE OF
THE WORLD

Chapter 7

Prophets, Priests and Kings

I simply argue that the cross be raised again at the centre of the market place as well as on the steeple of the church. I am recovering the claim that Jesus was not crucified in a cathedral between two candles, but on a cross between two thieves; on the town garbage heap; at a crossroad so cosmopolitan that they had to write his title in Hebrew and in Latin and in Greek . . . at the kind of place where cynics talk smut, and thieves curse, and soldiers gamble. Because that is where he died. And that is what he died about. And that is where churchmen should be and what churchmen should be about.

George MacLeod of the Iona Community[1]

The one great preacher in history, I would contend, is the church. And the first business of the individual preacher is to enable the church to preach.

P.T. Forsyth[2]

William Temple's oft-quoted words bear repeating. The church is the one institution that exists for those outside it. But it is much more. The church does not merely exist to bring in new members. It exists within the sending of God to be the primary agent for the Kingdom of God on earth. Many of the biblical images and metaphors reinforce this. The *laos* of God is a pilgrim people travelling

---

[1] G. MacLeod, *Only One Way Left* (Glasgow: Iona Community, 1956), 38, quoted in G. Harkness, *The Church and Its Laity*, 156.
[2] P.T. Forsyth, *Positive Preaching and the Modern Mind* (Grand Rapids: Eerdmans, 1964), 53.

toward a destination (the full coming of the Kingdom of God),[3] God's colony on earth (representing God's interests and sovereignty), the bride of Christ (as a betrothed waiting for the day of full consummation), and the body of Christ (offering its life for the world). So exploring as we will the threefold offices under the Old Covenant is not only a handy way of understanding the ministry of the whole *laos* in Christ; it is a biblically founded expression of the missionary *identity* of the people of God: prophets speaking God's word, priests mediating God's presence and kings extending the rule of God into all of God's creation.[4] The combination of these three roles was popularized in the sixteenth century but there is a long biblical history to the threefold offices.[5]

1. Three Leadership Roles

Moses and Samuel united all three offices, although neither is given all three titles anywhere in the text of the Old Testament.

---

[3] 'The Church . . . is a community *in via*, on its way to the ends of the earth and to the end of time . . . The Church is the pilgrim people of God. It is on the move – hastening to the ends of the earth to beseech all men to be reconciled to God, and hastening to the end of time to meet its Lord who will gather all into one . . . The Church cannot be understood rightly except in a perspective which is at once missionary and eschatological' (Lesslie Newbigin, *The Household of God: Lectures on the Nature of the Church* [London: SCM Press, 1953], 25).

[4] Another time-honoured pattern of considering the church's mission has developed in recent missiological thinking, especially through the works of Hans Hoekendijk and Hendrik Kraemer, namely the articulation of the church's mission as *kērygma*, *diakonia* and *koinōnia*. As George Hunsberger points out these three terms were instrumental in the 1961 New Delhi assembly of the WCC (witness, service and unity) and keep reappearing in various works as words of love, deeds of love and life of love (Tom Sine); the truth, the life and the way (Christans, Schipper and Smedes); prophet, priest and king (*Lumen Gentium* from Vatican II); being the witness, doing the witness and saying the witness (Guder). See Guder, *The Missional Church*, 102–9.

[5] Y. Congar makes the exposition of these three offices the grammar of his theology of the laity, though he comes short of expressing these offices fully as whole-people ministries. Congar, *Lay People*, 121–323.

Later, when Jeremiah wanted to demonstrate the universal decline into idolatry, he listed the three categories of stated leaders: 'At that time, declares the Lord, the bones of the kings and officials of Judah, the bones of the priests and prophets, and the bones of the people of Jerusalem will be removed from their graves' (Jer. 8:1). It is one of a few places where prophets, priests and kings are listed in Scripture together.[6] These three offices were leaders representing the people as a whole to God and representing God to the people – mediators and bridge builders.[7] They were also mediating points of connection between God and the world.

In Israel

Priests had several functions: maintaining the sanctuary and the sacrificial system (Num. 18:1), guarding and teaching the Torah (law, Deut. 27:9);[8] judging especially in matters of ritual uncleanness (Ezek. 44:24);[9] and finally, discerning the will of God (Ex. 28:30).[10] Priests built a community of faith that would be characterized by God's dwelling with his people.

Prophets spoke words to foretell the future (Is. 7:14; Jer. 31:31ff.) and to 'tell forth' God's purpose in concrete situations so bringing people to repentance and faith (Amos 2:6–8). They interpreted and reminded people about past events. Prophets were the 'watchpersons' of Israel (Hos. 9:8) assessing the true spirituality and morality of the society – faith barometers. They were also ministers of hope, proclaiming the ultimate rule of God: 'Surely the Sovereign Lord does nothing without revealing his plan to his servants the prophets' (Amos 3:7).[11]

---

[6] See also Jer. 2:26; 4:9; Neh. 9:32. A more typical Old Testament conjunction is priests, prophets and wise men, a division also reflected in the layout of the canon itself.

[7] G. Breshears, 'The Body of Christ: Prophet, Priest, or King?', *Journal of the Evangelical Theological Society* 37.1 (March 1994), 3–26.

[8] Lev. 10:11; Deut. 31:19; 33:10.

[9] Lev. 13–15; Num. 5:11–31.

[10] 1 Sam. 23:1–6; 30:7–8.

[11] See also Jer. 29:11–14; 31:17.

Kings were anointed representatives of God to bring order, justice and peace to the nation.

Israel needed all three.[12] The priests ministered to the personal and spiritual needs; the prophet to the public and social needs, and the king to the organizational and political needs. All three pointed beyond themselves toward the eternal purposes of God for Israel.[13] But they did more. They equipped Israel to accomplish God's purpose of being 'a kingdom of priests and a holy nation' (Ex. 19:6) and so fulfil God's promise to Abraham to bless all the nations. Not only Israel but the world needed all three.

In Christ

Not surprisingly the full messianic ministry of Christ was explained by the Reformers as the fulfilment of these three messianic offices, though, as Yves Congar explains, this famous sixteenth-century doctrine of the *munera* stems from a common tradition in the ancient liturgies that prophets, priests and kings were appointed to these offices by anointing, so making them 'christs' (anointed ones).[14] Long before the Reformation, Eusebius of Caesarea argued for Christ as prophet, priest and king from such passages as Deuteronomy 18:15; Psalm 110:4 ;and Zechariah 6:13. The reasons are understandable. Israel awaited a prophet (Deut. 18:15), a priest (2 Sam. 7:12–13; Ps. 110:4), and a king (Is. 9:6–7; Ps. 2:6; 45:6; 110:1–2), three roles Christ fulfilled in his own person.

Thus John Calvin emphasized the importance of the anointing of these servants of God with holy oil and elaborated on the meaning

---

[12] There were, of course, other kinds of leaders within the Old Testament including sages, professors (like Ecclesiastes), judges (charismatic saviours), shepherds and warriors.

[13] 'They provided a framework within which ancient Israel could organize and conduct itself as the elect people of God, but they also pointed toward the eternal purposes of Yahweh' (E.H. Merrill, 'Royal Priesthood: An Old Testament Messianic Motif', *Bibliotheca Sacra* 150.597 [January–March 1993], 50 [50–61]).

[14] See Congar, *Lay People*, 61. This Old Testament anointing is developed theologically in T.F. Torrance, 'The Ordering and Equipping of the Church for Ministry', in Anderson, *Theological Foundation for Ministry*, 410–12.

of Messiah as 'the anointed one'.[15] So Jesus fulfilled all three Messianic offices as prophet (Is. 61:1–2),[16] priest (Ps. 110:4)[17] and king (Ps. 89:35–7; 110:1).[18] Elaborating on this Karl Barth noted that the prophetic office was at work in Christ in Galilee, the priestly in the passion and the kingly in his exaltation.[19] Now what does this mean for the church and its leadership? Here we find a double tradition: one emphasizing Christ's fulfilment of the offices in the clergy and another finding expression in the whole people of God.

In the clergy

Starting with Christ as prophet, priest and king, the Roman Church, largely under the seminal influence of Cardinal Newman (1877), has considered how the threefold office works out in the church's government with specific roles being assigned to designated church leaders. This is justified on the basis of a long history of representing clergy in this way from the early church through

---

[15] Calvin, *Institutes*, II.15.1. Thomas Torrance uses these three ordinations as the basis of his theology of ministerial ordination for Christian leaders. See T.F. Torrance, 'The Ministry: Consecration and Ordination', in Anderson, *Theological Foundations for Ministry*, 405–29.

[16] 'Now it is to be noted that the title "Christ" pertains to these three offices: for we know that under the law prophets as well as priests and kings were anointed with holy oil. Hence the illustrious name of "Messiah" was also bestowed upon the promised Mediator. As I have elsewhere shown, I recognize that Christ was called Messiah especially with respect to, and by virtue of his kingship. Yet his anointings as prophet and priest have their place and must not be overlooked by us. Isaiah specifically mentions the former in these words: "The Spirit of the Lord Jehovah is upon me, because Jehovah has anointed me to preach to the humble . . . to bring healing to the brokenhearted, to proclaim liberation to the captives . . . to proclaim the year of the Lord's good pleasure", etc. [Is. 61:1–2; cf. Lk. 4:18]. We see that he was anointed by the Spirit to be herald and witness of the Father's grace . . . This, however, remains certain: the perfect doctrine he has brought has made an end to all prophecies' (*Institutes*, II.15.1).

[17] Ibid., 15.6.

[18] Ibid., 15.3–5.

[19] Karl Barth, *Church Dogmatics* (Edinburgh: T. & T. Clark, 1957), II.2.431.

Vatican II.[20] 'Knowledge flowed from the prophetic office, sovereignty over conscience from the kingly office, and endurance from its sacrificial priesthood.' Yet, as Joseph H. Crehan, SJ, admits, 'there remained a paradox: Catholic priests throughout history have been regarded as sharing in the priestly office of Christ, while the other two offices have been left to the bishop.'[21]

In the whole people of God

At the same time there is a parallel tradition that regards prophet, priest and king as pertaining to the whole Christian people. This dates from the patristic period and the Middle Ages, as well as the liturgies of both the Western and Eastern Churches.[22] Barth notes that the three offices of Christ 'all find their secondary continuation in those who are sent by Him'.[23]

In *Laity in the Church* Yves Congar makes the threefold office his grammar for explaining the ministry of the whole people.[24] There is a progressive concentration of anointed leadership under the Old Covenant in Christ and, after Christ, an expansive inclusion of the whole people in the prophethood, priesthood and Kingdom rule of all believers.[25] This is not merely theological inventiveness but clearly taught in the New Testament itself, as we will now see, though we must return to the question of prophets, priests and kings in church leadership.

---

[20] See the extensive research in Joseph H. Crehan, SJ, 'Priesthood, Kingship and Prophecy', *Theological Studies* 42.2 (June 1981), 216–31.

[21] Ibid., 217.

[22] See H. Rikhof, 'The Competence of Priests, Prophets and Kings: Ecclesiological Reflections about the Power and Authority of Christian Believers', in J. Provost and K. Walf (eds.), *Power in the Church* (Edinburgh: T. & T. Clark, 1988), 58 (53–62). Rikhof's article considers the implications of Vatican II for the question of authority in the church.

[23] Barth, *Church Dogmatics*, II.2.431.

[24] Congar reflects this double tradition in his massive volume but puts the weight on the lay fulfilment of the three offices.

[25] Congar, *Lay People*, 61–2. Congar cites in support, Thomas Aquinas, *Summa theologiae*, III, q.22.a.1, ad 3, and II–II, q.183, a.2.

2. The Prophetic People

It all started with the *crie de coeur* of the first prophet, Moses. Moses replied, 'Are you jealous for my sake? I wish that all the Lord's people were prophets and that the Lord would put his Spirit on them!' (Num 11:25–9). Joel had a more complete vision for the last days: 'And afterward, I will pour out my Spirit on all people. Your sons and your daughters will prophesy, your old men will dream dreams, your young men will see visions. Even on my servants, both men and women, I will pour out my Spirit in those days' (Joel 2:28–9).

The eschatological Spirit

So on the Day of Pentecost, Peter quoting these words, significantly changed 'and afterward' (Joel 2:28) into 'in the last days' since the whole of Joel's prophecy was about the 'end time' (Acts 2:17–18). The last days of fulfilment had arrived with the outpouring of the eschatological Spirit. These days began with the coming of Jesus as the Prophet of whom Moses spoke in advance: 'The Lord your God will raise up for you a prophet like me from among your own brothers. You must listen to him' (Deut. 18:15). Consequently the apostles declared that Jesus was the Prophet (Jn. 1:45; Acts 3:22). Then, through the outpouring of the Spirit, all believers were equipped to prophesy, not just a few special anointed messengers like Moses, Isaiah and Hosea. Now it is everyone's gift. Prophecy is not a 'spiritual' gift in the sense of an attribute, ability or endowment in a person; it is a Spirit gift – a direct expression of the empowering presence of God in God's people. Along with the 'priesthood of all believers' popularized in the Reformation, we could coin another phrase.

The prophethood of all believers

This empowering perspective is based on several important scriptural foundations. First, all believers in Christ know God and are enlightened, thus fulfilling the prophecy of Jeremiah that 'they will all know [God], from the least of them to the greatest' (Jer. 31:34). Second, all have an anointing for revelation so that authoritative teachers are in a final sense not needed. 'As for you, the anointing you received from him remains in you, and you do not need anyone to teach you' (1 Jn. 2:27).[26] Third, all Christians corporately are able to interpret Scripture through the Spirit. Apostolic authority is now vested in Scripture rather than in living eyewitnesses (or their successors).[27] Finally, the Holy Spirit continues to teach by leading people into all the truth of Christ (Jn. 16:14). So the church, taught by God through Scripture and Spirit, is a teaching[28] and a preaching church.[29]

---

[26] See also Jn. 6:45; Rom. 16:26; 1 Cor. 14:6, 26; 2 Cor. 12:1. Congar concedes that 'charisms of knowledge and unveiling of divine mysteries . . . do not, or need not, come from any hierarchical proceeding . . . but from an unpredictable direct visitation of God' (*Lay People*, 297).

[27] This is held in contrast to the Catholic belief in the 'infallibility of the Church's faith' (ibid., 288). Congar responds to Luther on this point arguing that Luther 'transpose[d] the exercise of the inward anointing, by which the faithful are enabled to grasp the sense of true doctrine, to the plane of the Church's doctrinal life; he uses it to replace the principle of apostolic function by an apostolicity of content that every man can judge for himself, and the community above all . . . Similarly with Calvin's notion of the inner witness of the Spirit' (ibid., 278–9).

[28] As he often does, Congar starts by exalting the universal ministry of all Christians and then defends the hierarchy. In this case he distinguishes between the teaching church (which all believers share) and the taught church (which apostolic delegates instruct) (*Lay People*, 276).

[29] With regard to the relation of prophecy and preaching: There are occasions when prophecy involves foretelling future events (Acts 11:28; 21:10–11). Most commonly, however, prophecy is telling-forth – speaking the Word of God with immediacy, directness, with anointed relevance. When Paul had to regulate the tendency of the Corinthians to exalt tongues as the superlative Spirit gift, he argued that they should desire 'especially the gift of prophecy' which is for strengthening, encouragement and comfort (1 Cor. 14:1,3).

Today there are two extremes that should be avoided: one is the reduction of all prophecy to preaching and the other is the rejection of preaching as a form of prophecy. Anointed preaching in the church or world speaks to the heart in such a way that people know they have heard from God. Amos's prophecies were like sermons carefully prepared and honed for maximum impact. But prophecy may also be spontaneous, on the spur of the moment, an inspired utterance that also speaks directly. Prophecy is not above Scripture but must be tested by Scripture. Indeed

Universal Word ministry

The church is God's greatest prophet/preacher in history.[30] All are spokespersons for the Gospel of the Kingdom through 'verbal signing'.[31] This is the burden of Jesus' teaching[32] and the preoccupation of early Christians.[33] And the first duty of the preacher-pastor is to equip the whole church to preach. This is part of building up the body of Christ so that believers will no longer be 'infants' (Eph. 4:11–14). Leaders do this by equipping all the people of God to be able to open God's Word and to hear God speak *for themselves*. Speaking to the inversion of the biblical vision, the radical missiologist Roland Allen said: 'It would be better to teach a few men to call upon the name of the Lord for themselves than to fill a church with people who have given up idolatry, slavishly and unintelligently, and have acquired a habit of thinking that it is the duty of converts to sit and be taught and to hear prayers read for them in the church by a paid mission agent.'[34] Who could have designed a system, as has surely happened, by which people can hear two sermons a Sunday for the whole of their lives and not be able to open up the Bible to others publicly?

---

[29] *(continued)* prophecy is not bringing new revelation about God and God's purposes since these have been finally declared in Christ and Scripture. What prophecy does is to bring Scripture 'home'.

That is indeed what good preaching does. Prophetic preaching is 'making present and appropriate the revelation of God' (Fred Craddock). It is a 'manifestation of the incarnate Word, from the written Word, by the spoken word' (Bernard Manning). What makes a speech a sermon (prophecy) and a sermon Gospel is 'the real presence of Christ crucified' (P.T. Forsyth).

[30] Congar surveys the significant and rich history of lay preaching which, he laments, was largely shut down in reaction to the 'excesses' of the Protestant Reformers. He does, however, note the considerable influence of non-clerical defences of the faith made by people like Pascal and G.K. Chesterton (*Lay People*, 298–301, 304).

[31] Guder, *The Missional Church*, 107.

[32] See Mt. 10:7; 24:14; Mk. 1:14–15; Lk. 4:21; 4:43.

[33] See, for example, Acts 8:12; 14:22; 19:8; 28:23,31.

[34] R. Allen, *Missionary Methods: St Paul's or Ours?*, 160–61.

What does this mean for the ministry of the people of God under the New Covenant? First, every believer is called and equipped by God to bear witness to the gospel and to bring God's Word to the world. A person does not need the 'gift' of preaching to be a witness.[35] Second, the prophethood of all believers means that each Christian should be ready to bring God's Word 'in season' (when prepared and expected) and 'out of season' (when the opportunity comes unexpectedly and inconveniently, 2 Tim. 4:2). Not only the apostles but all Christians are Christ's ambassadors – 'God . . . making his appeal through us' (2 Cor. 5:20).

Finally, the primary equipment of believers for the ministry of prophecy is the continuous inundation of the Holy Spirit (Eph. 5:18). The Holy Spirit convicts of sin, convinces, persuades, and reveals Jesus – 'not simply with words, but also with power, with the Holy Spirit and with deep conviction' (1 Thess. 1:5). The Holy Spirit is not given to the gifted, confident and ambitious but to the poverty stricken.

Thus far we have been considering how individual Christians can fulfil the prophetic function. But the people of God is not a mere collection of individual preacher/prophets. Corporately the church is a prophetic community.

The prophetic church

The church is not meant merely to be the ambulance of society – picking up the casualties – but the prophetic pioneer, caring for what God cares for. Speaking to this prophetic function E.H. Oliver says the church does this by acting as conscience to society, by educating and inspiring, by pioneering new ministries, by studying to prevent rather than to cure, by transforming the helped into helpers.[36] This is not merely the 'social gospel' as it was once called, which too often was like sowing grains of sand in the soil of the world. Rather it is a divinely inspired orthopathy. P.T. Forsyth had

---

[35] Preaching is not a gift but a means of communication (like writing, making films or drawing cartoons) through which other gifts, such as prophecy, exhortation, knowledge and leadership can be expressed. But the preacher-teacher is a gift.

[36] Oliver, *The Social Achievements*, 116.

the right emphasis when he said 'the largest and deepest reference of the gospel is not to the world and its social problems but to eternity and its social obligation'.[37] The church must be equipped to serve in the world precisely because it does not belong to the world. If we start with the world the church will lose its mission. If we start with God, the church cannot refrain from giving its life for the world.

Prophets, however, need priests and kings. And a prophetic church must also be a priestly church.

3. The Priestly People

The biblical basis of the revolutionary doctrine of the priesthood of all believers is one major reference in 1 Peter 2:9: 'But you are a chosen people, a royal priesthood, a holy nation, a people (*laos*) belonging to God,' and three minor references in the last book of the Bible, Revelation (1:6; 5:10; and 20:6).[38] But there is more to the priesthood of all believers than a few obscure verses in the New Testament. This intriguing idea gathers up many other New Testament themes such as universal ministry, universal empowerment in the Spirit, universal calling. It also fulfils the seminal idea planted in the infancy of Israel's story that God's people would be a 'kingdom of priests' (Ex. 19:6).

The priesthood of all believers was the watchword of the Protestant Reformation.[39] Luther said, 'All Christians are priests and

---

[37] P.T. Forsyth, *The Church and the Sacraments* (London: Independent Press, 1917), 29.

[38] See A.J. Bandstra, ' "A Kingship and Priests": Inaugurated Eschatology in the Apocalypse', *Calvin Theological Journal* 27.1 (April 1992), 10–25.

[39] The literature on the priesthood of all believers is extensive. Some important articles and books not referenced in footnotes are as follows: C. Eastwood, *The Royal Priesthood of the Faithful: An Investigation of the Doctrine from Biblical Times to the Reformation* (London: Epworth Press, 1963); J.L. Garrett, 'The Pre-Cyprianic Doctrine of the Priesthood of All Christians', in F.F. Church and T. George (eds.), *Continuity and Discontinuity in Church History*, 45–61; J.L. Garrett, 'The Biblical Doctrine of the Priesthood of the People of God', in H. Drumwright (ed.), *New Testament Studies: Essays in Honor of Ray Summers* (Waco, TX: Baylor University Press, 1975), 137–49; R. Hanson, *Christian Priesthood Examined*; G.D.

all priests are Christians. Anathema to him who distinguishes the priest from the simple Christian.'[40] Luther argued that the simple milkmaid or the tailor with the word of God in his or her hands was able to please God and minister the things of God as effectively as the priest, the prelate and the pope himself. 'Ordination does not make a priest, but a servant of priests . . . a servant and an officer of the common priesthood.'[41]

The priestly community

The idea that the whole Christian community was priestly was not itself an innovation. Even Augustine acknowledged that the baptismal anointing of all Christians made them priests: 'None of the faithful doubts that the priesthood of the Jews was a figure of that royal priesthood which is in the Church, to which are consecrated all who belong to the Body of Christ, the sovereign and true Head of all priests.'[42]

Augustine distinguished between the priesthood of ordinary Christians whom 'we call priests because they are members of the one Priest',[43] a lower level priesthood, from the hierarchical priesthood. But as we have seen, there is no *sacerdotium in sacerdotio*, no priesthood within the priesthood in the New Testament or the

---

[39] *(continued)* Henderson, 'Priesthood of Believers', *Scottish Journal of Theology* 7 (March 1954),1–15; E.G. Hinson, 'Pastoral Authority and the Priesthood of Believers from Cyprian to Calvin', *Faith and Mission* 7.1 (autumn 1989), 6–23; W.F. Scott, 'Priesthood in the New Testament', *Scottish Journal of Theology* 10 (December 1957), 399–415.

[40] Martin Luther, *Babylonian Captivity of the Church*, 2.283, *opera Latina Lutheri*, Frankfurt, 1986, X, quoted in P.F. Palmer, 'The Lay Priesthood: Real or Metaphorical?' *Theological Studies* 8 (1947), 574–613.

[41] Martin Luther, 'Answer to Goat Emser', iii, 322ff, quoted in R.H. Fisher, 'Baptists and the Ministry: Luther on the Priesthood of All Believers', *The Baptist Quarterly* 17 (July 1958), 303 (293–311).

[42] Augustine, *Quaestionum evangeliorum*, ii, 40 (PL XXXV, 1355), quoted in Paul F. Palmer, SJ, 'The Lay Priesthood: Real or Metaphorical?' *Theological Studies* 8 (1947), 583 (574–613).

[43] Augustine, *The City of God*, trans. M. Dodds (New York: Random House, 1950), XX.10.729.

first few decades of the church's life. All are priests, period.[44] It was this that Luther so passionately wanted reinstated and for several important reasons.

First, the ministry of the people of God derives from the permanent high priesthood of Jesus; it is not self-generated. Because of this every believer has direct access to God through Jesus and does not need the penances and absolution of a human priest. Jesus is enough. Because Jesus ever lives to intercede on our behalf, and because believers are joined to the Lord, the believing community is a priestly community in which every believer might well be called a priest.

Second, all believers participate in the continuing priestly ministry of Christ; it is not now undertaken representatively or vicariously by a select few. As the Letter to the Hebrews says, 'Since we have a great priest over the house of God, let us draw near to God with a sincere heart in full assurance of faith' (Heb. 10:21–2). 'Let us consider how we may spur one another on toward love and good deeds . . . let us encourage one another' (10:24–5). This priesthood is corporate as well as individual.[45]

Finally, the priesthood of believers is both ecclesial (in the gathered life of the church) and diasporic (in the dispersed life of the church). To show the missionary implications of the priesthood of Jesus, the author of Hebrews says in 13:13, 'Let us, then, go to him outside the camp, bearing the disgrace he bore.' L. Floor puts the

---

[44] 'We are all consecrated priests through baptism' (*Luther: Selected Political Writings*, trans. J.M. Porter [Philadelphia: Fortress Press, 1957], 40).

[45] It should be noted that the Anabaptist model of brotherhood church stressed that a believer cannot come to God in good conscience without his brother. In his thoroughgoing analysis of the general priesthood Ernest Best shows that while the majority of instances implicitly or explicitly relating to the doctrine in Scripture refer to Christians in general or a particular congregation, there are three clear instances that refer to individuals: Phil. 2:17; 2 Tim. 4:6; Rom. 15:16. He concludes, 'we are forced thus to reject both the individualism implied in the phrase "the priesthood of believers" and the false corporateness in "the priesthood of the church", and choose a phrase which suggests both the true individual and corporate nature of Christians as priests; for this purpose "general priesthood" seems a preferable term' (E. Best, 'Spiritual Sacrifice: General Priesthood in the New Testament', *Interpretation* 14 [July 1960], 273–99).

matter succinctly: 'From the Epistle to the Hebrews may be derived this most important thesis: the deeper we enter the sanctuary the further we will penetrate the world.'[46] It is precisely this last crucial *and missing* dimension of every member ministry which is expounded by the synergistic combination of 'priesthood' and 'regency' – this latter term describing the rule exercised on behalf of a monarch. Priesthood connotes the interiority of the ministry of the whole people of God. Royalty and prophethood connote the exteriority of every member ministry.

Misunderstanding priesthood

As it turns out both Catholics and Protestants have misunderstood this priestly rule. Catholics contained the priesthood in a sacerdotal and sacramental caste system of ministry which required that the faithful could only approach God through the priest. This loss, now widely recognized by Catholics themselves, is quite obvious. Not so obvious is how Protestants have lost the corporate priesthood completely in the granular individualism that has paralysed Western culture, so making each individual Christian his or her own priest, a do-it-yourself priesthood. In some Protestant churches the priesthood of all believers has degenerated into one vote per person as a way of finding God's will for a congregation, or allowing every male (!) to have a turn in the pulpit. As I will show in due course, the idea that the community as a whole is the royal priesthood, and that the community has this priesthood only in Christ (and not in itself) has largely been lost. The road to these deep and dangerous aberrations, traced in Chapter 3, was a long one.

Luther and the priesthood of believers

In his famous tractates of 1520 and in *de Instituendis Ministris* of 1523, Luther taught that 'All Christians are alike priests. Everything depends upon the Priesthood of Christ which is shared by us in virtue of our communion with Him through faith.'

---

[46] L. Floor, 'The General Priesthood of Believers in the Epistle to the Hebrews', in F. Fenshaw, et al., *Ad Hebraes: Essays on the Epistle to the Hebrews* (Pretoria: University of Pretoria, 1971), 80 (72–82).

Luther notes the analogy of the oneness of husband and wife which gives them all things in common. As fellow-priests with Christ we have access to God and may do all things which we see done and figured in the visible and corporeal office of the priesthood.[47] Luther discovered, what we now know to be the unequivocal truth, that the argument for a special or a clerical priesthood must be made on some other grounds than the New Testament.[48]

After Luther

In his detailed history of the priesthood of all believers from the Reformation to the present in the Western Church Cyril Eastwood documents how each denomination and Christian movement attempted to embody this doctrine.[49] Wolfgang Schäufele shows

---

[47] G.D. Henderson, 'Priesthood of Believers', *Scottish Journal of Theology* 7 (March 1954), 5 (1–15).

[48] On this issue Luther took his stand. But ironically 'Here I Stand' became in one sense the model for the individual Christian. Though Luther never intended this, his recovering of the priesthood of the faithful became in the cultural history of the West, the epitome of the individual standing alone before God. Unwittingly Luther paved the way for the situation in which we now find ourselves. Ernest Best cautions against both an extreme individualistic and an oppressive corporateness, which says that the priesthood belongs only to the church and not to the members (E. Best, 'Spiritual Sacrifice', 297 [270–93]).

[49] *The Priesthood of All Believers: An Examination of the Doctrine from the Reformation to the Present Day* (London: Epworth Press, 1960). After considering Luther, Calvin, Anglicanism, the Puritan Tradition, and Methodism, Eastwood offers the following summary: (1) No single church has been able to express in its worship, work and witness, the full richness of this doctrine. (2) It has been a living issue in each century since the Reformation. (3) It is a unitive, positive and comprehensive principle that springs directly from the evangelical concept of 'free grace'. (4) The doctrine affirms that the divine revelation is more important than the means God uses to mediate it. (5) It is an assertion that God's justifying activity is proclaimed in the lives of all believers. (6) It is intrinsically related to the high priesthood of Christ. (7) The doctrine is significant for an understanding of the word 'ministry'. (8) It is significant for current ecumenical studies. (9) The truths inherent in the doctrine should be

how the Anabaptists took the apostolate of the laity to its logical conclusion, claiming that the revivalistic character and sect sociology of
the Anabaptist brotherhood enabled them to have 'no distinction
between an academically educated ministerial class on the one hand
and the laity on the other. Each member was potentially a preacher
and a missionary.'[50] As lay missionaries the Anabaptists reached out to
near and far relatives, neighbours and to connections made through
their occupations. But this missionary activity was limited to the oral
proclamation of the Gospel as only office-bearers in the church were
authorized to baptize.[51]

Calvin, of course, admired the Anabaptists no better than did
Luther.[52] He refused to abandon the professional ministry. Even
though Rome had befouled the priesthood with corruption, the
right of honour proceeding from the calling of God remains. Calvin
did not use the word 'priest' for the ordained minister but he might
have by his insistence on the divine origin and permanent necessity
of the ministry of Word and sacraments. The priesthood of all
believers was not decisive for either Calvin's thinking or his practice
in congregational life.[53]

Each of the post-Reformation attempts to embody fully the
priesthood of all believers has been incomplete partly because of its
anti-Rome stance: no priest and no mediator. For example, speaking to the Baptist implementation of the doctrine William Pitts
identifies its implicit individualism and privatism: 'There is a powerful legacy of individual privilege associated with the priesthood

---

[49] *(continued)* incorporated into the worshipping life of the church. (10) It
anticipates the full participation of all Christians in the evangelistic action
of the church. (11) It leads to a fuller understanding of the doctrine of
divine vocation. (12) The doctrine [has] eschatological significance
(238–58).

[50] W. Schäufele, 'The Missionary Vision and Activity of the Anabaptist
Laity', *Mennonite Quarterly Review* 36 (April 1962), 100 (99–115).

[51] Ibid., 101.

[52] Calvin did draw more from the Anabaptists generally than did Luther,
and some regard him as a halfway house between the two, though not in
this respect.

[53] J.R. Crawford, 'Calvin and the Priesthood of All Believers', *Scottish
Journal of Theology* 21.2 (June 1968), 145–56.

of all Christians.'[54] Baptists have generally resolved the priesthood of all believers into the following practices: All Christians have the right to interpret Scripture for themselves; every member of a Baptist church possesses voting rights in the conduct of church business; all Christians have the authority and obligation to develop personally their own religious beliefs.[55] By and large denominations deriving from the so-called radical Reformation have succumbed to the clergy–lay distinction in one form or another. John Howard Yoder sadly concludes we cannot look to the radical congregationalists of the sixteenth century for special guidance on how to review ministerial patterns 'since this was not a matter concerning which they claimed any deep originality or any strongly biblical warrant for the patterns they did develop'. [56] So what would it be like to reinstate the priesthood of the people?

Experiencing priesthood

There are three dimensions of priestly ministry for the *laos* of God.[57]

First there is the priestly ministry of access to God through worship and intercession.[58] All believers have access to the Father and are enjoined to make 'prayers, intercession and thanksgiving' on behalf of every-one – 'for kings and all those in authority, that we may live peaceful

---

[54] W.L. Pitts, 'The Priesthood of All Christians in the Baptist Heritage', *Southwestern Journal of Theology* 30.2 (spring 1988), 45 (34–45). For a Baptist assessment of Luther's doctrine see R.H. Fisher, 'Luther on the Priesthood of All Believers', *Baptist Quarterly* 17 (July 1958), 293–311. For a practical perspective on applying the doctrine in local church life see D.L. Young, 'What Difference Does it Make, Anyway? The Priesthood of All Christians Applied to the Local Church', *Southwestern Journal of Theology* 30.2 (spring 1988), 46–54.

[55] T.D. Lea, 'The Priesthood of All Christians According to the New Testament', *Southwestern Journal of Theology* 30.2 (spring 1988), 15 (15–21).

[56] J.H. Yoder, *The Fullness of Christ: Paul's Vision of Universal Ministry*, 41. Yoder concedes that the Society of Friends (Quakers) and the Plymouth Brethren have the longest record of successfully functioning without a class of religious professionals.

[57] I am here following an outline suggested by Ernest Best.

[58] Acts 13:2; Heb. 13:15; Rev. 7:15; 5:8; 8:3–5.

and quiet lives in all godliness and holiness' (1 Tim. 2:1–2). Sins can and should be confessed to one another (Jas. 5:16). In such mutual confession we may offer a priestly word of absolution based on the promise of God. Each is a priest to God and to brothers and sisters. Together we bless God with worship and we bless the world with the presence of God.

Paul's 'one anothers' in 1 Thessalonians and his collection of newly coined words involving the word 'together' in Ephesians emphasize that there is no such thing as solitary ministry or individual Christians. Ministry happens at the point of real connection in the body. Most of the imperatives in Paul's letters (such as 'be filled with the Spirit' – Eph. 5:18) are addressed in the plural to the corporate experience of Christians.

This priesthood to 'one another' should be experienced not only on the micro level but also on the macro scale. Paul's great passion was not only to plant self-propagating churches throughout the Roman Empire but also to cultivate interdependence between Jewish believers with Gentile believers, thus bringing 'equality' (2 Cor. 8:14). Each was to contribute from their riches (Rom. 15:27) thus making a 'new man' (Eph. 2:15) a rich social unity, rather than a uniform, bland conformity. Paul described this ministry in priestly terms (Rom. 15:16) and claimed that he (and by implication we) could only know the fullness of Christ (Rom. 15:29) when people otherwise incapable of being together become profoundly interdependent in Christ. On a global scale this challenges any notion of mission as patronage. It is only 'together with all the saints' (Eph. 3:18) that we can know Christ fully or make Christ known fully.

Second, there is priestly ministry through service in the world.[59] There are obvious ways we may do this such as helping the helpless. There are also strategic ways such as asking why the poor are poor and dealing with the structures and powers of our societies that marginalize and depersonalize people; thus we become priests to the principalities and powers (Eph. 3:10), a matter taken up in Chapter 9. There are also earthy ways in which priestly ministry can touch people and places for God in homes, workplaces, neighbourhoods and whole societies. The priesthood of Adam and Eve

---

[59] Rom. 15:27; 2 Cor. 9:12–13; Heb. 13:16.

in the garden was an embodied ministry – naming, cultivating, integrating, releasing potential, envisioning, creating, offering what Robert Farrar Capon calls 'the oblation of things'.[60] This priestly ministry takes place in homes, schoolrooms, offices and factories, on planes and buses, in government offices and artists' studios, as well as in churches.

Third, there is priestly ministry in daily life.[61] Romans 12:1–2 describes the continuous priestly ministry of ordinary Christians as they offer up their everyday life to God as a spiritual ministry and live transformed lives in this world, conforming to the will of God rather than to the pressures of society (1 Pet. 2:1–3,11–12). Worship, praise and sacrifice are not now matters of sacred actions, sacred words in sacred places. Ordinary life is infused with God's presence and can be given back to God as 'spiritual worship' (Rom. 12:1).

Now we must turn to the intriguing and usually neglected first half of the phrase '*royal* priesthood' in 1 Peter 2:9. It is seldom noticed that in all but the final reference to the priesthood of believers in Revelation 20:6 the priesthood is linked with kingship or sovereign rule. The reinstatement of the royal dimension of the ministry of the people of God is critical for the ministry of the whole people of God especially in the world.

4. The Kingly People

There are several textual considerations. First, this phrase is a direct quotation of Exodus 19:6 in which both the Hebrew and the Greek translations communicate the idea of a kingdom and not merely a priesthood.[62] Second, whether *basileion* (royal) is an adjective or a

---

[60] See some of Capon's insightful statements about this priesthood: moving from clock time to significant time, from space to place, from information to mystery. Robert F. Capon, *An Offering of Uncles: The Priesthood of Adam and the Shape of the World*, 163.

[61] Rom. 12:1–2; Phil. 2:17; 2 Tim. 4:6; Rev. 6:9. See E. Best, 'Spiritual Sacrifice', 295.

[62] It is noteworthy that the Greek translation is *basileion* and not *basileia*, the first word meaning 'sovereignty' rather than a kingdom.

noun it is much more than a mere verbal peg for *hierateuma* (priest-hood). It is unclear whether the meaning of the Old Testament text is a kingdom (with God as king) whose subjects are all priests, or the sovereignty exercised by priests (a priesthood consisting of kings). But the idea of kingship/sovereignty does communicate the idea that leadership in the world and leadership in the sacrificial worship should ideally be in the same hands.[63] Christians are called to reign with Christ and share his sovereignty and kingship, especially in the light of Zechariah 6:13 (where the Branch 'will sit and rule on his throne. And he will be a priest on his throne') and Revelation 5:10 ('you have made them [the believers from every tribe, people and nation] to be a kingdom and priests to serve our God'). Third, the larger context of the New Testament suggests that Christians are royalty in the world in a real sense.[64] To grasp this we must consider the New Testament teaching about the Kingdom of God.

Understanding the Kingdom of God

It is not an overstatement to say that the Kingdom was the master thought of Jesus. It is used over a hundred times in the Gospels in comparison with only three references to the church. The Kingdom was the subject of his first sermon: 'The time has come. The kingdom of God is near. Repent and believe the good news' (Mk.

---

[63] On this point A. Gelston notes the several instances in the Old Testament where priests and kings are united in the same persons: Gen. 14:18; Ps. 110 (Melchizedek); Zech. 6:13 (the Branch), as well as references to the temporal rule of Israel. In the New Testament *basileion* is used in 1 Pet. 2:9 but in Rev. 1:5–6; 5:9–10; and 20:6 the word is *basileia* – kingdom (A. Gelston, 'The Royal Priesthood', *Evangelical Quarterly*, 31.1 [January–March 1959], 152–63).

[64] Rom. 5:17 (reigning in life); Jas. 2:5 and Lk. 12:31–2 (heirs of the Kingdom); Eph. 2:6 (seated with Christ in heavenly places); Mt. 19:28; Mt. 5:3,10; Lk. 6:20; 2 Tim. 2:12 (ultimately reigning and ruling with Christ and inheriting the earth). See also E. Best, '1 Peter 2:3–10 – A Reconsideration', *Novum Testamentum* (Leiden E.J. Brill, 1969), 270–93. Best offers the following meanings of *basileion* as a noun: royal residence, palace, tiara, diadem (a Hellenistic usage), kingdom and especially 'a body of kings' – this last he considers to be the best interpretation for reasons explained in the article.

1:15). It was also the subject of his last sermon on earth when the disciples asked, 'Lord are you at this time going to restore the kingdom to Israel?' (Acts 1:6).

The Kingdom is not a realm, a territory, but the rule of God as King (Lk. 19:12,15; Rev. 11:15; 1 Cor. 15:24). More accurately the Kingdom is the *rule of the sovereign* (God expressing his will and powerful presence) plus *the response of the subjects* (as they yield to the sway of the sovereign). Rule without response is less than the Kingdom. In this matter the Queen of England provides a graphic negative model of how many Christians inadvertently regard the King. Queen Elizabeth reigns but she does not rule. And many so-called Christians defer to the position of God as supreme ruler, but in actuality do not respond as subjects. The Kingdom involves both rule and response.

The emphasis in gospels and letters, however, is not on 'the Kingdom' but 'the Kingdom *of God*' (or in the more Jewish gospel of Matthew, 'the kingdom *of heaven*'). Richard T. France carefully shows that both the Hebrew/Aramaic *malkût(â)* and the Greek *basileia* refer to the *act* of being a king rather than to a concrete place such as a realm.[65] Various alternative phrases have been crafted to communicate this: 'God in strength', 'God's actual exertion of royal force' (B.D. Chilton), 'the saving sovereignty' (Beasley-Murray), and 'the divine government' (R.T. France).[66] France concludes:

> As God the king exercises his authority in his world, and people respond to it, there the 'kingdom of God' will be experienced in many ways. There can be no one place, time, event or community which *is* 'the kingdom of God', any more than 'the will of God' can be tied down to any specific situation or event. 'The kingdom of God' is God in saving action, God taking control in his world, or to use our title, 'divine government'.[67]

---

[65] See von Rad, Kuhn, '*Basileus/Basileia*', in Kittel and Friedrich, *Theological Dictionary of the New Testament*, I, 564ff.; Ceslas Spicq, '*Basileia*', in Ernest, *Theological Lexicon of the New Testament*, I, 256–71.

[66] R.T. France, *Divine Government: God's Kingship in the Gospel of Mark* (London: SCM Press, 1990), 12–13.

[67] Ibid., 15.

Jesus did more than teach about the Kingdom. He embodied *both* the rule of God in bringing liberation, peace and hope, and the response of the people which, throughout the history of Israel, was fitful and half-hearted, but in Jesus is total. Through the centuries Christians have considered Jesus to be the *autobasileia* – the Kingdom in his own person. So we can gratefully affirm that with Jesus the Kingdom has come. 'But if I drive out demons by the finger of God, then the kingdom of God has come to you' (Lk. 11:20).

The Kingdom is in the hearts of humankind as a new creation (Lk. 17:21; Mt. 12:28). It is in the world invisibly as the sway of God's rule in the affairs of people and nations. It is in the church visibly as an 'outcropping' of the Kingdom in the same way that outcroppings of strata in a highway cut through a hill reveal strata that extend in a hidden way beneath the soil. The church is not the Kingdom in totality (a mistake the Catholic Church has often made) but expresses, represents and serves as an agent for the Kingdom that is 'now'[68] and 'not yet' as we await final consummation.[69]

Regents of our God and King

A regent is a representative of the monarch. Christians serve as royalty representatives in several ways. They are royal rulers over themselves *personally* as they walk in the Spirit and triumph over the flesh – the self turned inward and away from God (Rom. 7:1–25; Gal. 5:16–26). Christians govern their passions, exercise self-control, put their lives in order and live as royal creatures.[70] They are also royal rulers *ecclesiastically* – in the church. They share Christ's rule as Head and King. Paul's ironic outburst to the Corinthians suggests that in putting the church in order relationally, socially and morally they should have been properly functioning as royalty: 'You have become kings – and that without us! How I wish that you really had become kings so that we might be kings with you' (1 Cor. 4:8). Believers in the family of God are not passive compliant followers but share in leadership, decision-making and

---

[68] Mt. 12:28; 21:31; 23:13; Lk. 4:17ff.; 10:23ff.
[69] Mt. 8:11; 24; 25:31ff.; Mk. 13; 14:25.
[70] 'Christian is king because he triumphs over sin, controls the enticements of the flesh, and rules body and soul' (Congar, *Lay People*, 235).

discerning the mind of the Head, Christ. A dramatic example of this is found in Acts 6 where the seven servants were proposed by the body and appointed by the apostles (Acts 6:3,6).[71]

They also share in the rule of the world *cosmically* in a prophetic, preliminary and anticipatory way through their daily work, social action and Christian mission as they live now in the Kingdom but wait, work and pray for the full coming of the Kingdom: now but not yet. As kings in the world, men and women are called to exercise dominion (Gen. 1:26,28), a distinctively royal role,[72] though in this partially redeemed world 'man is a toilful and anxious king, who has to subdue his realm inch by inch, with unceasing labour' (Congar).[73]

The church is the principal agency for the Kingdom on earth.[74] The purpose of the church is not to 'bring in' the church, but to 'bring in' the Kingdom of God. We do this through the mission of the church (the subject of the next chapter). We also do this in all the fields of service in the world: home, neighbourhood, civil society, politics and the environment, grappling with the powers,

---

[71] Panayotis Nellas offers an Orthodox perspective. He quotes Chrysostom in support of the kingly role of all believers in the administration of the church: 'We cannot leave everything to the priests but must ourselves take care of the whole Church which is our common body.' Nellas recalls the historic role of the laity in electing bishops and administering the life of the church through councils. See Nellas, 'The Ministry of the Laity', in I. Bria (ed.), *Martria/Mission: The Witness of the Orthodox Churches Today*, 60–65. Along these lines Congar laments that there never has been any power of ecclesiastical rule among the laity in the Catholic Church and pleads for its reinstatement.

[72] W.J. Dumbrell, *The End of the Beginning: Revelation 21–22 and the Old Testament* (Homebush West, Australia: Lancer Books. 1985), 42.

[73] Congar, *Lay People*, 237. The subject of 'kings in the church' – secular rulers functioning within the church to achieve Christendom (king and bishop being like two arms of the same body) and Luther's concept of the Christian participating in 'two kingdoms' cannot be considered here, but relate to the issue at hand (ibid., 251–6). For Luther's 'two kingdoms' see P. Althius, *The Ethics of Martin Luther*, trans. R.C. Schultz (Philadelphia: Fortress Press, 1972), 43–82.

[74] H. Snyder, *The Community of the King*, 12. See also Guder, *The Missional Church*, 183–220.

proclaiming the gospel, participating creatively in the structures of society and in parachurch mission structures, witnessing through suffering powerlessness, working to change evil systems and in extreme situations by laying down our lives in martyrdom.[75] The idea that believers are royalty opens up one of the most neglected areas of New Testament discipleship.

Three metaphors describe the Christian as a Kingdom person and the people of God as agents for the kingly rule of Christ. The first is salt, which preserves, protects and brings out taste. The second is light, which illuminates, draws out the meaning of life and points the way to God and his kingdom. The third is a spy. While this last metaphor is not directly suggested by Scripture, the twelve spies going into Canaan (Josh. 2:1; Heb. 11:31) provide a fascinating analogy for living in one world while spying out the next, being a citizen of one kingdom and sharing fully in its life while being subject to another kingdom and another King. The spy metaphor was proposed by Jacques Ellul:

> [The Christian] is the citizen of another Kingdom, and it is thence that he derives his way of thinking, judging and feeling. His heart and his thought are elsewhere. He is the subject of another State . . . He may also be sent out as a spy. In fact that is the situation of the Christian: to work in secret, at the heart of the world, for his Lord; to prepare for his Lord's victory from within; to create a nucleus in this world, and to discover its secrets, in order that the Kingdom of God may break forth in splendour.[76]

Kingly priests and priestly kings

Priesthood and royalty belong together. Even under the Old Covenant there was interdependence of prophet, priest and prince. When

---

[75] 'Martyrdom is the supreme achievement of spiritual kingship resisting worldly power, just as it is the supreme achievement of the spiritual-real priesthood of holiness' (Congar, *Lay People in the Church*, 241). Congar proposes two forms of kingly relation to the world, first engagement, and second refusal – by keeping independence of conscience, martyrdom and withdrawal. This last he defends (incorrectly in my view) as a sacred right for those specifically called to a 'total engagement in the work of God's Kingdom, *opus Dei*' (ibid., 242).

[76] J. Ellul, *The Presence of the Kingdom*, 45.

Hilkiah the high priest found the lost Book of the Law in the Temple, he read the Scripture to king Josiah. The king tore his robes in an expression of repentance for the people's neglect of the covenant. He ordered the priest Hilkiah to inquire of the Lord who did so by speaking to Huldah the prophetess (2 Kgs. 22:8–14). Then the prophetess declared the outcome of the matter – judgement on the nation and mercy to the king for his spiritual responsiveness: 'Because your heart was responsive and you humbled yourself before the Lord . . . and because you tore your robes and wept in my presence, I have heard you, declares the Lord' (22:19). The king then administered the law of God in the nation implementing the terms of the covenant (23:1–25). This same community of prophet, priest and king now forms a ministering whole under the New Covenant.[77] Now under the New Covenant the church is a royal priesthood.

Priesthood without kingship could easily degenerate into a new sacerdotalism – pure religiosity. Kingship without priesthood could easily degenerate into do-goodism without the touch of God, world-transformation without spiritual transfiguration. Together, the royal priesthood is able to praise God in acted words directed Godward in worship, and incarnational mission directed to the world to declare God's glory among the nations. Like common salt, which is composed of two deadly poisons, sodium and chlorine, which taken together are life-giving, so the *laos* of God must be both priestly and kingly. Together it salts the earth.

With great eloquence Luther pleads for the recovery of the royal priesthood, and for the faith without which it can never be realized:

> First, with respect to kingship, every Christian is by faith so exalted above all things that, by virtue of a spiritual power, he is lord of all things without exception, so that nothing can do him any harm. As a matter of fact, all things are subject to him and compelled to serve him in obtaining salvation. Accordingly, Paul says in Rom. 8[:28], 'All things work together for good for the elect,' and in 1 Cor. 3[:21–23], 'All things are yours whether . . . life or death or the present or the future, all are yours; and you are Christ's . . .' That is not to say that every Christian is placed over all things to have and to control them by physical power – a madness with which some churchmen are afflicted

---

[77] For an Orthodox expression of this see Nellas, 'The Ministry of the Laity', in Bria, *Martria/Mission*, 60–65.

– for such power belongs to kings, princes and other men on earth . . . The power of which we speak is spiritual. It rules in the midst of enemies, and is powerful in the midst of oppression. This means nothing else than that the 'power is made perfect in weakness' [2 Cor. 12:9], and that in all things I can profit toward salvation [Rom. 8:28], so that the cross and death itself are compelled to serve me and to work together with me for my salvation . . . Lo, this is the inestimable power and liberty of Christians.

Not only are we the freest of kings, we are also priests forever, which is far more excellent than being kings, for as priests we are worthy to appear before God to pray for others and to teach one another divine things.[78]

5. Prophets, Priests and Princes in the World

Taken together the threefold office expresses every member ministry in the church and the world. But it also illuminates the requirements for church leadership. All three are needed to serve the church in leadership, although it is unhelpful to identify in a rigid way (as an office) a pastor as equivalent to any one of the Old Testament anointed leaders. Yet a leadership team in a local church should embody all three, as these are rarely if ever embodied in a single individual like Moses.[79] This is a further argument for plural leadership in local churches rather than expecting an individual to embody in his or her person all the charismatic gifts and all the leadership functions. Among the people and in the leadership the three roles are found in the body together. Priests care, prophets proclaim and kings lead. Not only in the church, however, but in the world the threefold office also expounds dimensions of the ministry of God's *laos*.

---

[78] *Luther's Works: Career of the Reformer* I, Am. Ed., op. cit., 'The Freedom of a Christian, 1520' trans. W.A. Lambert, revised H.J. Grim, Vol. XXXI, 354–5 (pp. 327–77, 1957).

[79] J.R. Hardee, 'The Minister's Ministry Imagery', *Review and Expositor* 82.3 (summer 1985), 419–40. 'The staff ministers need not, in fact in most instances cannot, do all three alone – but they must see to it that all three are operating within the congregation' (424).

What do prophets do? Their work is discerning, communicating, exposing, seeing that justice is done, revealing outcomes – the very thing God's people can do in corporations and homes. What do priests do? Their work is bridge building, mediating, expressing meaning, evoking faith, blessing, bringing grace – again what the whole of God's people is able to do in the world. What do kings do? King work is ruling, organizing, planning, providing, nurturing, integrating, settling arguments, solving problems, co-ordinating, expediting, consummating – again ways that God's people serve in so-called secular occupations, in church and in the home. An executive in the banking industry, for example, has developed these three offices as they relate to business management: the prophet helping organizations discover what God intends for them to become, the priest caring for people and serving as a model, and the king acting as a faithful steward of people and resources.[80]

Luther concludes with the emphasis that all this comes from faith: 'Who then can comprehend the lofty dignity of the Christian? By virtue of his royal power he rules over all things, death, life and sin, and through his priestly glory is omnipotent with God because he does the things God asks and desires, as it is written, 'He will fulfil the desire of those who fear him; he will also hear their cry and save them' [cf. Phil. 4:13]. To this glory a man attains, certainly not by any works of his, but by faith alone.'[81]

---

[80] S. Herron, 'Reflecting Christ in the Banking Industry: The Manager as Prophet, Priest, and King', in R.J. Banks (ed.), *Faith Goes to Work* (Washington: Alban, 1993), 83ff (80–92). A Christian approach to environmental stewardship has been developed along similar lines: D.T. Williams, 'The Christian and the Environment: Prophet, Priest and King', *Evangelical Quarterly* 66.6 (April 1994), 158 (143–58).

[81] Luther, 'The Freedom of a Christian, 1520', 355.

For further study / discussion

1. Look at 1 Peter 2:4–10 again in the light of this chapter.

2. Analyse one non-ecclesiastical enterprise (a business, voluntary organization, or a school) in terms of the need for a practical expression of the threefold office.

3. Discuss and consider how important it is for there to be plural leadership in the church, as evidenced in most of the statements about leadership in the New Testament.

4. Discuss P.T. Forsyth's words: 'The one great preacher in history, I would contend, is the church. And the first business of the individual preacher is to enable the church to preach.'

Chapter 8

Mission – A People Sent by God

Christians can combat the oppressive structures of the powers of sin and death, which in our world cry out for God's world of justice and peace, as well as the false apocalypses of power politics, which assert themselves on both the left and the right, only by accounting for the hope that is in them (1 Pet. 3:15) and by being agitators for God's coming reign; they must erect, in the here and now and in the teeth of those structures, signs of God's new world.

David Bosch[1]

Momentous changes have taken place in the church's grasp of mission in this century, changes normally described by the term invented by Thomas Kuhn, 'paradigm shift'.[2] The West has lost its dominant position in the world; soon there will be more missionaries 'sent' from formerly 'receiving countries' than from the West. The centre of the Christian world has moved once again: from North America now to multiple focuses in Asia, Africa and South America. Post-Christian North America and Europe need to be re-evangelized and can rightly be called 'mission fields'. Mission is now conceived as something more than crossing salt water; it involves addressing oppressive structures at home and abroad. Since we are now capable of destroying the earth and wiping out humankind, mission must deal with creational stewardship. New theologies are emerging from the so-called developing world, theologies that challenge the neat Western systematic packages that

---

[1] David J. Bosch, *Transforming Mission: Paradigm Shifts in Theology of Mission*, 176.

[2] Ibid., 183.

owe much to the Enlightenment.[3] Fundamental questions are being asked.[4] Is the Christian faith unique? In a pluralistic global village do we have the right to assert the uniqueness and superiority of the Christian faith? Is it possible to bring the gospel to people without importing the cultural cocoon in which the gospel is couched?

1. The Sending God

Until the sixteenth century 'mission' was used in a way distinctly different from the common understanding in churches today: mission as human outreach. 'Mission' was the sending of Jesus by the Father and the sending of the Holy Spirit by the Father and the Son (Jn. 17:18), an explicitly trinitarian perspective.[5] So the term started as a theological term rather than an ecclesiastical one. It was the Jesuits who were the first to use the term ecclesiastically to describe the spreading of the Christian faith among people who were not members of the Roman Church (including the separated brethren: Protestants). In time, 'mission' came to be used, at least until the 1950s, as the sending of people across frontiers to propagate the faith, convert the heathen, plant churches and to do work of social uplift.[6] William Carey argued persuasively that it was unthinkable to refrain from taking the gospel to the ends of the earth since the invention of the mariner's compass made sea travel safe and predictable.[7] Thus mission came to be conceived of as the sending by the church.

In reality this represents a tragic decline in thinking about mission. The 'intrinsic interrelationship between christology, soteriology, and the doctrine of the Trinity, so important for the

---

[3] For an excellent summary of the influence of Enlightenment thinking on understanding mission and church life see Guder, *The Missional Church*, 21–76.

[4] See Bosch, *Transforming Mission*, 188–9.

[5] Ibid., 1.

[6] Ibid.

[7] *An Inquiry into the Obligation of Christians to Use Means for the Conversion of the Heathens.*

early church, was gradually displaced by one of several versions of the doctrine of grace'.[8] This Karl Barth, and soon others, would challenge.[9] So, as David Bosch notes, in the last century a subtle but important shift has taken place in missiology. Mission is much more than the this-worldly side of the church's life. Mission is what God is doing in the world through the church, and even without the church, to bring his creation to its consummation: unity and fullness Jesus Christ (Eph. 1:22–3; Col. 1:15–20).[10]

2. The Mission of God

Starting with the Brandenburg Missionary Conference in 1932, Karl Barth began to expound the truth that mission is the activity of God himself.[11] Then at the fifth International Missionary Council in Willingen, Germany (1952), the following statement was made:

> The mission is not only obedience to a word of the Lord, it is not only a commitment to the gathering of the congregation; it is participation in the sending of the Son, in the *missio Dei*, with the inclusive aim of establishing the lordship of Christ over the whole redeemed creation. The missionary movement of which we are a part has its source in the Triune God Himself.[12]

---

[8] Bosch, *Transforming Mission*, 389.

[9] K. Barth developed his entire ecclesiology in terms of mission: soteriology: the Holy Spirit and the gathering of the Christian community; sanctification: the Holy Spirit and the upbuilding of the Christian Community; and vocation, the Holy Spirit and the sending of the Christian community (Bosch, *Transforming Mission*, 373). Johannes Aagaard calls him 'the most decisive Protestant missiologist in this generation' (quoted ibid., 373).

[10] See D. Senior and C. Stuhlmueller, *The Biblical Foundations for Mission* (London: SCM Press, 1983).

[11] Bosch, *Transforming Mission*, 389.

[12] N. Goodall, *Missions Under the Cross* (London: Edinburgh House Press, 1953), 189, quoted in G.F. Vicedom, *The Mission of God: An Introduction to a Theology of Mission*, trans. G.A. Thiele and Dennis Hilgendorf.

Mission is thereby seen as a movement from God to the world in respect to creation, care, redemption and consummation. It is all that he is doing in his 'sentness' in the world. Not only does the Father send the Son, and the Father and Son send the Spirit, but the Father, Son and Spirit send the church into the world. Mission is the sending of God from first to last.

Mission within the triune God

The person who developed this truth most completely was George F. Vicedom. *Missio Dei* must be understood then as 'an attributive genitive'. God becomes not only the Sender but simultaneously the One who is sent. 'Thus,' notes Vicedom, 'Catholic dogmatics since Augustine speaks of sendings or the *missio* within the Triune God . . . Every sending of one Person results in the presence of the Other.'[13] So God is not only the One sent but is the content of the sending 'for in every Person of the deity God works in His entirety'.[14]

Mission is God's own going forth – truly an *ekstasis* of God. He is Sender, Sent and Sending (Jn. 17:18; cf. 16:5–16; 20:21–2).[15] And, in John 15:26, Jesus promises to send the Advocate, the Spirit of truth which was, nevertheless, the Spirit that baptized Jesus and led him into the wilderness. As Guder says, 'this mutuality in sending or "interprocession," if we may call it that, marks the divine communion as a communion of mission, and this in turn leaves its mark on the church'.[16] Howard Snyder says, 'Mission begins as the "overflow" of God's love in creating, sustaining and renewing the universe. Thus the power of the mutual love shared among Father, Son and Holy Spirit is the source of Jesus' own mission.'[17]

---

[13] Vicedom, *The Mission of God*, 7. Vicedom notes the reluctance of Evangelical theology to treat these sendings as an independent doctrine since it fears the essential unity of God would become unthinkable, though some of the intertrinitarian sending is preserved in hymns.

[14] Ibid., 8.

[15] C. Gunton, *The Promise of Trinitarian Theology* (Edinburgh: T. & T. Clark, 1991). See also L. Newbigin, *Trinitarian Faith and Today's Mission* (Richmond: John Knox Press, 1964).

[16] Guder, *The Missional Church*, 82–3.

[17] H.A. Snyder, 'Mission', in Banks and Stevens, *The Complete Book*, 646.

Incarnation: Sending by the Father and of the Father

God's specific sending involves, first of all, Adam and Eve as regents to fill the earth and bless it, then the election of Israel as a nation that belongs exclusively to himself. God's purpose is to bless all the nations, as promised to Abraham (Gen. 12:1ff.). Then God sends his Servant (Acts 3:13), the 'sent-one', the Apostle Jesus Christ (Heb. 3:1). In Jesus God is both the Sender and the One sent, both the revealer and the revelation. As revelation Jesus declares who God is, how he works, what his purposes are, how he wants to draw humankind into fellowship with Him, and what is his saving will for the world. Jesus not only declares the kingdom of God but also embodies that kingdom. Through his crucifixion, resurrection and exaltation Jesus is lord over all the powers and head of the church.

The last days: Sending by the Spirit and of the Spirit

Then God continued his sending through the gift of the Holy Spirit 'out of the onetime sending of His Son', so, through the Spirit making a continuing mission.[18] As Vicedom says, 'There would be no church, no congregation of God among the nations, and consequently no mission, if God did not Himself thus work among all nations through the gift of the Holy Ghost.'[19] The Spirit is sent (Jn. 14:26; 15:26; 16:7), proceeding from the Father and the Son in such a way that the triune God is present in the Spirit. The Holy Spirit is the true impulse for missions in this day of the eschatological Spirit.

The apostles: Sending by the Son and of the Son

God's continuous sending includes the selection and empowerment by Jesus of those who are sent out by him to expand his messianic work (Lk. 9:2; 10:7–9). This too is part of the *missio Dei*. With the final commissioning of the apostles after his resurrection,[20] forgiven, restored and freshly commissioned they were uniquely appointed witnesses to Christ. Their personal call and authorization by Christ

---

[18] Vicedom, *The Mission of God*, 54–5.
[19] Ibid., 55.
[20] Mt. 28:19; Mk.16:15; Lk. 24:46ff.; Jn. 20:21.

(a phenomenon that made Paul's Damascus road conversion/call unique[21]) was what made them apostles. Vicedom sums up the matter: 'The apostles have the duty and assignment to establish the church and thereby they become the foundation of the building upon which all other work was to be based (1 Cor. 3:9ff.) . . . This gives their work and proclamation the character of revelation. Such a claim cannot be made by the bishops.'[22] Elders and bishops are watchmen, not the foundation of the house.[23]

The continuing apostolate: Sending of the church by the triune God

The church is apostolic in a double sense.[24] First, it is built on the witness and faith of the apostles now contained in Scripture.[25]

---

[21] As noted earlier, Paul's conversion is shared with all who come to faith in Christ; his call to apostleship is not used by him in word or example as a model for the call to professional ministry. See Falk, 'A New Testament Theology of Calling', 129ff.

[22] Vicedom, *The Mission of God*, 64.

[23] O. Cullmann, *Peter: Disciple-Apostle-Martyr: A Historical and Theological Study* (Philadelphia: Westminster Press, 1953), quoted in Vicedom, *The Mission of God*, 64.

[24] For this reason Vicedom concludes that while it is not clear that Christ gave a distinctive missionary office to certain members of the church, he has given the church an office that should lead to missionary service – the ministry of the divine Word. 'Accordingly the pastoral office in the congregation in all its ramifications can have no other purpose than to lead the congregation to influence the world and to make her fit for missionary service' (*The Mission of God*, 90).

[25] This raises the question of whether there are apostles today, and whether such sent-out ones really constitute a missionary office. The listing of apostles in Eph. 4:11 along with prophets, evangelists and pastor-teachers, suggests that this rich diversity of word ministry still serves to equip the saints (as a whole) for the work of ministry, as does the reference to apostles in 1 Cor. 12:28 in the context of Spirit-working in the church today. As Vicedom notes, the New Testament authors themselves were quite cautious about calling anyone an 'apostle' and so should we be. Perhaps the term 'evangelist' is closer to something that could be called a missionary office, this term referring not so much to mass evangelists as to those specially gifted in bringing the gospel to new regions. This

Second it is the result of and the means of God's further sending into the world. Tragically when Christianity became Christendom, as Guder notes, 'apostolicity no longer described the action of the people of God in missional engagement. Instead it meant the succession in priestly authority'.[26]

Usually the view that the church is the instrument for God's mission has led to the practice of the church 'sending' missionaries. But there is more. There is church because there is mission, not vice versa. The church is not the sending agency; it is the sent agency. To participate in mission is to participate in the movement of God's love towards people, since God is a fountain of sending love.[27]

The church is born of mission, not the other way around.[28] The Bible came about through the mission of God in the world. Note how Paul hammered out justification by faith in the context of the Gentile mission. Mission is the mother of theology,[29] though there is little evidence of this today.

To sum up, theologically mission is not a human activity undertaken out of obligation to the great commission, or even simple gratitude. It is God's own mission in which we have been included. It is what God is doing to bless all the nations through the resurrection of Christ and the outpouring of the Spirit. Mission work itself is

---

[25] *(continued)* question of apostleship today must be entirely subordinated to the fact that the continuing *missio Dei* is not vested in the apostles but in the whole people of God, which people is apostolic.

[26] Guder, *The Missional Church*, 192.

[27] Bosch, *Transforming Mission*, 390.

[28] Bosch, quoting John Power, SMA, *Mission Theology Today* (Dublin: Gill & Macmillan, 1970, 41–2), says that mission is not a 'fringe activity of a strongly established Church, a pious cause that [may] be attended to when the home fires [are] first brightly burning . . . Missionary activity is not so much the work of the church as simply the Church at work' (*Transforming Mission*, 372).

[29] Martin Kähler suggests that 'theology was not a luxury of the world-conquering church but generated by the emergency situation in which the missionizing church found itself . . . However, as Europe became christianized and Christianity became the established religion in the Roman Empire and beyond, theology lost its missionary dimension' (Bosch, *Transforming Mission*, 489; see M. Kähler, *Schriften zur Christologie und Mission* (Munich: Chr. Kaiser Verlag, 1971), 189–90.

not motivated by the need of the world but by the sending God who calls and empowers. It is for this mission and in this mission that the whole people of God gains an apostolic (sent-out) status. Together the *laos* of God is the creation of God's sending and the means of his further sending.

3. The Sending

When we look to the Bible for a theology of mission we find not one theology but several, each contributing to a rich interdependent whole, each contributing to a wholistic transformative 'sentness' into the world.

God's mission in the Old Testament

The first eleven chapters of Genesis describe God's creation and covenant-making with humankind and the whole creation. People were mandated to fill the earth by scattering and by welcoming a rich diversity. Instead they built a monolithic city (Babel) with a homogeneous society – something God judged.[30] Then came the promise to Abraham, a promise of a presence, a people and the blessing of the nations (Gen. 12:3), really the patriarchal equivalent of the three dimensions of the human vocation we discovered in Genesis 1–2.

It is notable that the threefold human vocation elaborated in Chapter 4 is recapitulated in the 'call' implicit in the promise to Abraham, Isaac and Jacob. Essentially the patriarchs were called to *belong to God in communion*. To Jacob especially the promise 'I am with you' was repeatedly given (Gen. 28:15). They were called to *be God's people in community building*. The promise to Abraham was 'I will make you into a great nation . . . all peoples on earth will be blessed through you' (Gen. 12:2–3). And they were called to *do God's work through co-creativity and stewardship in the Land*. 'The

---

[30] In a sense Gen.11 is both judgement and fulfilment: judgement on the arrogant autonomous people of Babel, fulfilment of the promise and call to disperse and 'fill the earth'.

whole land of Canaan . . . I will give you as an everlasting possession' (17:8).[31]

The calling of the patriarchs was a focused call to the family of promise to recover the human vocation originally vested in Adam and Eve. The Christian vocation, as we have seen, fulfils this.

FULFILLING THE HUMAN VOCATION

THE HUMAN VOCATION	THE PROMISE	THE CHRISTIAN VOCATION
Communion	The presence of God	Belonging to God
Community-building	The people	Being God's people
Co-creativity	The land	Doing God's work

The main theme of the Pentateuch is really the advancement of this promise, a missionary promise, though balanced with God's special concern for Israel. Chris Wright in *God's People in God's Land: Family, Land, and Property in the Old Testament* shows how the vision of God for his people under the older covenant was both typological[32]

---

[31] The land is especially significant as the creation mandate can be understood as the command to expand Eden to encompass the whole earth. W. Dumbrell notes this with wonderful clarity, 'The Garden of Eden is best seen as a special sanctuary, quite unlike the rest of the world. In the Old Testament Canaan, which is significantly identified as a divine sanctuary in Exodus 15:17 and Psalm 78:54, and Eden are paralleled (Isa 51:3; Ezek 36:35), quite apart from the significance of the presence of God in the restricted space of Genesis 2–3. Moreover, Eden (itself necessarily evaluated as the source of the world river system) was clearly conceived of as a mountain sanctuary (Ezek 28:13–14), which is important since mountains in the ancient world were deemed basic points of contact between heaven and earth. Eden was the garden of God, the earth center where God was to be found (Isa 51:3)' (*The Search for Order*, 25).

[32] 'The New Testament concept and practice of fellowship, the local church community as a household or family, the principles of financial sharing and mutual support all have deep roots in the social and economic life of Old Testament Israel' (C.J.H. Wright, *God's People in God's Land: Family, Land, and Property in the Old Testament* [Grand Rapids: Eerdmans, 1990], xviii).

and paradigmatic.[33] The prophets,[34] especially Second Isaiah, and the Psalms pick up the mission thrust again that Israel was to be a light to the nations (Is. 42:6). The continual theme in Daniel is that God's purpose in choosing Israel is taken up in his dominion over all nations and his ultimate plan to accomplish the passing of these kingdoms into his own kingdom of love and righteousness (6:26).[35]

God's mission in the New Testament

Under the New Covenant Jesus comes as the missionary, the sent-out one by God who is also God. David Bosch does a masterful study of the great commission in Matthew 28:18–20 and shows us the contextual meaning for the disciple community: discipleship to Jesus involves witness.[36] Dr Luke, in Luke–Acts, pleads for solidarity with the poor and oppressed, offering a gospel that is both personal and social.[37] Some have called the words of Jesus in Luke 4:18–19

---

[33] 'The purpose of redemption is ultimately to restore the perfection of God's purpose in creation . . . Israel's socio-economic life and institutions, therefore, have a paradigmatic or exemplary function in principle. It is not simply that they are to be simply and slavishly imitated, but rather that they are models within a particular cultural context of principles of justice, humaneness, equality, responsibility, and so forth which are applicable, *mutatis mutandis*, to all people in subsequent cultural contexts' (ibid., xviii).

Wright summarizes his study of the Old Testament in this way: (1) the primary relationship is God and Israel; (2) Yahweh is the ultimate owner of the land; (3) the land is given to Israel as an inheritance; (4) the family is not only the basic social unit of Israelite society and kinship structure but also the basic unit of Israel's system of land tenure and the primary beneficiary of the inalienability principle; (5) these family-plus-land units were seen to be the basic fabric upon which Israel's relationship with God rests (ibid., 104).

[34] It is questionable whether Jonah is really a missionary tract, attempting to convince people to follow Jonah's example of reaching out to the pagan neighbours, since Jonah himself has no good news to bear. Rather this disturbing document is addressing exclusivity.

[35] See Marshall, *Thine Is the Kingdom*, 31.

[36] Bosch, *Transforming Mission*, 56–83.

[37] Ibid., 84–122.

the 'greater commission'. But perhaps John's gospel contains what might be called 'the *greatest* commission', 'as the Father has sent me I am sending you' (Jn 20:21; 17:18), proposing a fully incarnational mission of the disciples in the world.[38]

Paul's missionary vision was to see the church as the eschatological community of the Spirit. Frontiers are crossed by the outpouring of the Spirit enabling Jews and Gentiles *together* to share in the new humanity of God (Eph. 2:15). So Paul's missionary passion was not only to plant self-supporting, self-governing churches in every major centre of the Roman Empire but also to nurture the rich trinitarian unity of Jew and Gentile in Christ, expressly by raising the love gift from the Gentile Christians for the poor Jewish Christians in Judea.[39]

The final vision of the New Testament in the Revelation brings to fulfilment the mission mandate of the first two chapters of Genesis, the missionary promise to Abraham, as well as the prophetic vision of Ezekiel 40–48: a presence (the Lord dwelling with his people), a people (with all the tribes and people groups in rich perichoretic unity around the Lamb), and a place (the new heaven and the new earth). Mission must be bifocal, seeing 'up close' substantial salvation come to this life and world, while viewing 'in the distance' the ultimate goal of salvation *which is more than going to heaven*. It is nothing less than a consummated relationship with our God, a consummated people, and a consummated creation (new heaven and a new earth).[40] In a word, God's mission is wholistic.

---

[38] See L. Newbigin, 'Cross-currents in Ecumenical and Evangelical Understandings of Mission', *International Bulletin of Missionary Research* 6, (October 1982), 146–51.

[39] See Rom. 15:27–9. An important article on this subject is R.K. Orchard, 'The Significance of Ecumenical Travel', *Journal of Ecumenical Studies* 15 (summer 1978), 477–502. Also see K.F. Nickle, *The Collection: A Study in Paul's Strategy* (London: SCM Press, 1966).

[40] David Bosch notes how a single text seems to exemplify the concept of mission in each period of church history: Jn. 3:16 in the patristic period; Lk. 14:23 in the medieval Catholic missionary period; Rom. 1:16–17 in the Protestant Reformation; in the Enlightenment period three texts, Lk. 16:9 (among those who view the people of other races as living in darkness), Mt. 24:14 for premillenialists, and Jn. 10:10 for those embracing the social gospel. Bosch notes that while the Great Commission was used by

The full scope of God's mission

First, God's mission includes the individual person calling for the conversion of heart and mind on the basis of the good news announced and embodied in Jesus Christ (Mt. 4:17). Second, God's mission is directed to the whole of society, to structures of common life, bringing righteousness, justice, the empowerment of the poor and the liberation of the oppressed (Lk. 4:18–19). There is no place in the cosmos so demonized that a Christian might not be called to serve God there. Speaking to the endless debate about the relative priorities of evangelism and social justice, René Padilla says:

> Every human need . . . may be used by the Spirit of God as a beach-head for the manifestation of his kingly power. That is why in actual practice the question of which comes first, evangelism or social action, is irrelevant. In every concrete situation the needs themselves provide the guidelines for the definition of priorities. As long as both evangelism and social responsibility are regarded as essential to mission, we need no rule of thumb to tell us which comes first and when.[41]

Third, God's mission is directed to thought-forms and cultures that shape the way people think and act. Fourth, God's mission is concerned with the whole of creation, to conservation, sustainable development and the renewal of the earth (Jer. 22:29; Ezek. 36:1,8,9).[42] Yves Congar says, 'Ontologically, this is the world that, transformed and renewed, will pass into the Kingdom; so . . . the dualist position is wrong: final salvation will be achieved by a wonderful refloating of our earthly vessel rather than the transfer of the survivors to another ship wholly built by God.'[43] Finally, God's

---

[40] *(continued)* Orthodox Protestants, the person who placed this text in the centre of mission thinking was William Carey in his tract *An Enquiry into the Obligations of Christians to Use Means for the Conversion of the Heathen* (Bosch, *Transforming Mission*, 339–40).

[41] C. René Padilla, 'The Mission of the Church in the Light of the Kingdom of God', *Transformation* 1.2 (April–June 1984), 19 (16–20).

[42] See Snyder, 'Mission', in Banks and Stevens, *The Complete Book*, 647.

[43] Congar, *Lay People*, 92.

mission is directed to the powers, the full range of structures and fallen spiritual beings that hinder the advancement of the kingdom of God on earth.[44] It is personal and social, human and creational, temporal and eternal. It is concerned both with rehabilitation and with prevention.[45]

As we have seen above, God's people are spokespersons for the kingdom (prophets), servants of the kingdom (kings) and communal embodiments of the presence of the kingdom (priests). Put differently, the ministry in and on behalf of the kingdom of God involves *kērygma*, *diakonia*, and *koinōnia*. Words by themselves are not enough. As René Padilla says:

> Good works are not . . . an optional addendum to mission; rather, they are an integral part of the present manifestation of the Kingdom – they point back to the Kingdom which has already come and forward to the Kingdom which is yet to come. This does not mean, of course, that good works – the signs of the kingdom – will necessarily persuade the unbelievers concerning the truth of the gospel . . . Neither seeing nor hearing does always result in faith. Both word and deed point to the Kingdom of God, but 'no one can say, "Jesus is Lord" except by the Holy Spirit' (1 Cor. 12:3).[46]

My colleague Charles Ringma[47] expresses this graphically:

---

[44] See René Padilla, et al., 'The Church in Response to Human Need', *Missionalia* 11 (November 1983), 126–34.

[45] D. Bosch outlines the many dimensions of mission using the following concepts: mission as mediating salvation; mission as the quest for justice; mission as evangelism; mission as contextualization; mission as liberation; mission as enculturation; mission as common witness; mission as witness to people of other faiths; mission as theology; mission as action in hope (*Transforming Mission*, 393–510).

[46] Padilla, 'The Mission of the Church', 18.

[47] Lecture in 'Theology of the Laity', Regent College, Vancouver, 1997. Drawing used with permission.

GOD'S MISSION AND OUR MISSION

So mission is joining God in his caring, sustaining and transforming activity on earth. Mission is good news to the world. It is good news because it brings people into relation with Jesus. But it is also good news because it promises to bring *shalôm* into the world. The ultimate goal of mission is the sabbath *shalôm* of God: the threefold harmony of God, creation and humankind, which will finally obtain when Christ comes again and the kingdom is consummated.

4. The Sent People

David Bosch traces the complicated development of the *missio Dei* since the time when Barth first proposed it and developed it in the Willingen conference in 1952.[48] It underwent an important

---

[48] Bosch, *Transforming Mission*, 390.

transition in the years following, one which Barth had not antici-pated. If mission derives from the sending of God into the world, and God's own mission is larger than the mission of the church then the church could be considered unnecessary to that mission.

The mission of God and the mission of the church

Traditionally, the relationship of God to mission was conceived in a linear way: God, the sender, the church as the sent, the world as the recipient of the church's mission:

GOD——to——THE CHURCH——to——THE WORLD

Writing in the early 1960s a Dutch missiologist turned this around. J.C. Hoekendijk proposed that God works first with the world not the church:

GOD——to——THE WORLD——to——THE CHURCH

The church's mission then is to find out what God is doing in the world, celebrate it and embrace his mission.[49] The church has the character of an 'intermezzo' between God and the world,[50] and is an illustration (in word and deed) of God's involvement in the world.[51]

With considerable care Bosch examines whether these two images of the church (the one as sole bearer of God's mission, the other as an illustration of it) need be mutually exclusive.[52] Might not a triangle be a better way of describing the rich way God relates to both the church and the world?

---

[49] J.C. Hoekendijk, *Kirche und Volk in der deutschen Missionswissenschaft* (Munich: Chr. Kaiser Verlag, 1967), quoted in Bosch, *Transforming Mission*, 384.

[50] Bosch, *Transforming Mission*, 384.

[51] Ibid., 381.

[52] Ibid., 381–9.

RELATIONSHIP OF GOD, CHURCH AND WORLD

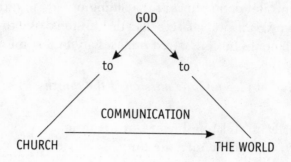

Significantly this takes us back to the covenantal triangle from the Old Testament (so well developed by Chris Wright):

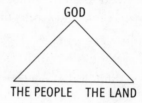

The sent church and the Kingdom of God

The key to resolving this tension of whether God works primarily through the church or the world is to grasp the relation of the Kingdom of God to the mission of the church. The church's mission is not to 'bring in' the church, or even to extend it. The Church's mission is to 'bring in' the Kingdom. In this way the people of God participates in, embodies and serves what God is accomplishing by creation, salvation, sanctification and consummation. But the church does not circumscribe God's work. The church is God's primary agency in fulfilling his sending.[53] But it also recognizes and welcomes the irruption of the Kingdom of God everywhere. The

---

[53] 'The exalted Lord transfers the sending to the church and makes her His messenger to the nations of the world. Within the framework of the divine *missio* she is the instrument of God's mercy. He transfers the apostolic function to her' (Vicedom, *The Mission of God*, 66).

church then serves as a lighthouse, an outcropping of the Kingdom, a visible manifestation of God's Kingdom on earth. The Orthodox theologian Alexander Schmemann says the church is the 'sacrament – the gift, the beginning, the presence, the promise, the reality, the anticipation of the Kingdom'.[54]

Trinitarian mission

The trinitarian approach is essential to a full understanding of the breadth of kingdom service. Mission must take many forms but in a rich interdependent whole. One conspicuous example is the duality of base communities (in South America) and the institutional Catholic Church, two faces of the church that Bosch explores under the paradigm of the divinity and humanity of Christ. Would not a trinitarian approach help us see the multiform but interdependent nature of the many faces of the church-in-mission? Denominational communities and parachurch 'missions' are not two opposing approaches to mission. They are the church in one of its trinitarian expressions! Trinitarian unity is unity *through* diversity. It was this vision that motivated the apostle Paul to tramp through the Roman world planting churches among the Gentiles *and* to raise money for the poor Jewish saints in Jerusalem. He was an ecumenical missionary.

All too often cross-cultural work is a one-way street, serving, saving and giving. We go (wrongly) into the world exclusively as patrons. There is little of Paul's vision of 'equality' (2 Cor. 8:14) between the Developing World and the First World, no grasp of the truth that the 'sending' church is also a receiving church, that the rich cannot be saved without the poor, or Gentiles without Jews. There is little sense that the missionary will be missionized, little of Paul's 1 Corinthians 12 celebration of diversity! Instead we 'grow' churches in fast-track ways so that they are composed of one ethnic and one economic group, and pride ourselves on quantitative growth that by biblical standards is not growth at all (Eph. 4:1–16)! It is a 'you-all' club – all speaking the same dialect. No Christ is confessed since such people would gather anyway, due to similarity of identity. The blessing of Christ (Rom. 15:29) is diluted. It is only 'together with all the saints' (Eph. 3:18) that we

---

[54] Schmemann, *For the Life of the World*, 113.

can know how 'wide and long and high and deep is the love of Christ, and to know this love that surpasses knowledge . . . [and be] filled to the measure of the fullness of God' (Eph. 3:18–19). But just how do the people of God share in the apostolate of God?

The apostolate of the people[55]

Mission, as we have seen, is not an occasional activity of the people of God of special interest for 'mission groups'. The church does not *have* a mission; it *is* mission. Under both covenants mission is the intended occupation and preoccupation of the whole people of God, not merely a few chosen representative or designated mission-aries. Put simply, the ordinary Christian is a missionary. And that mission is undertaken in societal occupations, in individual and per-sonal life (home and family), and through one's corporate life in the church.[56] As we have seen the church needs to be apostolic in a dou-ble sense. Its gospel and doctrine are founded on the testimony of the first apostles, the eyewitnesses of the risen Christ, and it exists in the carrying out of the apostolic proclamation, the missionary charge.

The problem is that it is largely on the theoretical level that the whole church is viewed as the primary expression of the mission of God. The church is still, by and large, configured in terms of clergy (missionary specialist) and laity (supporter of missions). Even recent documents from the Roman Church supporting the Lay Apostolate and Catholic Action, promising as these documents were, envi-sioned ordinary Christians being the arms and legs of the clergy into society. Pius XI, for example, deploring the lack of clergy says, 'it is for these reasons that the Church today appeals to lay people [and] asks them to unite and to help the hierarchy, by making themselves

---

[55] K. Barth expressed the matter in these words: 'On the one hand, "Apostolic" means that it exists by the ongoing work and word of the apostles, and, on the other hand, that it exists by itself in doing what the apostles did and are still doing, in virtue of the nature of their own works and words' II.2.431.

[56] With considerable wisdom Karl Barth begins his treatment of mission with the individual Christian and his or her calling/vocation and then proceeds to the church.

the right arm of the clergy; and the hierarchy, in its turn, forms them in long unbroken lines'.[57]

A more recent volume by James and Evelyn Whitehead takes some of the conclusions of Vatican II and explores what is involved in laypersons becoming co-heirs of Christ and equal partners in the church's ministry in the world. But their concern is with the dynamics of shared leadership in the church – the empowerment of lay leadership.[58] Other books explore the mission of ordinary Christians in the workplace[59] and in politics.[60] But there is little to help equip the church for mission except in the traditional sense of evangelistic events, procedures and cross-cultural ministries.

5. Equipping for Mission

The starting point in equipping the church for mission is the liberating truth that God is the ultimate equipper: giving vision and gifts, empowering through the Spirit's presence, motivating and guiding.

Mission motivation

The question of mission motivation is linked inextricably with the concept of mission. Bosch shows how after the Second World War the Great Commission had superseded all other texts as the definitive 'mission text'. The Dutch theologian Abraham Kuyper, responding to the attack of liberal theologians, stressed that all mission is essentially *obedience to God's command*.[61] While there can be no doubt that this widespread emphasis on obedience mobilized a mighty mission force, it had the disastrous effect of removing 'the

---

[57] *The Lay Apostolate: Papal Teachings*, trans. by a secular priest (Boston: St Paul Editions, 1960), 319. See also 'Notes on the Lay Apostolate', in K. Rahner, *Theological Investigations: Man in the Church*, trans. Karl-H. Kruger (22 vols.; New York: Crossroad, 1961–91), II, 319–52.

[58] J.D. Whitehead and E.E. Whitehead, *The Emerging Laity: Returning Leadership to the Community of Faith.*

[59] See Novak, *Business as a Calling.*

[60] Marshall, *Thine Is the Kingdom.*

[61] Bosch, *Transforming Mission*, 341.

church's involvement in mission from the domain of *gospel* to that of *law*.[62]

Paul's mission is a case in point. Paul was not motivated by the need of the Gentile world; he was motivated by a 'vision from heaven' (Acts 26:19). Significantly he was converted shortly after he held the coats of the people who stoned Stephen. That first martyr was probably the first missionary as he 'saw' Jesus as 'the Son of Man standing at the right hand of God' (Acts 7:56). Outside the gospels Stephen was the first to speak of Jesus as the Son of Man, that divine ruler of all peoples (Dan. 7:13–14) who was more than Jewish Messiah. Jesus as the Son of Man is already 'going' to all, determined to bless all the nations. Our mission work is not to get people to 'come to church' but to go with the Son of Man into the world. Tragically, it is sometimes noted that the church functions in a manner analogous with the Jewish nation at the time of Jesus: making proselytes.

It is common enough to speak of mission as worship and sometimes the glory of God is the prime motive of mission. Therefore, so it is argued, mission is an act of worship, a way of honouring and giving worth to God. But there is more to it than that. Mission is worship precisely because it is God's own outworking, outliving, outloving. Mission is worship because God is 'beside himself '. So Paul does not glory in himself or even his service; he glories in Jesus Christ (Rom. 15:17). He will speak of what Christ has accomplished (15:18). Evidence of God's work is not the apostle's own deeds but the signs and miracles through the power of the Spirit (15:19). It is God's work from first to last. So God is the ultimate mission equipper moving the hearts of Christians and the church as a whole. Our role in church leadership is to discern what God is doing and to be co-equippers.

Equipping principles[63]

First, the reality of the sovereign divine placement of ordinary Christians in workplaces, neighbourhoods and spheres of influence must

---

[62] Ibid.

[63] Conceptually Alan Roxburgh uses the sociological concepts of bounded sets and centred sets to establish a model for a missional church. A covenant community (bounded set determined by shared disciplines) is at the centre of the church's response to the kingdom, while the congregation (a centred set determined by shared values) is a larger community of

be recognized and supported in the communal life of the church. Hendrik Kraemer puts it this way: 'If the laity of the Church, dispersed in and through the world, are really what they are called to be, the real uninterrupted dialogue between Church and world happens through them. They form the daily repeated projection of the Church into the world. They embody the meeting of the Church and World.'[64]

So a fundamental strategy is simply not to disconnect people. The church, like the gathering and dispersion of blood in the body, is a rhythm of gathering (*ekklēsia*) and dispersion (*diaspora*). The only true picture of the church is a motion picture, perhaps an angiogram. The church gathered must not be separated from the church dispersed any more than the heart and lungs can be separated from the body. Gathered, the blood is cleansed and oxygenated. Sent out, it fights diseases and energizes. To do this the church must discern the body in dispersion, in other words, find out where in the world the people are. One church practices this systematically in commending various people to their weekday service. When Sunday school teachers are to be commissioned, the pastor also invites those teaching in the school system to rise and receive the commissioning prayers of the congregation.

In a fine volume on *The Missional Church*, Darrell Guder concludes that 'neither the structures nor the theology of our established Western traditional church is missional. They are shaped by the legacy of Christendom.'[65] More boldly still the Dutch theologian J.C. Hoekendijk proposes that if a church's structures thwart the possibility of its members serving relevantly in the world, we are to regard these structures as *heretical.*[66]

Second, 'go' structures must be developed alongside the 'come' structures. Most of our church structures are 'come' structures –

---

[63] *(continued)* people journeying toward a shared commitment. He argues that the missional church needs to be both bounded and centred. See Guder, *The Missional Church*, 204–13.

[64] Kraemer, *A Theology of the Laity*, 170.

[65] Guder, *The Missional Church*, 5. The main thrust of this fine multi-authored volume is to move from church with mission to missional church.

[66] Quoted in Bosch, *Transforming Mission*, 378.

they communicate by their existence and style 'come and hear', 'come and see'.[67] They invite people to join the believers, a legitimate expression of the church's mission (see Jn. 1:39; 10:40–42). As Michael Green has shown, house groups and home meetings are undoubtedly the basic 'come' structure to supplement the ubiquitous Sunday service.[68] What is needed is an equal interest in 'go' structures, ordered ways for believers to reach a particular part of society.[69] The most useful such structure is the mission house group. Gordon Cosby has developed this concept helpfully in his *Handbook for Mission Groups*.[70]

Third, we need to ordain/commission people with a proven mission in society with as much seriousness as we ordain people to the pastoral ministry of the church: politicians, stockbrokers, homemakers, schoolteachers, craftspersons, artists and musicians. As Alan Roxburgh says, 'the priesthood of all believers is continually undermined by the practices of ordination'.[71]

Fourth, Gordon Preece offers additional suggestions on how the church can equip people for mission in the workplace: by encouraging people to see the workplace, the primary place where people meet, as a natural place for evangelism (Acts 16:16–19; 17:17;

---

[67] Bosch notes how Newbigin has introduced the helpful distinction between the church's missionary *dimension* and its missionary *intention*. The church's missionary dimension is manifested in being a worshipping community that welcomes outsiders and equips them to serve in secular society. The church's missionary intention is revealed in direct involvement in society through engaging the world in evangelism and work for justice and peace (Bosch, *Transforming Mission*, 373; L. Newbigin, *One Body, One Gospel, One World* [London: International Missionary Council, 1958], 21, 43).

[68] M. Green, *Evangelism in the Early Church*.

[69] 'Kingdom people seek first the Kingdom of God and its justice; church people often put church work above concerns of justice, mercy and truth. Church people think about how to get people into the church; Kingdom people think about how to get the church into the world. Church people worry that the world might change the church; Kingdom people work to see the church change the world' (Snyder, *Liberating the Church: The Ecology of Church and Kingdom*, 11.

[70] Cosby, *Handbook for Mission Groups*, 131.

[71] Guder, *The Missional Church*, 195.

19:9–10,23–9). This can be done by using workplace terminology to share our faith; by connecting Sunday and Monday through interviewing people about their work, and praying for them; by extending pastoral care to the workplace, especially when there is injustice or unemployment; and dealing with workplace sins and temptations as part of church discipline in the same way as did the Puritan manuals. Finally, Preece advises

> creatively bridging the physical distance between churches and the workplace . . . We can use occasional fringe-work activities over meals or a few drinks to build relationships. Opening our homes in hospitality to fellow workers can lead to a new level of relationship. Where possible church buildings should be located near the commercial centre rather than be lost in suburban back streets.[72]

The goal is the whole people of God engaging in the whole mission of God in the whole world. That this will be difficult is obvious, as David Bosch says in the quotation with which we began this chapter.

It is the phenomenon of resistance (what makes the mission of the people of God so hard) that must now be considered: while engaging in the mission of God we wrestle with the principalities and powers.

---

[72] G. Preece, 'Work', in Banks and Stevens, *The Complete Book*, 1128–9.

For further study / discussion

1. Explore the possibility of being agents of the kingdom of God in a so-called secular business.

   - Does God call corporations as well as individuals?
   - What are the limits of change in a business that has both believers and not-yet-believers working in it?
   - What does kingdom consciousness mean for employee policies, pricing, promotion, products and services?

2. Consider the practical implications of moving from a church with a mission to being a missional church.

3. Discuss the Bosch quote at the beginning of the chapter.

4. Using the grid below place an x where you consider your church understands and practises the mission of God:

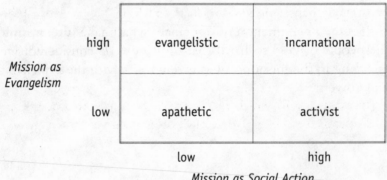

5. Discuss the 'greatest commission': 'as the father has sent me even so send I you' (Jn. 20:21).

Chapter 9

Resistance – Grappling with the Powers

We are without conviction about any worthwhile end to which
the travail of history might lead . . . The gospel is vastly more than
an offer to men who care to accept it of a meaning for their personal
lives. It is the declaration of God's cosmic purpose by which the
whole public history of mankind is sustained and overruled, and by
which men without exception will be judged . . . It is the invitation
to be fellow workers with God in the fulfilment of that purpose
through the atoning work of Christ and through the witness of the
Holy Spirit. It calls men to commitment to a worldwide mission
more daring and more far-reaching than Marxism. And it has –
what Marxism lacks – a faith regarding the final consummation of
God's purpose in the power of which it is possible to find meaning
for world history which does not make personal history meaningless, and meaning for personal history which does not make world
history meaningless.

Lesslie Newbigin[1]

Life in this world is not easy. Your child watches television in a
neighbour's home and you discover later that some of the material
was pornographic. Your church is denied the right to expand its
building because of an atheist lobby in the neighbourhood. Your
boss requires you to do graphic art for a business known to have
connections with the Mafia. The school system teaches a godless
approach to all subjects including the creation of the world. Your
purse seems to have holes in it and your money seems to purchase

[1] L. Newbigin, *Honest Religion for Secular Man* (Philadelphia: Westminster
Press, 1966), 42. Quoted with permission.

less and less because of global economic factors over which you have no power. These complexities come not simply from the perversity and sin of individual human beings but from something more systemic, more all-embracing. For every visible foreground to a person's life – family life, work life, community service, leisure life, citizenship, and church life – there is an invisible background, not seen with the human eye but profoundly influential. We want to do good, to serve God and our neighbour, to do an honest day's work that will contribute to the common weal, but we find ourselves confronted with resistance.

Ordinary Christians, like all citizens, in the world do not feel in control of the circumstances surrounding their service to God. They encounter unjust and unloving structures, principles of conformity (e.g. professionalism), cultural expectations, social patterns, law without moral foundations, customs and traditions, escalating pressures for performance, technology as master and not mere servant, intractable institutions, professionalism and careerism, images, the almighty dollar, red tape, spiritual forces, and spiritual personages. The last enemy is death. Those whose primary area of service is in the church are not free from resistance. They face principalities and powers in a disguised form: conformity, power structures, legalism, institutionalization and direct satanic attack. There is no escape from complexity in the church or the world.

1. Describing the Powers: Contemporary Confusion

The discussion of the powers has been extensive over the last century and is well documented by Peter T. O'Brien.[2] Put simply,

---

[2] P.T. O'Brien, 'Principalities and Powers: Opponents of the Church', in D.A. Carson (ed.), *Biblical Interpretation and the Church: Text and Context* (Exeter: Paternoster Press, 1984), 110–50. O'Brien's lucid article surveys the following trends: (1) Nineteenth-century theologians rejected the powers as antiquated mythology (Harnack). (2) Some recognized the value of the myths of principalities and powers as of value but only for the study of the history of religion (Dibelius). (3) Then came the existentialist approach of Bultmann, Käsemann and Schlier who treat the powers not as objective realities but self-understandings, projections of the attempt of humankind to explain the inability to control the world and

some think Paul and other New Testament authors did not know what they were talking about and that we are now in a better position to explain the difficulty we encounter in the world. The apostles accepted uncritically the apocalyptic world-view of their times, a world peopled with demons and spiritual hosts. This is one view. Others acknowledge that the New Testament authors knew what they were referring to, were fully cognizant of the complex

---

[2] *(continued)* the future – though O'Brien notes that Schlier later changes his theological position. O'Brien quotes Bultmann along these lines: 'He [Paul] is thereby only expressing a *certain understanding of existence*: The spirit powers *represent* the reality into which man is placed as one full of conflicts and struggle, a reality which threatens and tempts' (R. Bultmann, *Theology of the New Testament* [ET London 1952], I, 259; italics his). O'Brien notes, 'The objective, malevolent activity of Satan and his minions has been effectively reduced, even removed, through this demythologizing programme' (117). (4) The twofold, double-reference approach of Oscar Cullmann, Schmidt, Dehn and Karl Barth proposes that New Testament texts point simultaneously to both earthly rulers and superhuman influences. (5) Ethical and socio-political structures is a single-reference way of transferring Paul's references to contemporary realities in terms of tradition, convention, secular false gods, the idols of the marketplace, structures, law, authorities and even religion (Rupp, Wilder). Hendrikus Berkhof's influential *Christ and the Powers* takes this demythologizing approach and clearly influenced John H. Yoder and William Stringfellow, both influential figures in modern Western Christianity. (6) Structures and unseen spiritual forces – a viewpoint that adapts the 'double reference' approach by placing the emphasis on political structures – was promoted by John H. Yoder, who advises revolutionary subordination as the pattern of Christian involvement in politics, and Richard Mouw, who admits to an ontological and causal residue (of non-human powers) in Paul's language as he encourages our involvement in the political domain without fear of the powers since Christ has triumphed over them. (7) Principalities and powers: angels serving God, not hostile authorities, is an exceptional view which promotes the idea that the superhuman powers are good and positive (Wesley Carr), though this approach requires eliminating the clear sense of passages like Eph. 6:12. O'Brien carefully explores the hermeneutical assumptions that lead to these various viewpoints and concludes that we need to study the powers in the context of an integrated biblical theology in which the ultimate purposes of God for his creation are expounded.

systemic evil presumed in their world-view, but it is now impossible to explain this view to modern people except by reinterpreting principalities and powers into sociological and psychological terms: structures, political powers, cultural mores and systems at work in society.

Double reference

Still others argue for what has been called a 'double reference' approach, namely that when Paul refers to governing authorities in Romans 13:1 he is referring *both* to political leaders and the spiritual beings who wish to exploit earthly structures to frustrate or facilitate God's purpose on earth.[3] This, however, appears to force the text to say more than was intended. As Peter O'Brien says, 'The fact that nowhere in the New Testament is the relationship between civil rulers and spiritual powers explicitly affirmed . . . constitutes reason for doubting its presence.'[4]

An important point in this discussion is that the rejection of the primary spiritual, supernatural and non-human reference to the powers comes principally from Western theologians who are still reeling under the influence of the Enlightenment. John Stott expresses this crisply: 'We lose the demons and gain the structures, for the principalities and powers are structures in disguise.'[5] Third World theologians have relatively little difficulty grasping the New Testament world-view and conclude (as I do later) that the New Testament refers to both (though not necessarily in the same text) structures and non-human spiritual beings, both good and bad. This brief summary of the modern history of theological thought on the powers suggests that a study of the Bible itself

---

[3] This view has been chiefly promoted by M. Dibelius, O. Cullmann, K.L. Schmidt, G. Dehn and K. Barth. It is critiqued in O'Brien, 'Principalities and Powers', 117–18.

[4] Ibid., 119. The study of Daniel in this context is enlightening, both as a backdrop for the Revelation (where there is clearly reference both to earthly rulers and demonic presence) and for the New Testament generally.

[5] J.R.W. Stott, *God's New Society: The Message of Ephesians* (Downers Grove: InterVarsity Press, 1979), 271.

(including both Testaments) on the matter must be the starting point. The Bible says relatively little about the ultimate source of evil. Rather it concentrates on describing the complexity of our life in this world, and, most important of all, God's ultimate supremacy over all the powers that oppose the full inbreaking of his Kingdom.

Scriptural terms

What are called in Scripture 'principalities', 'powers', 'virtues', 'dominions', 'thrones', and 'names' are words used to describe the structured and ordered way that God has created the world. These terms imply government, human authorities, national structures, family and tribal structures, priorities within relationships of peers, and angelic realms. There are at least ten biblical terms that describe the powers – dimensions of visible and invisible realities that affect our life in the world:[6]

- 'the divine council' (Ps. 82:1) – a heavenly hierarchy
- 'angels' (Gen. 3:24; Rev. 1:1) – invisible spiritual beings who are messengers of God
- 'the devil/Satan' (Mt. 4:1) – a malevolent spiritual being who is totally opposed to God and God's purposes
- 'demons' (Jas. 3:15) – a variety of evil forces and beings operating under a single unified head
- 'the world' (Jn. 15:18) – the world system organized against God and his purposes

---

[6] Some resources on these include P.L. Berger, *The Sacred Canopy: Elements of a Sociological Theory of Religion* (Garden City, NY: Doubleday, 1967), ch. 1; J.H. Bietenhard, 'Angel', in Colin Brown (ed.), *The New International Dictionary of New Testament Theology* (Carlisle: Paternoster/Grand Rapids: Zondervan), I, 101–3; ibid., 'demon', 450–53; J. Ellul, *Money and Power*, trans. La Vonne Neff (Downers Grove: InterVarsity Press, 1984), 76–7, 81, 93; D.G. Reid, 'Principalities and Powers', *Dictionary of Paul and His Letters* (Downers Grove: InterVarsity Press, 1993), 746–52; G.C. Schoberg, 'The Human Predicament: An Examination of Four Biblical Perspectives on Evil' (ThM thesis, Regent College, Vancouver, 1992); T.F. Torrance, 'The Spiritual Significance of Angels', in J.I. Packer and Loren Wilkinson (eds.), *Alive to God: Studies in Spirituality* (Downers Grove: InterVarsity Press, 1992), 122–39.

- 'principalities and powers' (Eph. 6:12) – both socio-political and spiritual pressures
- 'mammon' (Lk. 16:9) – money that pretends to give security, the 'almighty dollar'
- 'the flesh' (Gal. 5:16–17) – the self turned in on oneself, life lived as though Christ had not come, died and been raised
- 'the law' (Rom. 7:12; 8:2) – the good gift of Torah that has been twisted by sin into a way of gaining righteousness
- 'death' (Heb. 2:15) – not merely the cessation of life but a power that holds people in lifelong fear

A fundamental question that arises even before we consider these theological themes, however, is the question of establishing what we are speaking of. Are these structures, or demons – or both?

2. Experiencing the Powers: Multi-level Resistance

On the one hand many authors understand our experience of resistance as primarily the structures of earthly life, structures that hold society together but have now gone wild. These powers can best be described by psychology and sociology.[7]

Fallen social structures

We experience these powers as political, financial and juridical rulers, traditions, doctrines and practices that regulate religion and life (Markus Barth[8]), images like Marilyn Monroe (William

---

[7] It is very popular today to see the principalities and powers as socio-political structures. Some, like Heinrich Schlier, accept the supernatural language used by Paul but argue for the demythologization of these powers to align Scripture with a scientific world-view. Others like Hendrikus Berkhof argue that Paul himself had already demythologized the powers. '[I]n comparison to the apocalypticists a certain "demythologizing" has taken place in Paul's thought. In short, the apocalypses think primarily of the principalities and powers as heavenly angels; Paul sees them as structures of earthly existence' (H. Berkhof, *Christ and the Powers*, trans. J.H. Yoder (Scottdale, PA: Herald Press, 1977), 23.

[8] *Ephesians* (Anchor Bible; 2 vols.; Garden City, NY: Doubleday, 1960), I, 365.

Stringfellow),[9] institutions like GM or IBM (Stringfellow),[10] ideologies like communism, capitalism and democracy (Stringfellow),[11] mammon (Jacques Ellul),[12] and the inner aspect of all the outer manifestations of power in society (Wink[13]). These authors are concerned with the hermeneutical question of how to identify powers in society today rather than the metaphysical question of the nature of their existence. The influence of Karl Barth on this matter is extensive.[14]

A long string of dependencies can be traced. William Diehl relies heavily on William Stringfellow in his analysis of competition.[15] Stringfellow, Ellul and Hendrikus Berkhof take a more psychological and sociological approach which was opened up by Karl Barth.[16] But there is another approach.

---

[9] '[T]he whole life of the person is surrendered to the principality and is given over to the worship of the image' (Stringfellow, *Free in Obedience* (New York: Seabury, 1964), 55; see also *An Ethic for Christians and Other Aliens in a Strange Land.*

[10] 'Everything else must finally be sacrificed to the cause of preserving the institution, and it is demanded of everyone who lives within its sphere of influence . . . that they commit themselves to the service of that end, the survival of the institution' (*Free in Obedience*, 56).

[11] Stringfellow notes how these principalities dominate life: (1) They deny the truth, replacing it with carefully engineered propaganda. (2) They are secretive, keeping their actions hidden from the masses and even loyal supporters. (3) They seek to become totalitarian by distracting people from important concerns (*An Ethic for Christians*, 97–106).

[12] Ellul, *Money and Power*, 75.

[13] W. Wink, *Naming the Powers: The Language of Power in the New Testament*, 5.

[14] See K. Barth's exposition of 'lordless indwelling forces' in III.3.519–31.

[15] W.E. Diehl, *Thank God It's Monday*, 3–16.

[16] 'Angels and demons are related as creation and chaos, as the free grace of God and nothingness, as good and evil, as life and death, as the light of revelation and the darkness which will not receive it, as redemption and perdition, as *kerygma* and myth' (*Church Dogmatics*, III.3.520). The approach to the powers taken by Barth, while a radical rejection of the demythologization programme of Rudolph Bultmann, opened the way for a more psychological and sociological approach to the powers. Barth deals with the powers in his section on 'God and Nothingness'. He does

Peter O'Brien notes the erroneous consequences of identifying the powers exclusively with secular structures: First, we do not have an adequate explanation of why structures so frequently become tyrannical. Second, we unjustifiably restrict our understanding of the malevolent activity of Satan. Third, we become too negative toward society and its structures. O'Brien notes, 'Advocates of the new theory may warn against defying the structures; they have to be warned against demonizing them. Both extremes are to be avoided.'[17] But if there are dangers in locating the powers exclusively in the human realm of structure and tradition, there are dangers as well in locating them exclusively in the angelic and demonic.

Personal spiritual beings

This approach assumes that the heart of our experience of multi-level resistance is the presence of personal spiritual beings who have intelligence and will, are capable of purposeful activity, but are determined to oppose the rule of God. Representing the cosmic perspective of the New Testament authors, Heinrich Schlier says:

> Satan and his hordes, those manifold developments and effusions of the spirit of wickedness with their combination of intelligence and lust for power, exist by influencing the world and mankind in every sector and at all levels, and by making them instruments and bearers of their powers. There is nothing on earth which is absolutely immune from their

---

[16] *(continued)* not regard demons or the devil as created godless beings. Thus when he comes to the principalities and powers he does not concern himself with metaphysics. Rather he speaks of the powers in terms of possibilities of human life or the negative side of creation. It has always been a myth, argues Barth, that when man lives outside the lordship of God he becomes lord of the possibilities of his own life. In trying to live independently from God man finds that his own capacities tend to take on a life of their own – a life which he cannot control but rather controls him. The lucid works of Peter Berger bring this approach to analysing our experience of powers to their consummation.

[17] O'Brien, 'Principalities and Powers', 141.

power. They can occupy the human body, the human spirit, what we call 'nature', and even the forms, bearers and situations of history. Even religions, including the Christian teaching, can become tools of their activity. Their spirit penetrates and overwhelms everything.[18]

A number of popular novels and treatments of spiritual warfare, notably the works of Frank Peretti and David Watson, take essentially this approach. A more scholarly approach is taken by Clinton Arnold in *Powers of Darkness: Principalities and Powers in Paul's Letters* (1992). Taken to the extreme these authors define the problem of the Christian too narrowly. They reduce opposition to the demonic and this mission is reduced to intercession and exorcism. There is little we can do, little for which we are responsible.

Having said this we must accept the important corrective offered by those who warn, as Stott did, that in locating the powers in structures we have lost the demonic. *Western society has largely rejected the spiritual interpretation of life.* Even the church turns to social analysis to find out what is going on, and leaves out the spiritual realities behind and within the visible and present. Years ago James Stewart traced the intellectual history of this demise of our biblical framework in these brilliant words:

> St. Paul's 'principalities and powers' – the 'spirit forces of evil' whose malignant grip upon the souls of men called forth 'a second Adam to the fight and to the rescue' – are now known, we are told, to have been mere apocalyptic imagination. To this result Newton, Darwin and Freud certainly contributed. For Newton's work left no room for an irrational principle in nature; and the devil is essentially irrational, teleologically indefinable – as St. John marks by his significant use of *anomia* and St. Paul by the phrase 'the mystery of iniquity' (1 John 3:4) . . . Darwin's picture of the biological struggle for existence was hailed as radically superseding the Biblical picture of the cosmic struggle between the demons and the kingdom of the Lord. Finally, Freud banished the powers of darkness from their last stronghold, the soul, by successfully dissolving them into psychological complexes, neuroses,

---

[18] H. Schlier, *Principalities and Powers in the New Testament* (New York: Herder & Herder, 1964), 28–9.

and the like: so that the good fight of faith becomes simply a matter of inner individual adjustment.[19]

Expressing this modern viewpoint Walter Wink states, 'We moderns cannot bring ourselves by any feat of will or imagination to believe in the real existence of these mythological entities that traditionally have been lumped under the category "principalities and powers".[20] Yet to be biblical Christians we must be converted to that which we may not be convinced about. As indicated in the survey of biblical words above, the Christian in the world must deal with both structures and beings. And Scripture witnesses to the complexity of systemic evil: structures, spiritual hosts, angels and demons, the devil, and the last enemy, death (1 Cor. 15:24–7) – all arenas of spiritual warfare. Even to speak of the 'spirituality' of institutions, as Wink does,[21] does not fully represent the complexity of evil encountered in the world.

Systemic evil

A truly biblical theology of the powers must include the gospels where Jesus clearly is encountering evil spiritual beings (Lk. 9:1) as well as structures. So in reality many of the seemingly autonomous powers are being influenced by Satan himself. The powers have been colonized: influenced and controlled by a foreign power. And in some cases the alien power (Satan) has 'home rule'.

The complex vision of the last book of the Bible reveals multiple (and systemically interdependent) levels of difficulty which can be pictured as concentric circles of interdependent influences: the

---

[19] J. Stewart, *A Faith to Proclaim* (London: Hodder & Stoughton, 1953), 76–7. Reproduced by permission of Hodder & Stoughton Limited, and SCM Press.

[20] Wink, *Naming the Powers*, 4.

[21] Walter Wink maintains that 'the "principalities and powers" are the inner and outer aspects of any given manifestation of power. As the inner aspect they are the spirituality of institutions, the "within" of corporate structures and systems, the inner essence of outer organizations of power. As the outer aspect they are political systems, appointed officials, the "chair" of an organization, laws – in short, all the tangible manifestations which power takes . . .' (*Naming the Powers*, 5).

red dragon (Satan) at the centre of it all (Rev. 12); the two beasts (Rev .13) representing diabolical authority and diabolical super-naturalism; the Harlot (Rev. 17) representing the sum total of pagan culture; and (in the outermost ring) Babylon (Rev. 18) as the world system. This elaborate picture shows that the Christian in the world not only encounters a multifaceted opposition but one in which there are interdependently connected dimensions. The Revelation shows us that the political power of Romans 13, the good servant of God in Paul's day, has become in Revelation 13 the instrument of Satan (in this case the same government but more colonized and corrupted) – thus showing the way in which supernatural and nonhuman forces and personages may influence and corrupt human institutions, structures and patterns of cultural and social life.[22]

It is impossible for human beings to function in this world with-out encountering these habitual, fallen patterns, which will be experienced in competition, compelling forces of conformity, and, in its worst form, in direct satanic attack through witchcraft and satanism. We must not jettison the demonic; nor must we jettison social structures and the need to participate in their transformation. We are now better positioned to gain a biblical theology of the powers.

3. Understanding the Powers: Biblical Theology

Good powers

Far from being the result of 'the fall' and a necessary restriction of man's fleshly nature to protect humankind from himself, these

---

[22] 'The major apocalyptic forces are, for him, those ontological powers that determine the human situation within the context of God's created order and that comprise the "field" of death, sin, the law, and the flesh. This field is an alliance of powers under the sovereign rule of death . . . The field operates as an interrelated whole; its forces cannot be geneti-cally delineated, and no power can be viewed in isolation from the others' (C.J. Beker, *Paul the Apostle: The Triumph of God in Life and Thought* [Philadelphia: Fortress Press, 1980], 189–90).

powers are part of God's *good* creation. They are not innately evil. They are made by Christ and for Christ! Paul claims that through Christ 'all things were created: things in heaven and on earth, visible and invisible, whether thrones or powers or rulers or authorities; all things were created by him and for him' (Col. 1:16). Hendrikus Berkhof describes this brilliantly, though his application is too narrow,[23] as the invisible background of creation, 'the dikes with which God encircles His good creation, to keep it in His fellowship and protect it from chaos'.[24] They were intended to form a framework in which we live out our lives for God's glory. They are the 'invisible weight-bearing substratum of the world, as the underpinnings of creation'.[25]

The narrative of creation (Gen. 1–2) shows us God's intention. Since this narrative takes us into the paradise of God it is beyond culture and therefore universal. In Eden there was order (seven days), boundaries for the garden, ethical structures (symbolized by the tree of the knowledge of good and evil), limited sovereignty (as expressed in Adam's naming the animals), the basic structure of covenant marriage (leaving, cleaving and one flesh, 2:24), and the cherubim to protect Adam and Eve from making their fallen state immortal (3:24). Family (1:28) and nation were part of God's purpose for humankind, frameworks to hold back chaos.

Four everyday frameworks are marriage, family, nation and law, each ordained by God for our good. Without marriage and family relationships would become meaningless, children would grow without the shelter of marriage. Karl Barth once said that coitus without covenant is demonic. In the same way tribe and nation provide contexts of belonging. But all these good structures can and have become tyrannized. An extraordinary example of how the state has become 'demonized' and tyrannical is given in the book of Daniel. Even marriage and family can become idolatrous, thence the striking demand of Jesus to 'hate' and 'leave' when (it is assumed) these loyalty structures displace wholehearted discipleship

---

[23] 'In short, the apocalypses think primarily of the principalities and powers as heavenly angels; Paul sees them as structures of earthly existence' (Berkhof, *Christ and the Powers*, 23).

[24] Ibid., 28.

[25] Ibid., 28–9.

(Lk. 14:26). Tribes, for example, are good; tribalism is demonic. And so on.

Fallen and colonized powers – human and nonhuman

These structures and the invisible ranks of God's servants have become broken, hostile, resistant to God's rule, intransigent. The New Testament notes that some superhuman and supernatural beings have fallen (Jude 6; 2 Pet. 2:4). Ephesians 6 claims we are engaging these fallen powers as a real factor in our daily existence. There will be no cessation of this spiritual conflict until Christ comes again, or we depart to be with Christ, whichever comes first. Some of these powers have taken on a life of their own, making idolatrous claims on human beings: government, religion, culture, isms, being symbolized by the names and titles that dominate the news (Eph. 1:21; Gal. 4:8–9). In Ephesians 6 Paul suggests these powers have been colonized (though the term is not used) by Satan himself. The orientation of these powers is parallel to the fall of man and woman. In each case the regent (the one responsible to fulfil the monarch's wishes) becomes a god. Heinrich Schlier notes, 'this power now operates as if it were self-ordained. He now has an autonomous nature. He and all the principalities now maintain as their own that which was given to them by God.'[26]

Overpowered powers

All too frequently the gospels are neglected in any consideration of the powers. There Jesus is seen as supreme over the evil spirits. He casts out demons by the finger of God (Lk. 11:20); he destroys the power of Satan (Mk. 3:23–6; Mt. 12:26; Lk. 11:18); he enters the strong man's house and plunders his goods (Mk. 3:27). No Old Testament passage is quoted as frequently in the New Testament as Psalm 110:1, a statement that all the powers have been subjugated by the Messiah-Christ. This extraordinary ability of Jesus to overpower the powers is delegated to his followers (Mk. 3:14f.; 6:7; Mt. 10:1; Lk. 9:1f.; 10:1). No consideration of the powers should neglect the strategic importance of the gospels and the demonstrated victory of

---

[26] Schlier, *Principalities and Powers*, 37–8.

Christ over the powers during his earthly ministry. Paul's further development of this elaborates the extensiveness of Christ's work now that he has died and been resurrected.

Paul uses several words to express how the hostile powers have been subjugated.[27] They have been abrogated, stripped, led in triumphal procession or into captivity, made to genuflect, pacified or reconciled.[28] Markus Barth comments that 'Most amazing is the use of the terms "pacified" and "reconciled"; everywhere except in Colossians (and Eph. 2:14) Paul has reserved them to describe Christ's work only for man.'[29] Christ's death put the principalities and powers in their place as instruments, subject to God's sovereignty. His cross was a victory not only over the sin of humankind but over the powers as well. The cross was both a political act and a cosmic victory.

Without the eye of faith, these powers still seem almost omnipotent. But to the eye of faith they are vanquished even though they continue to press their claims and therefore complicate even the Christian's life in this world. Oscar Cullmann compares the powers to chained beasts, kicking themselves to death. Between the resurrection of Jesus and the second coming they are tied to a rope, still free to evince their demonic character, but nevertheless bound.

---

[27] Berkhof elaborates Christ's work in pacification and reconciliation using the three phrases of Col. 2:15. (1) Christ made a public example of them. What once were considered fundamental realities are not seen as rivals and adversaries of God. As divine irony the title 'king of the Jews' was placed over the cross in the three languages that represent the powers that crucified Jesus: Hebrew, the language of religion; Latin, the language of government; and Greek, the language of culture. By volunteering to be 'victimized' by the powers through his death, and 'using' the powers to accomplish a mighty saving act, Jesus put the powers in their place as instruments of God rather than regents, showing how illusionary are their pretended claims. (2) Christ triumphed over them, the resurrection being proof that Jesus is stronger than the powers. He put death to death. (3) Christ disarmed the powers, stripping them of the power and authority by which they deceived the world, namely the illusion that they are godlike and all powerful, and that devotion to them is the ultimate goal of life (*Christ and the Powers*, 38).

[28] 1 Cor. 15:24–6; Col. 1:20; 2:15; Phil. 2:10; Eph. 1:22.

[29] Barth, *Ephesians*, I, 182. See also I, 170–76; II, 800–803.

Cullmann uses a helpful analogy to explain the tension. D-Day was the day during the Second World War in which the beaches of Normandy were invaded and the battle was turned. One could say the war was 'won' that day even though there were months of battling ahead, and many lives lost. VE day was the day of final victory. Christ's coming and death is D-Day. But we must still live in the overlap of the ages as we wait for the final consummation of the Kingdom at the second coming of Christ.[30] This experience of the 'overlap of the ages' can be represented visually in this way:

LIVING IN THE OVERLAP OF THE AGES

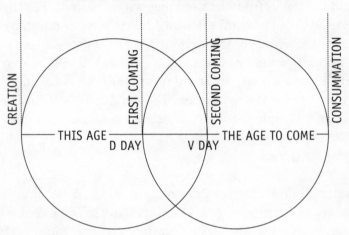

---

[30] 'The expectation thus continues to exist just as in Judaism. What the Jews expected of the future is still expected of the future; but the future event is no longer the center of redemptive history; rather, that center lies now in a historical event. The center has been reached, but the end is still to come. I may illustrate this idea by an example: the decisive battle in a war may already have occurred in a relatively early stage of the war, and yet the war still continues. Although the decisive effect of the battle is perhaps not recognized by all, it nevertheless already means victory. But the war must still be carried on for an undefined time, until "Victory Day"' (O. Cullmann, *Christ and Time: The Primitive Christian Conception of Time and History*, trans. F.V. Filson [London: SCM Press, 1951], 84).

Gerald Schoberg comments that the danger of this analogy is that it leaves open-ended the question of how much of the battle lies ahead, diminishing the importance of the second coming of Christ by focusing so much on the work of the cross ('The Human Predicament', 238).

4. Grappling with the Powers: Mission and Ministry

The world, the flesh and the devil, is the handy summary offered by the prayer book of the Church of England concerning the complexity of dealing with systemic evil. But how do we deal with evil?

We deal with the world through nonconformity with the world and conformity with the will of God (Rom. 12:2). We deal with the flesh by mortification (identifying with Christ's crucifixion) and aspiration (breathing in the Spirit). We deal with the devil by resisting and fleeing (Jas. 4:7). It is a multi-front battle: the world, the flesh and the devil. And our Lord meets us at each of these fronts: transfiguring us from within (Rom. 12:2) so we can transform the world, rather than be conformed to it as we penetrate it in our work and mission; bearing Spirit fruit through us (Gal. 5:22,25) as we determine to walk in the Spirit and regard the flesh as crucified; and overcoming the evil one, the devil (Rev. 12:10–11) through all kinds of prayer (Eph. 6:13–18) as we put on Christ's armour.

Preaching the gospel

The first and most effective strategy against the false claims of the powers is preaching the gospel. Our duty is not to bring the powers to *our* knees: this is Christ's task. Our duty is to arm ourselves with Christ (Eph. 6:10–18) and to preach his cross. As far as possible Christians should bring God's kingdom peace to the powers through involvement in creational tasks: subjecting the resources of the world in education, politics and culture to serve man as defined by God's intention. Some powers will be shown to be unmasked by the martyrdom of faithful believers (Rev. 12:11). But Christians and the church must be under no illusion. As Markus Barth says: 'The power of filling, subjugating, and dominating "all things", including these powers is reserved to God and Christ alone. But the function of demonstrating God's dominion and love is entrusted to the church. She is appointed and equipped to be a public exponent of grace and unity . . . the beginning of a new heaven and a new earth.'[31] Preaching will be central to our strategy. But there is more.

---

[31] Barth, *Ephesians*, I, 365.

Public discipleship

The four historic approaches to the powers can be represented graphically as follows:

WAYS OF GRAPPLING WITH THE POWERS

	EXORCISM INTERCESSION	SUFFERING POWERLESSNESS	CREATIVE PARTICIPATION	JUST REVOLUTION
VOCATION	spiritual liberation	witness to fallenness	regents	social change
MEANS	prayer	powerlessness	work/politics	civil disobedience
METAPHYSIC	demonic	colonized structures	fallen and colonized structures	none (Marxian)
DENOMINATIONS	charismatic	anabaptist	mainline	liberation theology
AUTHORS	Watson Wimber Schlier?	Yoder	Mouw Berkhof Ellul	Bonino Gutierrez

In the way of exorcism the assumption is that our role is to continue the liberation of individuals from bondage to Satan by preaching and prayer. The powers are much more than social structures. The social structures are merely fronts for Satan's grand plan to woo people away from God.

The way of suffering powerlessness is patterned after the way of the cross.[32] John Howard Yoder, representing the Anabaptist tradition, takes this approach. Our role is not to change society directly but our role is to witness. When we do this, even at the loss of our own lives, we expose the fallenness of all human rule and witness to God's action in the cross and the coming Kingdom. The powers have been colonized by Satan and can only be overthrown by God

---

[32] J.H. Yoder, *The Politics of Jesus.*

himself. When the world is off centre, it takes a lever with a fulcrum outside the world to move it. Christians, according to this approach, believe that the lever to move the world is a wooden cross.[33]

The way of creative participation assumes that our role is to be regents on earth. According to the creation mandate we are called to order and 'husband' all the dimensions of societal and creational life. The structures have been colonized by Satan (according to some) or merely reflect the fallen condition of human beings (according to others). But it is possible, indeed it is our vocation, to bring these structures into conformity to the rule of Christ. We do this through our daily work, social action and mission.[34] The danger in taking this approach exclusively is to minimize the demonic and the nonhuman forces and personages that we encounter in our public discipleship. The further limitation was expressed simply by Jacques Ellul: 'In reality all solutions, all economic, political and other achievements are temporary.'[35]

The final option is the way of the cleansed temple, with Jesus as the model revolutionary. It has been promoted actively by liberation theologians both Catholic and Protestant, though Jacques Ellul has identified a gentler form of Christian revolution. Indeed civil disobedience is a legitimate missional approach in some situations.[36]

---

[33] O'Brien offers three cogent criticisms of Yoder as a comprehensive approach to the powers: (1) We cannot consistently and universally imitate the work of Christ on the cross. (2) It may be questioned whether Christ's death provides a universal pattern for political involvement. (3) Yoder's idea of revolutionary subordination applies to the Son's relationship to the Father, not to Christ's relation to the powers which was one of victory through a victorious clash ('Principalities and Powers', 123–4).

[34] R. Mouw, *Politics and the Biblical Drama*.

[35] Ellul, *The Presence of the Kingdom*, 48.

[36] Civil disobedience can be understood as a form of subordination to government because it recognizes the claim of government and seeks to bring law and morality into greater congruence. Stephen C. Mott outlines the qualifications for civil disobedience: (1) the law opposed is immoral; (2) every possibly nondisobedient resource has been exhausted; (3) the protest is not clandestine; (4) there is likelihood of success; (5) there is willingness to accept the penalty (*Biblical Ethics and Social Change* [New York: Oxford University Press, 1982], 161–6).

Ellul says that when the essential structure of our civilization is flawed 'it is utterly useless to try to discover remedies for our present distress without altering this framework'.[37] One such Christian revolutionary summarized the dilemma implicit in taking this approach with these searching words: 'When I feed the hungry they call me a saint. When I ask why the poor are poor they call me a communist.' J.M. Bonino, speaking of the Columbian priest, Camilo Torres, said, 'In today's world there is only one way to feed the hungry, clothe the naked, care for the sick and imprisoned – as Christ invited us to do: to change the structures of society which create and multiply every day those conditions. This is revolution.'[38]

Which viewpoint is right? Indeed all are right,[39] and all have strong support in Scripture and may be chosen in particular circumstances. The church as a whole must engage in a full-orbed approach. As with the gifts for ministry in 1 Corinthians 12, we dare not say, 'I have no need of thee!'

Social justice and public discipleship must be more than good works. It must be theologically founded, rooted in the City of God and oriented to the Kingdom of God. The deepest reference to the gospel, as Forsyth said, 'is to eternity and its social obligations'.[40] We are not likely to keep this reference point without prayer.

---

[37] Ellul, *The Presence of the Kingdom*, 34. Ellul argues that the so-called revolutions of Marxism and Fascism are mere extensions of the linear direction of our present civilization, careening as it is to dissolution from within. Christians are called to radical nonconformity and a truly revolutionary stance. He equates this with an apocalyptic perspective (32) which alters our framework for thinking and acting. The Christian belongs to two cities (44). So the Christian plunges into social and political problems not in the hope of making it paradise but simply to make it tolerable (47). He warns against thinking that by making some progress in this order of things we will be able to attain the Kingdom of God. 'In reality all solutions, all economic, political and other achievements are temporary' (48). 'It is quite useless for Christians to give exclusive attention to social or political problems' (60).

[38] J.M. Bonino, *Doing Theology in a Revolutionary Situation* (Philadelphia: Fortress Press, 1975), 44.

[39] A remarkable fact is that whenever these options have been presented by the author in a South American context to evangelical Christians, the majority accept the revolutionary options as a Christian alternative.

[40] Forsyth, *The Church and the Sacraments*, 29.

Prayer

Paul uses an elaborate metaphor for arming ourselves in Ephesians 6:10–18 by using the pieces of armour worn by a Roman soldier. Perhaps he was chained to one as he wrote this. The belt of truth means living with integrity. The breastplate of righteousness involves having right relations with God and living righteously. The 'go' of the gospel implies that we are ready and 'on the way' to share the gospel – there is more than defence here! The shield of faith deflects the enemy's attacks, and the helmet of salvation brings assurance to our minds that we belong to a God who will never divorce us. The sword of the Spirit is the Word of God, read, obeyed and spoken. All these are ways of 'putting on Christ': Christ's righteousness, Christ's message, Christ's faith, Christ's finished work on the cross, and Christ's word. All of these are put on by prayer: prayer on all occasions and all kinds of prayer (6:18).

Paul ends his magnificent metaphor of donning the armour with this simple request: 'pray also for me' (Eph. 6:19). Karl Barth once said that 'to clasp the hands in prayer is the beginning of an uprising against the disorder of the world'.[41] It is also the beginning of an uprising against the disorder we see in ourselves and in others. Intercessory prayer is hard work but Ephesians 1:15–23 and 3:14–21 offer helpful patterns. It is hard to hold people in our hearts and then to take them to God in our praying hearts. But calculated from the perspective of the New Jerusalem some very important things happen when we pray for others.

First, we get God's mind about the person or the situation we are holding before God. Second, we piggyback on the Spirit's intercession since our prayers, even the most eloquent ones, are mere groans and babblings in comparison to the eloquence of the Spirit (Rom. 8:26). Third, in some mysterious way that offends the secular mindset, we get in touch with persons on a deeper level than we might otherwise. Bonhoeffer explains that direct relationships between people are impossible. But Jesus as our mediator puts his hand on each and brings both together. So the most direct way to our brother is indirect – through Christ. Finally, something happens

---

[41] Quoted in Kenneth Leech, *True Prayer: An Invitation to Christian Spirituality* (San Francisco: Harper & Row, 1980), 68.

when we pray for people. Pascal said that 'prayer is God's way of providing man with the dignity of causality'.[42] P.T. Forsyth agrees that the earth is shaken daily by the prayers of the saints. 'The real power of prayer in history is not a fusillade of praying units of whom Christ is the chief, but it is the corporate action of a Saviour-Intercessor and His community, a volume and energy of prayer organized in a Holy Spirit and in the Church the Spirit creates.'[43]

Martyrdom

This is not an attractive subject to contemporary Christians. But the twentieth century has known more martyrs than any previous century including the first. And, in the last book of the Bible the martyr is the model Christian. Indeed there are very few living Christians pictured in the Revelation. Those who overcome the devil are those who 'did not love their lives so much as to shrink from death' (Rev. 12:11). Some give their life in one extravagant act of obedience; others in day-to-day obedience to the gospel, paying the price of finding their life in God rather than in this age. In the Celtic Church several kinds of martyrdom were recognized:

> white martyrdom, green martyrdom, and red martyrdom. White martyrdom consists in a man's abandoning everything he loves for God's sake . . . Green martyrdom consists in this, that by means of fasting and labour he frees himself from his evil desires; or suffers toil in penance and repentance. Red martyrdom consists in the endurance of a Cross or death for Christ's sake.[44]

5. The Final Pacification of the Powers: Eschatology

As far as now possible Christians should Christianize the powers, to 'peace' the powers through involvement in education, government and social action, all the while knowing that the task of subjugating

---

[42] Blaise Pascal, *Pensées* (New York: The Modern Library, 1941), 166.

[43] Quoted in E. Peterson, *Reversed Thunder: The Revelation of John and the Praying Imagination* (San Francisco: Harper and Row, 1988), 87.

[44] J. Ryan, *Irish Monasticism* (London, 1931), 197, quoted in T. Ware, *The Orthodox Church* (Harmondsworth, UK, Penguin Books, 1985), 23.

the powers is reserved for Christ alone (Eph. 1:10; Phil. 2:10–11). We do this, as we have seen, through vocation, work and ministry. We are taken up in God's mission. We work on the problems of pollution, food distribution, injustice, genetic engineering, and the proliferation of violence and weaponry, knowing that this work is ministry and holy.

Romans 8:19–21 *pictures a continuum of the present in which creation 'groans' with a future without groaning.* As John Haughey puts it, 'Creation's hopes will not be mocked by annihilation any more than ours will be.'[45] The present will be factored into the future. The God who created with no materials will one day recompose the first creation with that materials of that creation over time including the work of human beings.[46]

---

[45] J. Haughey, *Converting Nine to Five: A Spirituality of Daily Work* (New York: Crossroad, 1989), 104.

[46] Volf argues that, 'if the world will be annihilated and a new one created *ex nihilo* then mundane work has only earthly significance for the well-being of the worker, the worker's community, and posterity – until the day when "the heavens will pass away with a loud noise, and the elements, will be dissolved with fire." Since the results of the cumulative work of humankind throughout history will become naught in the final apocalyptic catastrophe, human work is devoid of direct ultimate significance.'

As Volf shows, eschatological annihilation and responsible social involvement may be logically compatible but they are theologically inconsistent. He offers several arguments for the *transformatio mundi* (transformation of the world): (1) the earthly locale of the kingdom of God in Rev. 21–2 fulfils the earthly hopes of the Old Testament prophets (Is. 11:6–10; 65:17–25); (2) the Christian doctrine of the resurrection of the body makes little sense in a non-earthly future eschatological existence; (3) the New Testament explicitly promotes the vision of a liberation of the world – animate and inanimate which could not be accomplished through its destruction (Rom. 8:21); (4) finally, the Bible shows that ultimately creation is good, even though polluted with sin. Volf stresses that this is not merely projecting the survival and transformation of individual works but the cumulative work of the race, and that human work creates a home in the environment that is permanent. Further, he posits that the statement in Revelation that the saints 'rest from their labour, for their deeds follow them' (Rev. 14:13; cf. Eph. 6:8) 'could be interpreted to imply that earthly work will leave traces on resurrected personalities' Volf, *Work in the Spirit*, 89–96.

How this will be done we are not told, but we are invited to consider *which of our works will last* (1 Cor. 3:12–15). In view of the scope of recreation envisioned, these works cannot simply be ecclesial (or religious). Ironically, Paul envisions a situation in which the person's works are burned in the final fire, but the person himself is saved (1 Cor. 3:15).

We are told, however, what will last: 'And now these three remain: *faith, hope and love*' (13:13). Haughey comments:

> It seems that it is not acts of faith, hope and love in themselves that last, but rather works done in faith, hope and love: it is not the pure intention alone, nor is it faith, hope and love residing unexercised as three infused theological virtues in a person that last. What lasts is the action taken on these virtues, the praxis that flows from the intention, the works the virtues shape. These last![47]

We leave our mark on the cosmos and our environment, on government, culture, neighbourhoods, families, on the principalities and powers. The Bible hints that in some way beyond our imagination our marks are permanent. All the visions of the new heaven and the new earth are in terms of what we know and do now (Rev. 21:26). Our environment is going to heaven. Christ is the first-born of all creation (Col. 1:15) and first born from the grave (1:18). But his resurrected body bore scars in historical continuity with his life in the flesh, though the scars were not now merely signs of faith but a means of faith (Jn. 20:27). These are powerful biblical visions of the way this life and the next is connected. Our violent acts against nature and culture will not be erased by the final Armageddon and the final consummation at the second coming of Jesus, but may, by God's grace be transfigured. This is our hope.

This brings new meaning to those whose toil is in so-called secular work: the arts, education, business and politics. They too are shaping the future of creation in some limited way just as are missionaries and pastors. Most people think that only religious work will not be in vain (1 Cor. 15:58) but if Christ is the first-born of all creation and first born from the grave, then all work has eternal consequences, whether homemaking or being a stockbroker. We look

---

[47] Haughey, *Converting Nine to Five*, 106.

forward to a time of exquisite transfiguration. We are invited to leave beautiful marks on creation, on the environment, family, city, workplace and nation. And when we cannot do this, and cannot undo the violence we have committed against the cosmos, we have faith in Jesus that one day he will transfigure even the environmental, social, cultural and political scars we have left through our work. In the short run our work, ministry and mission may seem unsuccessful, but in the long run we are co-operating with what Christ wants to do in renewing all creation.

We cannot wrestle with the powers faithfully without a vision of the final pacification of the powers when Christ comes again and establishes the new heaven and the new earth. Jürgen Moltmann spoke of eschatology as the most pastoral of all theological disciplines because it shows us that we are living not at the high noon, nor the sunset of life but, as Moltmann says, 'at the dawn of a new day at the point where night and day, things passing and things to come, grapple with each other'.[48]

Drawing heavily on the imagery of Ezekiel and Isaiah (65:17–25), John envisions for Christians in Rev. 21–2 an even greater hope: a completely renewed creation. Jesus says, 'I am making everything new' (Rev. 21:5). That final renewal vision involves the pacification of the powers – both structures and angelic beings. Satan and his minions are thrown into the lake of fire. There is no more sea. But there are tribes, the city, beauty and creativity, kings and nations, aesthetics, and order. This is the ultimate goal of the whole people of God. This is what vocation, work and ministry are for, what it will become and why it has meaning now. Only heavenly-mindedness can make us of earthly use and save us from despair about work in the world, even Christian service. Lesslie Newbigin comments on this with great depth:

> We can commit ourselves without reserve to all the secular work our shared humanity requires of us, knowing that nothing we do in itself is good enough to form part of that city's building, knowing that everything – from our most secret prayers to our most public political

---

[48] J. Moltmann, *Theology of Hope: On the Grounds and Implications of a Christian Eschatology*, trans. J.W. Leitch (New York: Harper & Row, 1967), 31.

acts – is part of that sin-stained human nature that must go down into the valley of death and judgement, and yet knowing that as we offer it up to the Father in the name of Christ and in the power of the Spirit, it is safe with him and – purged in fire – it will find its place in the holy city at the end.[49]

---

[49] Newbigin, *Foolishness to the Greeks*, 136.

For further study/discussion

Case Study: Grappling with the Powers at the News Desk. Typing at a personal computer terminal an hour from the deadline, Gary Bayer's quick temper was on the verge of erupting. A reporter for the *Messenger*, an English-language daily in the capital city of a Latin American country, his editor had just told him to reduce any negative coverage of the national oil company NAC.

Gary had spent weeks tracking a growing conflict between the oil-workers' union and the management of NAC, run by the government. The conflict had come to a head that afternoon at a press conference in which leaders from several oil-worker unions had criticized NAC for pay that lagged behind the inflation rate and for strong-arm tactics in labour negotiations. The press conference, attended by a few reporters from local Spanish-language newspapers, was followed by a protest march.

Gary had managed to get comments from an NAC (management) spokesman defending the oil company against the accusations, but the story could clearly focus primarily on the worker grievances and march. His editor, an expatriate like himself from the United States, explained to him that orders had come from the president of the publishing company that owned the *Messenger* to reduce all news that could reflect poorly on NAC, which was still reeling from adverse publicity from an explosion at a storage centre in which hundreds of workers and nearby residents had died.

The editor didn't need to say more; Gary knew that the government was the sole supplier of newsprint, and that newsprint prices would go up to untenable levels for the *Messenger* and its major daily, Spanish-language sister publication if the government were to be alienated by the publishing company that owned these dailies.

Gary began to object – he couldn't imagine how to write the story in a way uncritical of NAC management even if he'd wanted to – but his editor said he didn't have time to argue and returned to his office. The *Messenger* was read by US and other diplomats, government officials of the Latin American expatriate community. It would be a glaring omission not to run a story on the labour dispute. A story soft pedalling the union grievances, however, would not only reflect poorly on him as a reporter and the *Messenger* as a newspaper, but do disservice to the public, and could also damage his relations with a key source within the union.

The story Gary would have to rewrite was already three-quarters finished. While he had a burning desire to write the truth and let the chips fall where they may he also felt an obligation to be culturally flexible, put US press standards aside and be loyal to his editor, who had defended him against publishing company brass and government objections to his stories in the past. Deadline was fast approaching.

1. How would you answer the following questions?

   • What are the powers Gary was encountering?
   • How could he grapple with them?
   • What resources did Gary have as a follower of Christ to cope with these pressures?
   • What can the church do to equip people like Gary to engage in ministry and mission in the workplace?

2. Consider advertising as one of the 'powers' with which we must wrestle, and in which world some Christians are rightly employed. Discuss how one might grapple with this all-encompassing area both from within the profession and as a Christian citizen.

   Years ago Marshall McLuhan said, 'Ours is the first age in which many thousands of our best trained minds made it a full-time business to get inside the collective public mind . . . to manipulate, exploit, and control'. Some anthropologists view advertising in terms of rituals and symbols – incantations to give meaning to material objects and artefacts. Advertising defines the meaning of life and offers transcendence in the context of everyday life. Our commercial-religious education begins early with jingles, slogans and catchphrases – the total commercial catechism – so that children learn the 'rite words in the rote order'. So direct exhortations are employed, literally a series of commandments, a secular litany that Jacques Barzun identified as 'the revealed religion of the twentieth century'. 'You get only one chance at this life; therefore get all the gusto you can!' – is a theological claim and a moral injunction. Toward this end advertising appeals to the traditional seven deadly sins: greed, lust, sloth, pride, envy and gluttony, with anger only infrequently exploited or encouraged. Since these words are frowned upon in the advertising community they must be given a different spin. Lust becomes the desire to be sexually attractive. Sloth becomes the desire for leisure. Greed becomes the desire to enjoy the good things of this life. Pride becomes the desire for social status. In this way advertising cultivates what Paul called 'the works of the flesh' (Gal. 5:17–21; 6:8). Morality is subverted; values are revised; ultimate meaning is redefined.

3. Reflect on how you personally and how your church corporately are encountering the powers.

4. Re–read Ephesians 6:10–20.

Epilogue

Living Theologically

I believe in Christianity as I believe that the Sun has risen not only because I see it but because by it I see everything else.

C.S. Lewis

Living theologically![1] This title is an oxymoron like black light, constructive criticism, fried ice, or servant leadership – two ideas that normally do not belong together. What has theology to do with everyday life?

Theology is usually considered an abstract discipline. It is rational, reducible to propositions, and capable of being categorized (liberal, conservative, evangelical, Reformed, liberation). It is not usually thought of as practical. People in business, law, the professions and the trades often regard the study of theology as a process of becoming progressively irrelevant. Theology! God-words. God-study. God-thought.

Then there is life! Everyday life. Getting-up-in-the-morning life. Paying-the-bills life. Watching-a-hockey-game life. Trying-to-find-a-job life. Trying-to-say-'I love you'-to-your-spouse life. Raising-a-family-in-a-postmodern-culture life. Computers, credit cards, motorways, gridlock, virtual reality, running a small business, films, the economy, racial tension, sexual appetite, recession, radar imaging from satellites, fashion, television, ambition, workaholism, debt, prayer, Bible study, theological discourse – what do these have in common?

---

[1] Much of the epilogue was first published in *Themelios* 20.3 (May 1995), 4–8.

We have considered in this book how the church is a people without laity or clergy, summoned and equipped by God for the life of the world. It should be obvious that I have been pleading for a different kind of theology than what is commonly thought, one closer to the Bible. Such is supplied by the Puritan William Perkins, who said, 'Theology is the science of living blessedly forever.' For example, James Houston recently suggested at a pastors' conference that the curriculum vitae of a pastor is usually written on the face of his wife. There was a stunned silence among the predominantly male audience.

In this final section I will explore the life-theology connection by looking through three lenses, each providing a way of looking at the rich connection designed by God but largely fragmented in contemporary theological education.

1. Orthodoxy

Orthodoxy is made up of two Greek words, the first, *orthos*, meaning 'straight' or 'right' (from which we get the English word 'orthodontist', the person who makes straight teeth); and the second, *doxa*, meaning 'glory' or 'worship'. Doctrine that lines itself up (*orthos*) with Scripture is designed to be a blessing to everyday life and, at the same time, to bless God (*doxa*) in life itself. It aims, as J.I. Packer says, at true godliness that is true humanness.

Redeeming the routines[2]

The whole of our life has the glorious prospect of living out the great doctrines of the faith. The doctrine of the Trinity, for example, directs God-imaging creatures to live relationally. Those who proclaim that God is love are invited to be included in the love life of God and so become lovers themselves (Jn. 17:21). To believe in God the creator is to accept trusteeship of the earth. The incarnation revolutionizes our attitude to things and promotes a radical Christian materialism. The atonement equips us to live mercifully.

---

[2] This is the title of an excellent book authored by my friend, Robert Banks.

Ecclesiology evokes the experience of peoplehood, living as the *laos* of God rather than a bouquet of individual believers (one of the themes of this book). Eschatology teaches us to view time as a gift of God rather than a resource to be managed.

All of this involves straight thought. Far from denigrating thought, the Bible invites us to love God with our minds (Mt. 22:37) by thinking comprehensively (taking the whole into consideration, including paradox, ambiguity and the aesthetic), thinking critically (not allowing our minds to be conformed to this age), thinking devotedly (by taking captive every thought to make it obedient to Christ, 2 Cor. 10:5). The fruit of such thinking should be a blessing for everyday life. Thinking in a Christian way is part of the 'science of living blessedly forever'.

The danger of unapplied theology

But orthodoxy involves more than merely speaking correctly *about* God. We could do that and still be damned, like the friends of Job – Eliphaz, Bildad and Zophar – who spoke with impeccable correctness about God (according to the theology of the day) but in the end received God's judgement: 'I am angry with you [Eliphaz] and your two friends, because you have not spoken of me what is right, as my servant Job has' (Job 42:7). Remarkably God judged Job as orthodox and his friends were condemned. Why? This is not only a fascinating question but a vital one.

A careful study of the book of Job reveals that the only authentic theologian in the book was Job himself. The reason is sublimely simple: while the friends talked *about* God, Job talked *to* God. P.T. Forsyth says that 'the best theology is compressed prayer'.[3] While Job's friends delivered their lectures about God, Job talked to God, and in so speaking – with all his holy boldness – he spoke well of God. His theology was orthodox. We will return to this later.

The danger of mere intellectual orthodoxy is that we are tempted to think we can manage God. Our doctrines then become idols – static, fixed and inflexible. According to Psalm 115:8, 'those who make [such idols] will be like them'. They will become people who are static, inflexible and unsurprising. In contrast the Lord

---

[3] P.T. Forsyth, *The Soul of Prayer* (London: Independent Press, 1954), 11.

'does whatever pleases him' (115:3). And those who worship the
Lord become free and spontaneous. God can never be contained by
the human mind. The point of theology is to under-stand God (to
stand *under* God in reverent awe) not to over-stand him by attempting to control him through theological discourse. Much that passes
for theological education is the extension of the tree of knowledge
of good and evil through history offering the temptation to transcend our creatureliness. True worship is the opposite invitation.
Orthodoxy welcomes mystery and confesses with Job 'these are but
the outskirts of his ways' (Job 26:14 KJV). As Robert Capon said:
'The work of theology in our day is not so much interpretation as
contemplation . . . God and the world need to be held up for oohs
and ahhs before they can be safely analyzed. Theology begins with
admiration, not problems.'[4] So orthodoxy is about worshipful
living.

Truthful living for God's glory

Doctrine that does not lead to doxology is demonic (Jas. 2:19).
That is why those who set out merely on a theological education
experience are on a dangerous journey. We must make sure we are
heading in the right (orthodox) direction. The goal of biblical
theological education is to increase our love for God and to make
us more human. For this reason the academy must work in partnership with the church and the marketplace since there is in these
real-life ministry and life situations a built-in reality check. More
important there is a built-in love check. We cannot learn to love
the church as Christ does (Eph. 5:25) without being in both Christ
and the church. The church cannot be loved *in absentia* the way
some people get their degrees. The congregation is essential for
our God-given goal of forming people who will worship God
through preaching, examining a balance sheet, preparing a family
meal, praying with or pruning the rose bushes of a friend, and
equipping the saints. According to Ephesians the purpose of congregation and life-based education is that the saints will live for the
praise of God's glory (1:12,14), that is, live doxologically.

---

[4] Capon, *An Offering of Uncles*, 163.

So, looking at the theology and day-to-day life connection through the lens of orthodoxy, we see that the great doctrines of the faith beg for application. They bless everyday life. They point us simultaneously to the adoration of God and to the possibility of living a genuinely human existence. But we must now look through a second lens – orthopraxy – to discover what is involved in the connection of theology and daily life. Orthopraxy literally means 'right or straight practice'.

2. Orthopraxy

The church (and especially we evangelicals) is in desperate need today of a theology of good works. We are saved by grace and not of works – that is the gospel. But faith without works is dead – and that is part of the gospel too. But how can people saved by grace work? What is right practice? When is a deed Christian?

Humanizing theological living

Is it Christian because it is a work of evangelism, preaching, pastoral care, counselling – all the subjects loosely called 'applied theology' or 'ministry division' courses? On the most basic level orthopraxy is about practices that are in harmony with God's kingdom in the church and world, that bring value and good into the world.

The Bible invites us to wholistic living that embraces propositional truth, as well as truth learned through image, imagination and action, forming a seamless robe. For example, the apostle Paul hammered out his doctrine of justification by faith in the context of the Gentile mission. He was a missionary theologian. Ray S. Anderson notes, 'Paul's theology and mission were directed more by the Pentecost event which unleashed the Spirit of Christ through apostolic witness rather than through apostolic office. This praxis of Pentecost became for Paul the "school" for theological reflection.'[5] The gospels point to the same unity of knowledge. Many of the commands of Jesus link revelation with obedience. 'If you obey my commands, you will remain in my love' (Jn. 15:10). 'If you hold to

---

[5] Anderson, *Praxis of Pentecost*, 163.

my teaching, you are really my disciples' (8:31). 'If anyone keeps my word, he will never see death' (8:51). Sometimes Jesus invited people to 'believe this'; more often Jesus said 'do this and you will live' (Lk. 10:28, see also Mt. 19:21).

Every action has implicit theory just as every theory has implicit action. So theological reflection *in* ministry or a societal occupation is essential to living theologically. But in these things we are not trying to squeeze blood from a rock. Daily life is bursting with theological meaning just as theological truth is laden with blessing for daily life. God can be known and loved through praxis in the realities of everyday life. What a strange marriage psychology would require one to love fully and only then to kiss, rather than to kiss in order to love! What a strange perversion of the Christian life that would forbid one to act until one knows, and not act in order to know! We are formed theologically not only by reading, and reasoning but by action and by service. Indeed, as Eberhard Jüngel said, 'Everything can become the theme of theology on the basis of its relation to God.'[6] In this we have a clue to our basic question: what makes practice Christian?

Inside Christian practice

What makes an activity Christian is not the husk but the heart. Preaching, caring for the flock and equipping the saints can be profoundly secular. Listening to a child, designing a software package, and examining a balance sheet can be profoundly Christian. What makes a work Christian is faith, hope and love. This is a crucial point. Orthopraxy is not merely accomplished by the skilful performance of ministerial duties like leading Bible studies, praying for the sick and doing acts of justice. This misunderstanding has seduced many non-clergy laity to aspire to ministerial duties in order to be 'doing ministry'. They become paraclergy instead of regarding their ordinary service in the world as full-time ministry. It is not the religious character of the work that makes service Christian but the interiority of it. I can preach a sermon to impress people; I can fix

---

[6] Eberhard Jüngel, *The Freedom of a Christian: Luther's Significance for Contemporary Theology* (Minneapolis: Augsburg Press, 1988), 22.

our shower door at home for the glory of God. I have probably done both. The difference is faith.

Luther deals with this brilliantly in his *Treatise on Good Works*. He uses the analogy of husband and wife as an example of the Christian practices that spring from gospel confidence. Where the husband is confident of his acceptance he does not have to do big things to win his wife's favour. In the same way the person who lives by the gospel 'simply serves God with no thought of reward, content that his service pleases God. On the other hand, he who is not at one with God, or is in a state of doubt, worries and starts looking about for ways and means to do enough and to influence God with his many good works.'[7] Faith defines orthopraxy. Faith by definition cannot be calculating, or even self-evaluative, just as the eye cannot look at itself, designed as it is for looking at another. When the eye is single or sound the whole of one's bodily life is filled with the light of Christ (Lk. 11:34–6). Life centred on God transforms the ordinary into the extraordinary so we discover what Alfons Auer described as 'the sense of *transparency in worldly matters*'.[8]

The unselfconsciousness of such faith is the matter raised by the disturbing parable of the sheep and goats (Mt. 25:31–46). The unrighteous protest that if they had seen Jesus in the poor, hungry or stranger, even if they had known Jesus was disguised in the poor, they would gladly have done a service directly to the Lord. So the unrighteous are surprised that their failure to love their neighbour was a failure to love Jesus. They would gladly have done Christian practices for Jesus but not for others! Apparently that is not enough. In contrast the righteous found to their exquisite surprise that what they did not regard as a ministry to Jesus (but just loving their neighbour) turned out to be a Christian practice approved by the Lord. They too protest, 'Lord, when did we see you, hungry, naked and thirsty, and feed you?' Jesus says, 'Whatever you did for one of the least of these brothers of mine, you did for me' (25:40). We onlookers are caught up in the parable and are surprised also by the implication that compassionate actions (surely

---

[7] Luther, 'Treatise on Good Works', *Luther's Works*, XVIV, 27.

[8] Alfons Auer, *Open to the World: An Analysis of Lay Spirituality*, trans. Dennis Doherty and Carmel Callaghan (Baltimore: Helicon Press, 1966), 230 (emphasis mine).

intrinsically Christian practices) are Christian precisely because they did not have a spiritual reward in view! They are Christian, Luther would say, because they arise from gospel confidence, from the generosity of a heart set free by acceptance in Christ. It is this element of surprise for which we are least prepared when we ponder the parable. Perhaps the purpose of theological education is to set us up to be surprised as the righteous on the day of judgement to discover we acted in love without knowing it was for and to Jesus.

True Christian action – orthopraxy – is gratuitive, free from contrivance, free from a calculating spirit, free from contract: I do this for God and God does that for me. Orthopraxic living is essentially spontaneous. With Jesus in our hearts we love because there is someone in need, not to gain approval by God or to receive the benefits of Christian action.

This is the issue behind the question that dominates the book of Job. Satan said, 'Does Job serve God for nothing?' (Job 1:9). In the end our own service to God can be tested by the same probing question. One of the great lessons of the book of Job is this: Job proves that faith is not for the this-life benefits of having faith: not for healing; not for the restoration of his fortunes (this comes after he meets God again). Faith is for the glory of God. Christian practice, whether developing a compensation package for a business or empowering the poor, is for God's glory. The South American liberation theologian Gustavo Gutiérrez comments on this insightfully (and remarkably in view of his theological orientation):

> The truth that [Job] has grasped and that has lifted him to the level of contemplation is that justice alone does not have the final say about how we are to speak of God. Only when we have come to realize that God's love is freely bestowed do we enter fully and definitively into the presence of the God of faith . . . God's love, like all true love, operates in a world not of cause and effect but of freedom and gratuitiveness.[9]

---

[9] Gustavo Gutiérrez, *On Job: God-Talk and the Suffering of the Innocent* (Maryknoll, NY: Orbis Books, 1987), 87.

Orthopraxy is action in harmony with God's purposes in which we can discover God and his truth. Orthopraxy is not necessarily clerical, though it includes the work of the pastor. Whether washing dishes or preaching, being a cobbler or an apostle, 'all is one, as touching the deed, to please God', as Tyndale said. Orthopraxis is not measured by excellence, by efficiency or by its religious character, but by faith, hope and love. We must cultivate the heart and not merely the husk of such action. But that points to a third lens through which to investigate the theology–life connection: orthopathy.

3. Orthopathy

The word orthopraxy was coined by Richard Mouw and derives from the writings of the Jewish theologian Abraham Heschel who said the prophets embodied the divine pathos, that is, what God cares for. They had the heart of God. Their passion was inspired by God's passion. 'He has showed you, O man, what is good. And what does the Lord require of you? To act justly and to love mercy and to walk humbly with your God' (Mic. 6:8). Jürgen Moltmann develops the idea of the pathos of God as a 'free relationship of passionate participation'.[10]

The cultivation of the heart – a more wholistic way of knowing – is the very thing our postmodern culture invites. But the biblical response to the postmodern challenge is not to abandon reason but to allow God to evangelize our hearts as well as our heads, to care for what God cares for. As a practical knowledge of God unifying head and heart, theology has the character of wisdom. But where do we get wisdom?

Educating the heart

It is often conceded that the academy cannot be a solo educator, but there is little evidence that the academy needs the home, the congregation and the marketplace, though all four are linked by God in a daily life system for learning. The first school, of course, is the

---

[10] Moltmann, *The Trinity and the Kingdom*, 25.

home. The congregation and the academy are poor substitutes when it comes to the education of the heart.

Though my parents never intended it, their spiritual nurturing included exposing me to the ministry of the poor to the rich. They built our lovely family home on a three-acre plot next door to a one-room shack without water, electricity, indoor plumbing, or a furnace. Albert Jupp lived with his aged and ill mother in that smelly, dank shack. As he was occupied with the care of his mother, Albert was unable to hold down a steady job. Somehow he eked out an existence beside the Stevens, his rich next-door neighbours. Today the rich hardly see the poor except on television or from an air-conditioned coach.

Each night Albert would get a pail of water at our outside tap, which was always kept running, even in the dead of winter when our neighbours had their taps safely protected from freezing. My mother was one of the most generous souls on earth, and her sensitive conscience would not allow her to place a fine meal before our family without thinking of Albert and his mother. So night after night I was asked to make a pilgrimage up the hill to the shack with two portions from our table for our poor neighbours. I confess that as a teenager I usually resented doing this. But what I think was bothering me was how that nightly visit to the Jupps made me think about my own existence as a rich young man. Daily I was confronted existentially with the truth that the rich cannot know God well without relating to the poor. My neighbour made an evangelical invitation to my heart.

In a remarkable series of seven sermons on the parable of the rich man and Lazarus, the fourth-century church father, John Chrysostom addressed the illusions of wealth. In these prophetic sermons, Chrysostom argues that the rich are not owners of their wealth but stewards for the poor.[11] Appealing to the prophets of the Old Testament (Mal. 3:8–10) Chrysostom warns about the spiritual dangers of the rich. 'The most pitiable person of all,' he says, 'is the one who lives in luxury and shares his goods with nobody.'[12] In contrast, '*by nourishing Christ* in poverty here and laying up great

---

[11] St John Chrysostom, *On Wealth and Poverty* (Crestwood, NY: St Vladimir's Seminary Press, 1984), 50.
[12] Ibid., 57.

profit hereafter we will be able to attain the good things which are to come'.[13] In this last quotation Chrysostom hints that ministering to the poor simultaneously heals the hearts of the rich and nourishes Jesus. What should be observed is the truth that God has provided for the education of our hearts in love and compassion through our everyday family experiences and through our neighbour. Both are a means of grace.

Neighbour as educator

As we have already seen the neighbour becomes a means of grace precisely when the neighbour is taken seriously as neighbour and not as a means of grace! We cannot simply deal with the poor, the stranger and the outsider in principle, or engage in theoretical or strategic considerations of how to care for our global neighbours. It is in the context of actual neighbour relationships that we are invited to live the life of faith. It is precisely in the unplanned and uncontrollable circumstances of our lives that we can find God and be found by him. Bonhoeffer spoke to this with great depth in a conversation he reports he had with a young French pastor: 'I discovered later, and I'm still discovering right up to this moment, that it is only by living completely in this world that one learns to have faith . . . By this-worldliness I mean living unreservedly in life's duties, problems, successes and failures, experiences and perplexities. In so doing we throw ourselves completely into the arms of God.'[14] We find God (and get our hearts educated) in the centre of life rather than the circumference. This was the case for Job.

Passion for God

Job is a stunning example of orthopathy. His school was his life. He, like David was a man after God's own heart. As he went through test after test, sometimes with obvious weariness, Job began to want God more than he wanted health. Indeed – and this is a seldom

---

[13] Ibid, 55 (emphasis mine).

[14] Dietrich Bonhoeffer in a letter from Tegel prison, 1944, quoted in Melanie Morrison, 'As One Who Stands Convicted', *Sojourners* (May 1979), 15.

noted – Job never asked for healing. What he wanted was the friendship of God (Job 29:4). So most of Job's speeches are directed to God, inquiring of God, challenging God, exploring God, demanding of God, confronting God with holy persistence (Jas. 5:11). At times I think his orthodox friends with degrees from a prestigious theological college may have hid under the table expecting God to liquidate him for his impertinence. But in the end the God-talkers were condemned and Job was justified, being blessed with a first-hand experience of God (42:5). Was this because Job spoke well of God (the primary theological task) *by speaking to him boldly, with passionate faith* (the primary theological method)?

Job used his experience of the absence of God in order to know God better. P.T. Forsyth once said, 'Prayer is to the religious life what original research is for science – by it we get direct contact with reality.'[15] Job was not a half-hearted researcher. He took God on, like Abraham pleading, Jacob refusing to let God go until he had blessed him, like the Syro-Phoenician woman begging for crumbs under the table, like Paul asking three times for the thorn to be removed, like – dare we say it? – Jesus in the garden exploring his own heart options with the Father until he could freely do the Father's will through submission rather than compliance. Job withstanding God, wrestling with God, extracting revelation from God and in the end knowing God – is this orthopathy? Is this proof positive that the Kingdom of God is not for the mildly interested but the desperate? God-knowers (orthodox, orthopractic theologians) will 'take' the Kingdom by violent, passionate (orthopathic) faith (Mt. 11:12). Caring for what concerns God, caring for God's concerns in daily life, and caring for God above all. This is orthopathy.

Orthodoxy, orthopraxy, orthopathy. All three point to the marriage of theology and everyday life: theology and life linked in praise (orthodoxy), practice (orthopraxy) and passion (orthopathy). What God therefore has joined together let no theological institution put asunder.

Might not the most pernicious heresy in the church today be the disharmony between those who claim to be theologically approved but live as practical atheists? Is the greatest challenge not graduating from a theological college or seminary, but in the end, at the

---

[15] Forsyth, *The Soul of Prayer*, 78.

conclusion of our lifelong theological education, having the Lord say, 'I know you'? Would not the most fearful failure be to have God say, 'I never knew you' (Mt. 7:23; 25:12)?

One of the desert fathers[16] was approached by an eager young student who said, 'Abba, give me a word from God.' The wise mentor asked if the student would agree not to come back until he had fully lived the word. 'Yes,' the eager young student said. 'Then this is the word of God: "You shall love the Lord your God with all your heart, soul, strength and mind."' The young man disappeared, it seemed, forever.

Twenty-five years later the student had the temerity to come back. 'I have lived the word you gave. Do you have another word?' 'Yes,' said the desert father. 'But once again you must not come back until you have lived it.' 'I agree,' said the student. 'Love your neighbour as yourself,' said the desert father.

The student never came back.

---

[16] This story was cited by James Houston in a lecture. The source is unknown.

Select Bibliography

1. History

Bainton, R.H., 'The Ministry in the Middle Ages', in *The Ministry in Historical Perspectives*, ed. H.R. Niebuhr and D.D. Williams (New York: Harper Brothers, 1956), 82–109.

Banks, R., 'Lay Theology and Education Since 1945', in *All the Business of Life: Bringing Theology Down to Earth* (Sutherland, Australia: Albatross Books, 1987), 119–47.

Bliss, K., *We the People: A Book About Laity* (London: SCM Press, 1963).

Chrisman, M.U., 'Lay Response to the Protestant Reformation in Germany, 1520–1528', in P.N. Brooks (ed.), *Reformation Principle and Practice* (London: Scholar Press, 1980), 35–52.

Every, G., 'Sacralization and Secularization in East and West in the First Millennium after Christ', *Concilium* 47 (1969), 27–38.

Faivre, A., *The Emergence of the Laity in the Early Church* (New York: Paulist Press, 1990).

Green, M., *Evangelism in the Early Church* (London: Hodder & Stoughton, 1970).

Guitton, J., 'Clergy and Laity in the Early Church', in idem, *The Church and the Laity: From Newman to Vatican II* (Montreal: Palm Publishers, 1965), 165–76.

Harkness, G., *The Church and its Laity* (Nashville: Abingdon Press, 1962).

Hertz, K.H., 'The Role of the Laity in American Christianity', *Mid-Stream* 22 (July–October 1983), 326–41.

Kraemer, H., *A Theology of the Laity* (Philadelphia: Westminster Press, 1958).

Küng, H., 'The Laity in Conciliar History', in *Structures of the Church* (New York: Thomas Nelson and Sons, 1964), 74–92.

MacLean, A.J., 'The Position of Clergy and Laity in the Early Church in Relation to the Episcopate', in Claude Jenkins and K.D. MacKenzie (eds.), *Episcopacy Ancient and Modern* (London: SPCK, 1930), 47–66.

Marshall, P., *A Kind of Life Imposed on Man: Vocation and Social Order from Tyndale to Locke* (Toronto: University of Toronto Press, 1996).

Meslin, M., 'Ecclesiastical Institutions and Clericalization from 100 to 500 AD', *Concilium* 47 (1969), 39–54.

Neill, S., and H.-R. Weber (eds.), *The Layman in Christian History: A Project of the Department on the Laity of the World Council of Churches* (Philadelphia: Westminster Press, 1963).

Newman, J., 'Historical Development of the Role of the Laity in the Church', in idem, *The Christian in Society: A Theological Investigation* (Baltimore: Helicon Press, 1962), 9–61.

Niebuhr, H.R., and D.D. Williams, *The Ministry in Historical Perspectives* (New York: Harper & Brothers, 1956).

Oliver, E.H., *The Social Achievements of the Christian Church* (Toronto: United Church of Canada, 1930).

Rowthorn, A., 'The Clerical Captivity of the Church', in idem, *The Liberation of the Laity* (Wilton, CT: Morehouse-Barlow, 1986), 27–49.

Russell, A., *The Clerical Profession* (London: SPCK, 1980).

Strayer, J., 'The Laicization of Society', in B.D. Hill (ed.), *Church and State in the Middle Ages* (New York: John Wiley & Sons, 1970), 174–84.

Williams, G.H., 'The Ministry of the Ante-Nicene Church (c. 125–325)', in H.R. Niebuhr and D.D. Williams (eds.), *The Ministry in Historical Perspectives* (New York: Harper Brothers, 1956), 27–59.

—, 'The Ministry in the Later Patristic Period (314–451)', in H.R. Niebuhr and D.D. Williams (eds.), *The Ministry in Historical Perspectives* (New York: Harper Brothers, 1956), 60–81.

—, 'The Role of the Layman in the Ancient Church', *Greek and Byzantine Studies* 1 (1958), 9–42. NB An edited version of this article also appears in *Ecumenical Review* 10 (1957–58), 225–48.

2. Theology

Amirtham, S., 'Theology by the People: Some Issues, Some Questions', *Ministerial Formation* 28 (October 1984), 19–25.

Amirtham, S., and J.S. Pobee (eds.), *Theology by the People: Reflections on Doing Theology in Community* (Geneva: World Council of Churches, 1986).

Anderson, J.D., and E.E. Jones, *Ministry of the Laity* (San Francisco: Harper & Row, 1986).

Anderson, R.S. (ed.), *Theological Foundations for Ministry: Selected Readings for a Theology of the Church in Ministry* (Grand Rapids, MI: Eerdmans, 1979).

Ayres, F.O., *The Ministry of the Laity: A Biblical Exposition* (Philadelphia: Westminster Press, 1962).

Banks, R., *God the Worker: Journeys into the Mind, Heart and Imagination of God* (Sutherland, Australia: Albatross Books, 1992).

Baptism, Eucharist and Ministry, Faith and Order Paper No. 111, World Council of Churches, Geneva, 1982 (Toronto: Anglican Book Centre, 1983).

Best, E., *One Body in Christ: A Study in the Relationship of the Church to Christ in the Epistles of the Apostle Paul* (London: SPCK, 1955).

Butt, H., and E. Wright, *At the Edge of Hope: Christian Laity in Paradox* (New York: Seabury Press, 1978).

Callahan, D., 'Freedom and the Laity', in idem, *The New Church: Essays in Catholic Reform* (New York: Charles Scribner's Sons, 1966), 89–103.

Congar, Y.M.J., *Lay People in the Church: A Study for a Theology of the Laity*, trans. D. Attwater (Westminster, MD: Newman Press, 1957).

—, *A History of Theology*, trans. Hunter Guthrie, SJ (Garden City, NY: Doubleday, 1968).

Doohan, L., *The Lay-Centered Church: Theology and Spirituality* (Minneapolis: Winston Press, 1984).

Fee, G.D., '*Laos* and Leadership Under the New Covenant', Crux 25.4 (December 1989), 3–13.

Garlow, J.L., *Partners in Ministry: Laity and Pastors Working Together* (Kansas City, MO: Beacon Hill Press, 1981).

Gasque, W.W., 'Must Ordinary People Know Theology?' *Christian Ministry* 29.2 (February 1985), 32–4.

Gaymon, D.M., 'The Christian Layman's Role', *Study Encounter* 3.3 (1967), 128–36.

Gibbs, M., 'The Christian Laity Today', *Laity Exchange* 29 (October 1986), 1–9.

Gibbs, M., and T.R. Morton, *God's Frozen People* (London: Fontana, 1964).

—, *God's Lively People: Christians in Tomorrow's World* (London: Wm Collins Sons, 1971).

Gillespie, T.W., 'The Laity in Biblical Perspective', *Theology Today* 36 (1979–80), 315–27.

Grimes, H., *The Rebirth of the Laity* (Nashville: Abingdon Press, 1962).

Hadden, J.K., 'Some Prerequisites for Lay Involvement', *Pastoral Psychology* 22 (June 1971), 7–13.

Haney, D., *The Idea of the Laity* (Grand Rapids: Zondervan, 1973).

Hardy, L., *Fabric of This World* (Grand Rapids: Eerdmans, 1990).

Harkness, G., *The Church and its Laity* (Nashville: Abingdon Press, 1962).

Kraemer, H., *A Theology of the Laity* (Philadelphia: Westminster Press, 1958).

Lewis, D., and A. McGrath, *Doing Theology for the People of God: Studies in Honor of J.I. Packer* (Downers Grove: InterVarsity Press, 1996).

Loeffler, P., 'Bonhoeffer versus Congar', *Frontier* 7 (summer 1964), 130–33.

Macquarrie, J., *The Faith of the People of God: A Lay Theology* (New York: Charles Scribner's Sons, 1972).

Moltmann, J., *The Trinity and the Kingdom*, trans. Margaret Kohl (San Francisco: Harper & Row, 1991).

Morawska, A., 'Introduction to a Theology for Laymen', *Cross Currents* 17 (1967), 5–14.

O'Connell, L.J., 'God's Call to Humankind: Towards a Theology of Vocation', *Chicago Studies* 18 (1979), 147–59.

Pittenger, N., *The Ministry of all Christians: A Theology of Lay Ministry* (Wilton, CT: Morehouse-Barlow, 1983).

Rademacher, W.J., *Lay Ministry: A Theological, Spiritual and Pastoral Handbook* (New York: Crossroad, 1991).

Richards, L.O., and Gib Martin, *A Theology of Personal Ministry: Spiritual Giftedness in the Local Church* (Grand Rapids: Zondervan, 1981).

Rowthorn, A., *The Liberation of the Laity* (Wilton, CT: Morehouse-Barlow, 1986).

Volf, M., *Work in the Spirit: Toward a Theology of Work (New York: Oxford University Press, 1991).*

Vos, N., *Seven Days a Week: Faith in Action* (Laity Exchange Books Series; Philadelphia: Fortress Press, 1985).

Wingren, G., *The Christian's Calling: Luther on Vocation*, trans. C.C. Rasmussen (Edinburgh: Oliver and Boyd, 1957).

3. The Priesthood of the People

Best, E., 'I Peter II 4–10 – A Reconsideration', *Novum Testamentum* 11.4 (1969), 270–93.

—, 'Spiritual Sacrifice: General Priesthood in the New Testament', *Interpretation* 14 (July 1960), 273–99.

Birch, P., 'Priesthood of the Laity', *The Furrow* 30 (1979), 80–90.

Capon, R.F., *An Offering of Uncles: The Priesthood of Adam and the Shape of the World* (New York: Crossroad, 1982).

Crawford, J.R., 'Calvin and the Priesthood of all Believers', *Scottish Journal of Theology* 21 (June 1968), 145–56.

Eastwood, C., *The Priesthood of All Believers: An Examination of the Doctrine from the Reformation to the Present Day* (London: Epworth Press, 1960).

—, *The Royal Priesthood of the Faithful: An Investigation of the Doctrine from Biblical Times to the Reformation* (London: Epworth Press, 1963).

Fischer, R.H., 'Baptist and the Ministry: Luther on the Priesthood of All Believers', *Baptist Quarterly* 17 (July 1958), 293–311.

Floor, L., 'The General Priesthood Of Believers in the Epistle to the Hebrews', in F. Fensham, et al., *Ad Hebraes: Essays on the Epistle to the Hebrews* (Pretoria: University of Pretoria, 1971), 72–82.

Garrett, J.L., Jr, 'The Biblical Doctrine of the Priesthood of the People of God', in H. Drumwright (ed.), *New Testament Studies: Essays in Honor of Ray Summers* (Waco, TX: Markham Press Fund, 1975), 137–49.

—, 'The Pre-Cyprianic Doctrine of the Priesthood of All Christians', in F.F. Church and T. George (eds.), *Continuity and Discontinuity in Church History* (Leiden: E.J. Brill, 1979), 45–61.

Hanson, R., *Christian Priesthood Examined* (Guildford, UK: Lutterworth Press, 1979).

Henderson, G.D., 'Priesthood of Believers', *Scottish Journal of Believers* 7 (March 1954), 1–15.

Hyatt, M.A., 'The Active and Contemplative Life in St John Chrysostom's Treatise on the Priesthood', *Diakonia* 15.2 (1980), 185–92.

Kjeseth, P.L., 'Baptism as Ordination', *Dialog* 8 (summer 1969), 177–82.

Küng, H., 'The Priesthood of All Believers', in idem, *The Church* (Garden City, NY: Image Books, 1976), 465–95.

Leclercq, J., 'The Priesthood in the Patristic and Medieval Church', in N. Lash and J. Rhymer (eds.), *The Christian Priesthood* (London: Darton, Longman & Todd, 1970), 53–75.

Nellas, P., 'The Ministry of the Laity', in Ion Bria (ed.), *Martyria/ Mission: The Witness of the Orthodox Churches Today* (Geneva: World Council of Churches, 1980), 60–65.

Norris, R.A., 'The Beginnings of Christian Priesthood', *Anglican Theological Review* 66, supplementary series 9 (1984), 18–35.

Palmer, P.F., 'The Lay Priesthood; Real or Metaphorical', *Theological Studies* 8 (1947), 574–613.

Ryder, A.R., *The Priesthood of the Laity: Historically and Critically Considered* (London: Hodder & Stoughton, 1911).

Schaufele, W., 'Missionary Vision and Activity of the Anabaptist Laity', *Mennonite Quarterly Review* 36 (April 1962), 99–115.

Scott, W.M.F., 'Priesthood in the New Testament', *Scottish Journal of Theology* 10 (December 1957), 399–415.

Werdt, J.D. von, 'What Can the Layman Do without the Priest?' *Concilium* 34 (1968), 105–14.

4. In the Church

Afanassieff, N., 'The Ministry of the Laity in the Church', *Ecumenical Review* 10 (1957–58), 255–63.

Allen, R., *The Case for Voluntary Clergy* (London: Eyre & Spottiswoode, 1930).

—, *The Compulsion of the Spirit: A Roland Allen Reader*, ed. David Paton and Charles H. Long (Grand Rapids: Eerdmans, 1983).

—, *The Ministry of the Spirit: Selected Writings of Roland Allen*, ed. David Paton (London: World Dominion Press, 1960).

Collins, P., and R. Paul Stevens, *The Equipping Pastor* (Washington, DC: Alban Institute, 1993).

Doohan, L., *Laity's Mission in the Local Church: Setting a New Direction* (San Francisco: Harper & Row, 1986).

Fenhagen, J.C., *Ministry and Solitude: The Ministry of the Laity and the Clergy in Church and Society* (New York: Seabury Press, 1981).

Feucht, O.E., *Everyone a Minister* (St Louis: Concordia, 1979).

Garlow, J.L., *Partners in Ministry: Laity and Pastors Working Together* (Kansas City, MO: Beacon Hill Press, 1981).

Gibbs, M., 'The Laity and the Institutional Churches', *Laity Exchange* 29 (October 1986), 1–8.

—, 'Ministries Outside the Parish', *Laity Exchange* 29 (October 1986), 1–3.

—, 'Myths about Ministry', *Laity Exchange* 13 (November 1981), 1–4.

Green, M., *Freed to Serve: Training and Equipping for Ministry* (Dallas, TX: Word, 1983).

Hull, B., *Jesus Christ Disciple-Maker: Rediscovering Jesus' Strategy for Building His Church* (Minneapolis, MN: Free Church Publications, 1984).

—, *The Disciple-Making Pastor: The Key to Building Healthy Christians in Today's Church* (Old Tappan, NJ: Revell, 1988).

Hunt, G., 'Vocation and Ministry', *Theology* 87 (May 1984), 190–96.

King, P.M., 'Learning from the Laity', *Theology Today* 36 (1979–80): 368–74.

Leckey, D.R., *Laity Stirring the Church: Prophetic Questions* (Laity Exchange Books Series; Philadelphia: Fortress Press, 1987).

Lindgren, A.J., and N. Shawchuck, *Let My People Go: Empowering Laity for Ministry* (Nashville: Abingdon Press, 1980).

Martin, G., and R., Lawrence, *Lay Ministry: Empowering the People of God* (Grand Rapids: Zondervan, 1981).

Niebuhr, H.R., *The Purpose of the Church and Its Ministry* (New York: Harper & Brothers, 1956).

O'Connor, E., *Eighth Day of Creation: Gifts and Creativity* (Waco, TX: Word Books, 1971).

—, *The New Community* (New York: Harper & Row, 1976).

Oden, T.C., *Pastoral Theology: Essentials in Ministry* (San Francisco: Harper & Row, 1983).

Ogden, G., *The New Reformation: Returning the Ministry to the People of God* (Grand Rapids, MI: Zondervan, 1990).

Page, P.N., *All God's People Are Ministers: Equipping Church Members for Ministry* (Minneapolis: Augsburg, 1993).

Richards, L.O., and Clyde Hoeldtke, *A Theology of Church Leadership* (Grand Rapids: Zondervan, 1980).

Schillebeeckx, E., *Ministry: A Case for Change*, trans. John Bowden (London: SCM Press, 1981).

—, *Ministry: Leadership in the Community of Jesus Christ*, trans. John Bowden (New York: Crossroads, 1985).

Stedman, R.C., *Body Life* (Glendale, CA: Regal Books, 1972).

Stevens, R. Paul, *Liberating the Laity: Equipping all the Saints for Ministry* (Downers Grove: InterVarsity Press, 1985).

—, *The Equippers Guide to Every Member Ministry* (Downers Grove: InterVarsity Press, 1992).

Stott, J.R.W., *One People: Helping Your Church Become a Caring Community* (Old Tappan, NJ: Revell, rev. edn, 1982).

Wagner, C.P., *Your Spiritual Gifts Can Help Your Church Grow* (Ventura, CA: Regal Books, 1979).

Warkentin, M., *Ordination: A Biblical, Historical View* (Grand Rapids: Eerdmans, 1982).

Weber, H.R., 'The Laity: Its Gifts and Ministry', in Robert C. Mackie and Charles C. West (eds.), *The Sufficiency of God* (Philadelphia: Westminster Press, 1963), 187–206.

Whitehead, J.D., and Evelyn Eaton Whitehead, *The Emerging Laity: Returning Leadership to the Community of Faith* (Garden City, NY: Doubleday, 1986).

Yoder, J.H., *The Fullness of Christ: Paul's Vision of Universal Ministry* (Elgin, IL.: Brethren Press, 1987).

5. In the World

Allen, R., *Missionary Methods: St Paul's or Ours?* (London: Robert Scott, 1912; Grand Rapids: Eerdmans, repr. 1962).

—, *The Spontaneous Expansion of the Church* (Grand Rapids: Eerdmans, 1962).

Almen, L.T., 'Vocation in a Post-Vocational Age', *Word and World* 4.2 (spring 1984), 131–40.

Anderson, J.D., and E.E. Jones, *Ministry of the Laity* (San Francisco: Harper & Row, 1986).

Anderson, R.S., *The Praxis of Pentecost: Revisioning the Church's Life and Mission* (Downers Grove: InterVarsity Press, 1993).

Banks, R., *All the Business of Life* (Sutherland, Australia: Albatross Books, 1987); reprinted as *Redeeming the Routines* (Wheaton: Victor Books, 1993).

— (ed.), *Faith Goes to Work* (Washington: Alban Institute, 1993).

Banks, R., and R. Paul Stevens, *The Complete Book of Everyday Christianity* (Downers Grove: InterVarsity Press, 1997).

Bernbaum, J.A., and S.M. Steer, *Why Work? Careers and Employment in Biblical Perspective* (Grand Rapids: Baker Book House, 1986).

Bosch, D.J., *Transforming Mission: Paradigm Shifts in Theology of Mission* (Maryknoll, NY: Orbis Books, 1996).

Carey, W., *An Inquiry into the Obligation of Christians to Use Means for the Conversion of the Heathens* (London: Carey Kingsgate Press, 1961).

Catherwood, Fred (C. F. R), *On the Job: The Christian 9–5* (Grand Rapids: Zondervan, 1983).

Catherwood, C.F.R., *The Christian in Industrial Society* (London: InterVarsity Press, 19662).

Cosby, G., *Handbook for Mission Groups* (Waco, TX: Word Books, 1975).

Diehl, W.E., *Christianity and Real Life* (Philadelphia: Fortress Press, 1976).

—, *Thank God, It's Monday* (Laity Exchange Books Series; Philadelphia: Fortress Press, 1982).

Doohan, L., *Laity's Mission in the Local Church: Setting a New Direction* (San Francisco: Harper & Row, 1986).

Ellul, J., *The Presence of the Kingdom* (New York: Seabury Press, 1967).

Fenhagen, J.C., *Ministry and Solitude: The Ministry of the Laity and the Clergy in Church and Society* (New York: Seabury Press, 1981).

Geaney, D., *Emerging Lay Ministries* (Kansas City, MO: Andrews & McMeel, 1979).

Guder, D.L. (ed.), *The Missional Church: A Vision for the Sending of the Church in North America* (Grand Rapids: Eerdmans, 1990).

Hall, C.P., *Lay Action – The Church's Third Force: A Strategy for Enabling Lay Ministry in Secular Institutions* (New York: Friendship Press, 1974).

Hunt, G., 'A Gap that needs Closing', *Theology* 86 (March 1983), 96–103.

Hybels, B., *Christians in the Marketplace* (Wheaton: Victor Books, 1986).

John Paul II, *On Human Work* (Washington, D.C.: Office of Publishing Services, United States Catholic Conference, 1981).

Kinast, R.L., *Caring for Society: A Theological Interpretation of Lay Ministry* (Chicago: The Thomas More Press, 1985).

Kolden, M., 'Luther on Vocation', *Word and World* 3.4 (autumn 1983), 382–90.

Kromminga, Carl G., 'The Role of the Laity in Urban Evangelization', in R.S. Greenway (ed.), *Discipling the City: Theological Reflections on Urban Mission* (Grand Rapids: Baker Book House, 1979).

Leckey, D.R., *Laity Stirring the Church: Prophetic Questions* (Laity Exchange Books Series: Philadelphia: Fortress Press, 1987).

Lowery, J.L. (ed.), *Case Histories of Tentmakers* (Wilton, CT: Morehouse-Barlow, 1976).

Marshall, P., *Thine is the Kingdom: A Biblical Perspective on the Nature of Government and Politics Today* (Hants, UK: Marshall, Morgan & Scott, 1984).

Marshall, P., et al., *Labour of Love: Essays on Work* (Toronto: Wedge Publishing Foundation, 1980).

Milliken, D., 'What is the Theology of Everyday Life?' *Laity Exchange* 33 (September 1987), 1–5.

Mouw, R., *Called to Holy Worldliness* (Laity Exchange Books Series; Philadelphia: Fortress Press, 1980).

—, *Politics and the Biblical Drama* (Grand Rapids: Baker Book House, 1976).

—, *When the Kings Come Marching In: Isaiah and the New Jerusalem* (Grand Rapids: Eerdmans, 1983).

Nelson, J.O. (ed.), *Work and Vocation: A Christian Discussion* (New York: Harper & Brothers, 1954).

Niebuhr, H.R., *Christ and Culture* (New York: Harper & Row, 1951).

Peabody, L., *Secular Work is a Full-Time Service* (Fort Washington, PA: Christian Literature Crusade, 1974).

Peck, G. and J.S. Hoffman (eds.), *The Laity in Ministry: The Whole People of God for the Whole World* (Valley Forge, PA: Judson Press, 1984).

Preece, G., *Changing Work Values: A Christian Response* (Melbourne: Acorn Press, 1995).

Raines, J.C., and D.C. Day-Lower, *Modern Work and Human Meaning* (Philadelphia: Westminster Press, 1986).

Reber, R.E., 'Vocation and Vision: A New Look at the Ministry of the Laity', *Laity Exchange* 31 (March 1987), 1–6.

Roy, P., *Building Christian Communities for Justice* (New York: Paulist Press, 1981).

Rylen, L., *Work and Leisure in Christian Perspective* (Portland, OR: Multnomah Press, 1987).

Schmemann, A., *For the Life of the World: Sacraments and Orthodoxy* (Crestwood, NY: St Vladimir's Seminary Press, 1988).

Schumacher, E.F., *Good Work* (New York: Harper & Row, 1979).

Slocum, R.E., *Ordinary Christians in a High-Tech World* (Waco, TX: Word Books, 1986).

Snyder, H.A., *The Community of the King* (Downers Grove: InterVarsity Press, 1977).

—, *Liberating the Church: The Ecology of Church and Kingdom* (Downers Grove: InterVarsity Press, 1983).

Stevens, R. Paul, *Disciplines of the Hungry Heart: Christian Living Seven Days a Week* (Wheaton: Harold Shaw, 1993).

Stringfellow, W., *A Private and Public Faith* (Grand Rapids; Eerdmans, 1962).

—, *An Ethic for Christians and Other Aliens in a Strange Land* (Waco, TX: Word, 1973).

Tillapaugh, F.R., *The Church Unleashed* (Ventura, CA: Regal Books, 1982).

Todd, J. (ed.), *Work: Christian Thought and Practice* (London: Darton, Longman & Todd, 1960).

Trueblood, E., *The Company of the Committed* (San Francisco: Harper & Row, 1961).

—, *Your Other Vocation* (New York: Harper & Row, 1952).

Tucker, G., *The Faith-Work Connection: A Practical Application of Christian Values in the Marketplace* (Toronto: Anglican Book Centre, 1987).

Vicedom, G.F., *The Mission of God: An Introduction to a Theology of Mission* trans. Gilbert A. Thiele and Dennis Hilgendorf (St Louis: Concordia, 1965).

Vos, N., 'Laity in the World: Church at Work', *Word and World* 4.2 (spring 1984), 151–8.

—, *Seven Days a Week: Faith in Action* (Laity Exchange Books Series; Philadelphia: Fortress Press, 1985).

Watson, D., *Called and Committed: World Changing Discipleship* (Wheaton: Harold Shaw, 1982).

Wentz, F.K., *The Layman's Role Today* (New York: Abingdon Press, 1963).

White, J., and M.E. White, *Your Job: Survival or Satisfaction?* (Grand Rapids: Zondervan, 1977).

Wilson, J.C., Jr, *Today's Tentmakers: Self-Support – An Alternative Model for Worldwide Witness* (Wheaton: Tyndale House, 1979).

Wingren, G., *The Christian's Calling: Luther on Vocation*, trans. C.C. Rasmussen (Edinburgh: Oliver & Boyd, 1957).

Wink, W., *Naming the Powers: The Language of Power in the New Testament* (Philadelphia: Fortress Press, 1984).

Wyszynski, Stefan Cardinal, *All You Who Labor: Work and the Sanctification of Daily Life*, trans. J. Ardle McArdle (Manchester, NH: Sophia Press, 1960/95).

Yoder, J.H., *The Politics of Jesus* (Carlisle: Paternoster/Grand Rapids: Eerdmans, 1972).

Zikmund, B.B., 'Christian Vocation – In Context', *Theology Today* 36 (1979–80), 328–37.

Index of Authors

Index of Biblical References

Subject Index

The names of individuals who are the subject of the text rather than authors whose works are being referred to are included in the subject index.